CW00403210

Kevin Flinn's book on *Leadership Development* is an important antidote to the usual literature on leadership and leadership development. Instead of simply reinforcing largely mythical accounts of some idealised story about what leadership should be, Flinn's book insightfully reflects on the actual experience of leading and proposes useful approaches to developing that experience.

Ralph Stacey, Professor of Management, Hertfordshire Business School, UK

A timely insight into the theory and practice of leadership and leadership development in a world characterised by complexity and uncertainty. In this book Kevin Flinn provides a refreshingly frank take on the limitations of traditional approaches and a thorough and illuminating exploration of an alternative, rooted in the insights of over a decade's experience working with students and practising managers to understand how things really get done in groups and organisations.

Richard Bolden, Director of Bristol Leadership and Change Centre,
University of the West of England, UK

In this gem of a book, you will find no best practices and no short cuts but a spirited writer reflecting upon his extensive practice of leadership development. If you are sceptical of prescriptions, but want to be introduced to tools and techniques for reflexivity, this book is for you. In addition, you will get a comprehensive overview of current management literature. I can highly recommend it.

Henry Larsen, Professor of Participatory Innovation, University of Southern Denmark

Kevin Flinn's book is a welcomed addition to the still very small number of books written on the topic of Complexity and Management. Kevin builds on the tremendously important work of Ralph Stacey and his colleagues and adds his own story creating an important contribution to the study of management both in theory and in practice.

Esko Kilpi, Founder, Esko Kilpi Company, Finland

LEADERSHIP DEVELOPMENT

Drawing on the complexity sciences and personal narrative accounts of experience from practitioners based in the UK, Germany, Denmark and North America, this book examines conventional leadership development methodologies with a view to identifying what is useful and what is not. It proffers an alternative perspective on leadership and organisation for business schools, consultancies and corporate training functions to adopt in their development of leaders.

Leadership Development: A Complexity Approach is essential reading for advanced students and researchers of leadership development, leadership studies, human resource management and organisational development. It will also be of interest to management educators and practising managers whose experience of, or aspirations for, working life are not represented in mainstream academic texts and popular management literature.

Kevin Flinn is Head of Leadership and Organisational Development at the University of Hertfordshire, UK, a Visiting Lecturer at Hertfordshire Business School, an Associate with the Leadership Foundation for Higher Education and an Associate Member of the Institute of Group Analysis.

LEADERSHIP DEVELOPMENT

A Complexity Approach

Kevin Flinn

Routledge
Taylor & Francis Group

LONDON AND NEW YORK

First published 2018
by Routledge
2 Park Square, Milton Park, Abingdon, Oxon OX14 4RN

and by Routledge
711 Third Avenue, New York, NY 10017

Routledge is an imprint of the Taylor & Francis Group, an informa business

© 2018 Kevin Flinn

The right of Kevin Flinn to be identified as the author of this work has been asserted by him in accordance with sections 77 and 78 of the Copyright, Designs and Patents Act 1988.

All rights reserved. No part of this book may be reprinted or reproduced or utilised in any form or by any electronic, mechanical, or other means, now known or hereafter invented, including photocopying and recording, or in any information storage or retrieval system, without permission in writing from the publishers.

Trademark notice: Product or corporate names may be trademarks or registered trademarks, and are used only for identification and explanation without intent to infringe.

British Library Cataloguing in Publication Data
A catalogue record for this book is available from the British Library

Library of Congress Cataloging in Publication Data
Names: Flinn, Kevin, author.
Title: Leadership development : a complexity approach / Kevin Flinn.
Description: 1 Edition. | New York : Routledge, 2018. | Includes index.
Identifiers: LCCN 2017045929| ISBN 9781138934023 | ISBN 9781138934030
  | ISBN 9781315678269 (eISBN)
Subjects: LCSH: Leadership. | Career development.
Classification: LCC HD57.7 .F5955 2018 | DDC 658.4/092–dc23
LC record available at https://lccn.loc.gov/2017045929

ISBN: 978-1-138-93402-3 (hbk)
ISBN: 978-1-138-93403-0 (pbk)
ISBN: 978-1-315-67826-9 (ebk)

Typeset in Bembo
by Taylor & Francis Books

CONTENTS

LIST OF ILLUSTRATIONS

Figure

Tables

ACKNOWLEDGEMENTS

This book would not have been possible without the help and support of a number of colleagues/friends who continue to push my thinking/practice every time I have the pleasure and privilege of working with them.

Thank you to …

Professors Chris Mowles and Ralph Stacey, my doctoral supervisors, who encouraged me to take my everyday experience seriously, and introduced me to ways of thinking that not only provided me with a more reality congruent understanding of leadership and organisation, but also the antidote to my growing disillusionment with mainstream thinking.

Professors Doug Griffin and Patricia Shaw, who along with Ralph developed, over a quarter of a century ago, the perspective of Complex Responsive Processes of Relating (Stacey, 2010; Griffin, 2001; Shaw, 2002; Mowles, 2011); the *complexity approach* of this book's title. Doug will not get to read this, but his influence can be found on every page.

Eric Wenzel (Chapter 4), Henry Larsen (Chapter 5), Sam Talucci (Chapter 6) and Chris Mowles (Chapter 7), who have generously allowed me to share elements of their doctoral theses and/or publications for a number of the vignettes that appear here. Chris Rodgers (Chapter 3) for permission to share his 'Management in five acts' framework.

Sally Graham, who introduced me to relational coaching (de Haan, 2008) and developed the Leading Through Coaching programme explored in Chapter 4; a solid foundation that my colleagues, Helen Charlwood and Jill Lees, continue to build on.

Macarena Mata, Dawn Hudson and Alastair Snell, my fellow collaborators in the development of the conversational approaches to leading that are explored in Chapter 5.

My Hertfordshire Business School MBA programme colleagues – Jana Filosof, Rachelle Andrews, and Yasmin Imani – with whom I work on the Leadership and Change module.

The Leadership Foundation for Higher Education colleagues with whom I have worked directly – Paul Gentle, Glyn Jones, Lawrie Phipps, Heather Thornton and Alison Halstead – and the many others who I am lucky enough to engage with on development events.

The many managers who have participated in the management and leadership development programmes that I have been involved in during the past twenty years, especially those who have afforded me the privilege of reading (and assessing) their reflective narrative accounts of experience. These reflections illustrate the influence that involvement in the programmes that I lead has had on their thinking and practice, some examples of which can be found in Chapters 6 and 7.

The baristas of St Albans, Trebarwith, Mousehole and Liverpool who served up the flat whites and lattes that fuelled many a writing session.

My wife, 'tricia, for her unstinting support through my doctoral studies and the writing of this book, activities that have interrupted far too many weekends and holidays for my own liking let alone hers.

References

de Haan, E. (2008) *Relational Coaching: Journeys towards Mastering One-to-One Learning*. Chichester: Wiley and Sons.

Griffin, D. (2002) *The Emergence of Leadership: Linking Self-Organisation and Ethics*. London: Routledge.

Mowles, C. (2011) *Rethinking Management: Radical Insights from the Complexity Sciences*. London: Gower.

Shaw, P. (2002) *Changing Conversations in Organizations: A Complexity Approach to Change*. London: Routledge.

Stacey, R. (2010) *Complexity and Organizational Reality: Uncertainty and the Need to Rethink Management after the Collapse of Investment Capitalism*. London: Routledge.

FOREWORD

In contemporary organisational life it would be easy to come away with the idea that every organisational problem and every question of organisational authority turns on the topic of leadership. It has become a ubiquitous notion in most HR departments that everyone in an organisation, whether they have responsibility for managing others or not, needs leadership training. At my own university I have been asked to offer a session on leadership for researchers, as though the average researcher requires this kind of development in their thinking in order to carry out their research. And the requirement for leadership development is understood to be different, and more privileged, than requiring management training: whereas managers keep things stable and transactional, leaders are capable of 'transforming' things and people. So leadership development in organisations often involves these quite grandiose ideas about transformation, passion, courage and vision which are on the one hand most edifying, yet on the other they may be totally impractical, perhaps unreasonable, for the average manager working in an ordinary organisation. If you are a manager heading up a sales team is it really necessary to wonder what Nelson Mandela or Martin Luther King would do?

In this important book on leadership development Kevin Flinn teases apart these accepted notions of what we might mean by leadership, and questions whether it is so different from management. He then offers an alternative perspective on what might constitute leadership development if organisations are still committed to doing it, by weaving together theory, practical suggestions and deep insight gained from more than twenty years spent developing leaders in organisations in many different sectors of the economy. Each chapter treats a taken-for-granted method for developing leaders and questions how they are taken up in practice. He deals with theatre techniques, reflective practice, coaching, action learning, among other methods, and then offers a persuasive critique of them. To do so he draws on insights from the complexity sciences, process sociology, pragmatic philosophy and his training at the Institute of Group Analysis, as well as his experience as a student on the Doctorate of Management Programme at Hertfordshire Business School. Kevin has run scores of groups for hundreds of managers in many different organisations. This book shows the gentle but critical ways in which he encourages a deep reflexivity in the participants on his programmes. The book models the generative tension between, on the one hand, accepting that leadership development programmes are here to stay, but on the other hand pointing out that they may then become vehicles for inquiring purposefully into the experience of trying to get things done together. It is an exemplar of the critical open-mindedness which he is encouraging in the participants on his leadership programmes. For these reasons this is an important book for anyone put in charge of such development programmes, for managers who undergo leadership development, as well as for researchers interested theoretically and practically in what we can do to make leadership development more critical.

Chris Mowles,
Oxford, July 2017

ABBREVIATIONS

CAS	Complex Adaptive Systems
CEO	Chief Executive Officer
CLS	Critical Leadership Studies
CMS	Critical Management Studies
DMan	Doctorate in Management
HE	Higher Education
IGA	Institute of Group Analysis
L-A-P	Leadership-as-Practice
LEG	Leadership Experience Group
LTC	Leading Through Coaching
MBA	Master of Business Administration
MSc	Master of Science
MSOL	Making Sense of Leading
OMD	Outdoor Management Development
PhD	Doctor of Philosophy
RCL	Responding to the Challenges of Leading
RPG	Reflective Practice Groups
RPO	Reflective Practice in Organisations
TQM	Total Quality Management
UH	University of Hertfordshire

INTRODUCTION

Why (yet) another book about leadership development?

> Traditionally, researchers instructed practitioners how to do their work better. If we are to hold the assumption that practitioners best know the context of their work, this tradition must end.
>
> *Barbara Czarniawska (2014)*

There is a gap in the literature on management and leadership development. This is because mainstream academic texts and popular management books tend to:

- sacrifice depth for breadth;
- take methods and techniques at face value, offering little, if any, exploration and critical evaluation of the attendant assumptions and ways of thinking that underpin them;
- focus, almost exclusively, on the development of the knowledge and skills that the authors deem it necessary to have in order to make it as a chief/executive officer (C/EO) in a large corporation;
- ignore, and in some instances actively avoid, the contingent, lived experiences of leader-managers and the plurality of contexts in which they find themselves;
- view organisations as systems that are manipulated and controlled at will by a CEO, with or without the additional support of a small group of executive officers.

However, the vast majority of people who choose a management career will never get to be a C/EO, whether they aspire to be or not, nor will they necessarily get (or desire) to work for a big, global corporation.[1] Indeed, as Wilson *et al.* argue:

> [F]irst-line managers are far and away the most numerous amongst the managerial ranks. They typically have less organizational authority in terms of decision making than their more senior colleagues … however, they usually have the greatest amount of day-to-day contact with the non-managerial employees, who themselves normally constitute the bulk of an organization's workforce. Supervisory managers are, therefore, the most numerous and direct source of potential influence upon employees and, hence, leadership. Their importance [has] been largely neglected in leadership studies.
>
> *(2018: 62)*

Moreover, the 'more abstract organizational issues' that mainstream authors and practitioners in the 'leadership industry' focus on – 'culture, identity, vision and strategy' (Alvesson *et al.*, 2017) – are not in reality the issues that managers, including C/EOs, actually find themselves struggling with on a daily basis. In my experience, the participants on leadership development programmes, whether C/EOs or first-time supervisors, are exercised by the everyday political challenges of how to rub along with the dozen or so people with whom they most regularly interact (Flinn, 2011). Identity, strategy and culture, and the artefacts that purport to capture and articulate these things, emerge in and from such interactions. Local interactions influence, and are simultaneously influenced by, the multitudinous patterns of local interaction that constitute the global patterning that we call organisation. This patterning can neither be predetermined nor controlled at will by anyone, irrespective of the degree of influence they may exercise at any one time (see Chapter 3).

Consequently, this book sets out to fill this void by exploring, in depth, a number of conventional development interventions that I, and the thousands of managers with whom I have worked over the years, have found useful for enhancing the capabilities that might help one to more adeptly navigate the everyday political contexts that one finds oneself in. Rather than perpetuating fantasies of heroic leadership and abstract conceptions of how leaders and organisations *ought to be*, I explore leadership as a social, relational, interdependent phenomenon and focus on how one might go about helping managers to deal with *how things are*. A complexity approach to leadership development involves supporting leader-managers to pay attention to what they are more or less already doing. That is, making sense of the context in which they find themselves, reflexively thinking about what they and others are thinking and doing in that context, and making practical judgements as to appropriate next steps. Sense-making, reflexivity and practical judgement (see Chapter 3) are capabilities that are available and useful to all, irrespective of the context in which we find ourselves or the seniority of role we currently hold or aspire to.

Why now?

> Leaders of every sort are in disrepute [and] the tireless teaching of leadership has brought us no closer to leadership nirvana than we were previously ... we don't have much better an idea of how to grow good leaders, or how to stop or at least slow bad leaders, than we did a hundred or even a thousand years ago.
>
> *Barbara Kellerman (2012)*

This myth of heroic leadership – a myth that business school educators, management consultants and corporate training facilitators have played no small part in creating and maintaining (see Chapter 1) – has long been problematised by Critical Management Studies (CMS) thinkers and those authors proffering a social and relational understanding of human interaction. Similarly, the dominant view of organisation as system, a machine-like entity that can be manipulated at will by a small group of powerful managers (see Chapter 1), has long been contested by authors looking for more reality congruent understandings of the uncertainties and complexities that characterise their experience of organisational life. Given the threat that these views pose to the orthodoxy, it is no surprise to find them confined to the margins of the academy. However, recent events have seemingly brought them to the fore.

The endless stream of scandals, crises and catastrophes in private, public and charitable sector organisations over the last two decades has forced some mainstream academic and popular management authors to question the approaches to leadership development that they have been advocating, and the corresponding conceptions and practice of leadership that such approaches have helped to create (Kellerman, 2012; Pfeffer, 2015). Some have even gone so far as to accept that leaders, however powerful they may appear, do not (get to) control corporate futures. On the face of it, these two acknowledgements constitute massive shifts in mainstream thought and one would be forgiven for thinking that this signals an accordance between conventional, critical and complexity perspectives. Job done! Consensus reached! Unfortunately, nothing could be further from the truth.

If this soul-searching signalled a true shift in orthodox thinking, it would be welcome, but scratch the surface and little, if anything, has changed. The old ways of thinking are still plain to see. So, rather than letting go of individualistic views of leadership and the illusory cause and effect certainties of some systems-thinking perspectives[2] on organisation, which are consistently and continually negated by real world events, mainstream authors are merely recasting them in the language of shared/distributed/collective leadership and/or uncertainty/complexity. The arguments that accompany these seemingly huge shifts in thought tend to go something like this: command and control approaches that were appropriate in the industrial age are no longer fit for purpose in the new complex, global, knowledge-based, technological era. Consequently, something needs to change. However, I argue that this is not merely old wine in new bottles (de Haan, 2005), but rather the original wine, in the original bottles, with the addition of new words on the labels. The marketing (rhetoric) may have changed, but the content (regurgitation of illusory recipes for success) remains the same.

Take an author like Jim Collins[3] for instance. For more than two decades Collins has been researching and writing, often in collaboration with others (see the list of references at the end of this chapter), about what it is that makes businesses and business leaders 'great'. You do not need to know a great deal about the content of each of Collins' publications as the titles alone more than sufficiently illustrate the point that I am looking to make:

1992 *Beyond Entrepreneurship: Turning Your Business into an Enduring Great Company*
1994 *Built to Last: Successful Habits of Visionary Companies*
2001 *Good to Great: Why Some Companies Make the Leap and Others Don't*

It is worth noting the wording on the dust jacket of *Good to Great* because it ably demonstrates the pervasiveness of this way of thinking on academic and popular management thought:

> Jim Collins is the co-author of *Built to Last: Successful Habits of Visionary Companies*, a fixture on the *Business Week* bestseller list for more than five years with nearly 1,000,000 copies sold worldwide. A recipient of the Distinguished Teaching Award at the Stanford School of Business, Jim jettisoned a traditional academic career in 1995 and now works from his management laboratory in Boulder, Colorado. A student of enduring great companies, Jim has been and continues to be a teacher of executives in the private, public and social sectors.

2006 *Good to Great and the Social Sectors*

Then, following the credit crunch and the banking crisis of 2008, and several articles pointing out that many of Jim's 'great companies' had ceased trading, Collins publishes:

2009 *How the Mighty Fall: And Why Some Companies Never Give In*

And most recently:

2011 *Great by Choice: Uncertainty, Chaos and Luck – Why Some Thrive Despite Them All*

If ever there was a set of book titles that tell their own tale, this is it. Collins cannot ignore the fact that many of the companies that he categorised as 'great' subsequently ceased to trade. Nor can he ignore the fact that the characteristics which he identified as guaranteeing long-term corporate success have, for many of the organisations involved in the research, patently failed to achieve this. Consequently, in *Great by Choice* the authors acknowledge the uncertainties and complexities of organisational life. However, they cannot let go of the illusion of control, and this is aptly illustrated by the advice that they give in the opening lines of Chapter 1 on how to navigate uncertainty and chaos:

> WE CANNOT PREDICT the future. But we can create it.

In contrast, this book explores what it means to take seriously a social understanding of leadership and a complexity approach to leadership and organisation development. This involves living with the uncertainty and doubt of not knowing a little longer, examining the underlying thinking and assumptions that inform one's sense-making, engaging with perspectives that are not found in the mainstream, and comparing and contrasting these theories and ideologies with one's lived experience – a process that I describe as *reflexive curiosity*, a way of thinking/working that I explore in detail in Chapter 3 and hope to model throughout.

Why me?

> There are no "barriers to entry" into the leadership industry; no credentials, rigorous research, knowledge of the relevant scientific evidence, or anything else required to pass oneself off as a leadership expert. Anyone and everyone can write a book, be a leadership speaker or a blogger, offer consulting and advice, or start a leadership-development or consulting firm. And there are days when it seems that virtually everyone does.
>
> *Jeffrey Pfeffer (2015)*

In the following chapters, I will be drawing on my experience of working with mainstream and critical thought and taking a complexity approach to leadership development from my perspective as (i) a lecturer in a business school; (ii) an internal and external leadership development consultant in public, private, and charitable sector organisations; and (iii) a participant-manager. This last role is important because it means that I have experienced all of the ways of thinking, the learning methodologies, and the tools and techniques discussed here from both sides of the flip chart, that is, as trainer/facilitator/consultant, and as a student/practising manager. This first-hand student perspective is often overlooked by, or is simply not available to, most authors in this field and I think it provides me with a somewhat unique view. Ultimately, of course, you will judge whether this is the case.

My working life spans thirty years. I spent the first ten years in various management roles and for the best part of the last two decades I have been a leadership and organisational development specialist working with managers and management teams across private, charitable and public sector organisations in the UK and overseas.

As a young first-time manager trying to make sense of my new role, I completed a Post-graduate Certificate in Management Studies, before going on to complete the Diploma. Later, during my early career in management development, I completed an MSc in Managerial Psychology. I spent the first half of my career trying to match my practice, as a leader-manager and more latterly as a leadership/management developer, with the conventional discourse on how things ought to be. Sometimes events conspired to convince me that I had somehow managed to do this, but more often than not they, and I, fell woefully short. Thankfully, before my growing disillusionment with the recipes, prescriptions and latest fads contained in the dominant academic and popular management discourse peaked, I stumbled[4] upon a perspective that helped me to make a better (and more reality congruent) sense of what I was being asked to do as a manager and as a leader of leadership and organisational development interventions – the perspective of complex responsive processes of relating (Stacey, 2001; Stacey *et al.*, 2000; Shaw, 2002; Mowles, 2011; Stacey and Mowles, 2016). This is the perspective that informs the *complexity approach* of this book's title.

In 2008 I enrolled on the programme that takes this perspective seriously, the Doctorate in Management (DMan) at the University of Hertfordshire (UH), and was lucky enough to have Professor Chris Mowles (the director of the DMan programme) as my principal supervisor and Professor Ralph Stacey (who developed the perspective along with Doug Griffin and Patricia Shaw) as my second supervisor. The DMan draws on group analytic thinking (Foulkes, 1984) and in order to gain some understanding of this, I spent a year as a participant in an Experiential Group (2009) at the Institute of Group Analysis (IGA) in London. More recently I completed the National Foundation Course in Group Analysis (2014), was part of the inaugural cohort on the Diploma in Reflective Practice in Organisations (2016), and by the time that this book is published I will have commenced two further years of study on the inaugural Creating Large Group Dialogue in Organisations and Society programme.

I am currently Head of Leadership and Organisational Development at UH, a member of Faculty on the Hertfordshire Business School MBA Programme, an Associate with the Leadership Foundation for Higher Education, Director of my own, one-man management consultancy business and, along with my good friend Sally Graham, I am co-founder of Connect to Lead, a not-for-profit organisation that supports people to lead, whatever their position in the local community. In sharing all of this, I am not looking to impress, but rather to illustrate that my challenge to the dominant discourse on leadership and organisation is based on many years of involvement and immersion in it, both as a practitioner and researcher. Consequently, my critique of mainstream conceptions of leadership and leadership development is not merely an intellectual exercise, it stems from the practical failure of mainstream thinking to explain my lived experience. Similarly, I hope to show that my engagement with the perspective of complex responsive processes and more latterly group analytic thinking has been anything but superficial. Thus, my advocacy of a complexity approach to leadership and organisation is based on ten years of research, engagement and practice.

So, in answer to the question 'why me?', I would say that after a decade of working from the perspective of complex responsive processes of relating, I am able to offer a radically different perspective on leadership development than that found in the mainstream. The complexity approach to leadership development that I explore here is a direct challenge to those programmes and perspectives that purport to take complexity seriously, but in my opinion abjectly fail to do so (Flinn and Mowles, 2014).

Some caveats

> I'm suspicious of all those people who say, "I've got this great unifying philosophy of life and this is what it is all about"… I think they just make up that shit to sound good. I don't really have any philosophy. Life is just something that you muddle through using whatever tools come to hand at the time.
>
> *Irving Welsh (2016)*

Caveat 1. I am not looking to convince you that the complexity approach that I describe here is the right approach for you. That is, there's no hope or misapprehension on my part that reading this book will provoke in you some form of conversion to my way of thinking. Dennis Smith argues that the 'game of intellectual exploration is most productive when the personal honour of the players is not tied to the particular model of reality they bring to the game' (2001: viii). He recommends that we 'should all be prepared to revise any aspect of our thinking at any time' and this 'means keeping our minds receptive and the "game" open' (ibid.). For Smith:

> Writers are most interesting when they are in 'search mode,' when they are becoming gripped by a strong sense of what matters in the world or how the world 'is', but have not resolved matters to their own satisfaction or become the agents for a formula.
>
> *(Ibid.: ix)*

I am not the 'agent for a formula', I remain in 'search mode' and I would ask you to adopt this mode too.

Caveat 2. I am under no illusions that my practice is in any way an exemplar for leadership development in general, nor indeed for a complexity approach to leadership development in particular. I am not offering the ways of working described here as some form of 'how to' guide, nor am I suggesting that you should adopt any aspect of my way of working as your own. What I find myself doing with the people with whom I work, in the contexts in which I operate, is not something that you can take and apply to the contexts in which you work with the people with whom you find yourself interacting. Consequently, I am not inviting you to adopt my praxis, but rather to examine, question and make sense of your own.

In the introduction to her book about rewriting the rules of relationships, the sociologist, Meg Barker (2013) argues that when we become aware of the limitations of the existing rules, we often rush to replace them with new ones. However, she suggests an alternative that does not involve 'either grabbing onto existing rules or desperately seeking new ones [and] this involves staying in the uncertainty of not having clear rules and finding a way to go on which doesn't require grabbing hold of anything' (ibid.: 4). I am not offering any recipes – there aren't any. You will have to find your own way, and this can only be done in relation to those you work with – your fellow practitioners, colleagues, students and collaborators on leadership development programmes. In short, I am suggesting that as leadership developers we have a responsibility to continually enhance and consciously draw on the capabilities that I am looking to support leader-managers to develop: namely, the capacities for sense-making, reflexivity and practical judgement (see Chapter 3).

So, in the chapters that follow, you will find no 'best practice'. Instead, there is incitement to challenge conventional thinking/practice, and this is a stimulus that I hope will act as a catalyst for a review of your own praxis. However, should you also discover something that is generalisable to your own thinking/practice as a manager, student, teacher, developer (or any combination thereof), then that's a bonus that I will be happy to have contributed to.

Caveat 3. There are no short cuts. Developing oneself as a leader, and as a leader of leadership development, takes time. This does not mean that one has to enrol on a three-year doctoral programme like the DMan, or complete three years of training in group analytic ways of working, but it does entail engaging in more than one or two workshops and the occasional conference. For example, as part of the work I do with leader-managers, I lead a programme that is spread over a year, with participants having the option of continuing for a further one or two years. Of course, I still find myself responding to requests from colleagues and clients for 'bite-sized' and 'one-off' leadership development events. And I am not saying that it is impossible to do something useful in these spaces, but one has to be realistic about what can be achieved during such short engagements.

Caveat 4. I have to accept that I cannot cover everything in this book. The thoughts shared here are based on my research, reading and experience. I have not, and of course could not, read every single book, article, blog and tweet that might be of some relevance to the themes and methods under discussion here. Indeed, having a chapter (or part thereof) to cover topics and techniques to which others have dedicated whole books (research careers!), means that I have not even been able to include all that I have to offer, let alone cover all that is currently available. Consequently, I have chosen to focus on the thinking that has influenced and continues to influence my practice, and the practice that has influenced and continues to influence my thinking. Any omissions are mine and mine alone, but I do hope to (i) do justice to the thinkers and thinking that I draw on here, and (ii) provide you with sufficient and sufficiently different provocation to stimulate your reflexive curiosity.

Who might find this book useful?

> Business schools should – with urgency – adopt approaches to leadership education that are more critical, relational and reflective.
>
> *Dennis Tourish (2013)*

This book is aimed at leadership and organisational development specialists, students, researchers and practicing managers whose experience of, and aspirations for, working life are not congruent with the accounts that can be found in mainstream academic and popular management literature.

It does indeed explore how we might go about incorporating the more critical, relational and reflective approaches to leadership development that Tourish calls for above, but for me this focus is far too narrow. In numerical terms, business schools play only a minor role in the education of managers. Most managers do not have the time or inclination to enrol on lengthy academic programmes, nor the financial wherewithal to attend the burgeoning number of executive programmes that business schools now offer as an alternative. The majority of managers who engage with any kind of formal learning access their leadership development via in-house training and development events, led not by business school academics, but by internal and external consultants working as, or procured by, staff in human resources departments. A minority of managers, usually those in more senior positions, additionally get to attend open programmes and events, run by specialist leadership development providers. And a select few, usually very senior or self-funding managers, will get to experience some combination of all three – business school, in-house, and specialist external provision.

Consequently, this book challenges not only business schools, but all those involved in leadership development – business school lecturers/researchers, leadership development/organisational development specialists, coaches, and participant-managers – to re-examine their praxis. This does not mean abandoning traditional development practices and ways of thinking out of hand, but rather paying attention to those elements of conventional thinking and practice that are helpful and being prepared to let go of those that are not. As a catalyst for this, I take a broadly critical look at a selection of the common tools, techniques and methods of leadership development that business schools, organisations and consultancies have been working with for many years, with a view to drawing attention to what is useful in helping managers to develop their capacities for sense-making, reflexivity and practical judgement (Chapter 3).

I say *broadly critical*[5] to differentiate the complexity approach that informs my practice from the critical (management studies) perspective taken by scholars like Tourish, quoted above. Tourish, for example, is critical of transformational leadership as it cedes more power to the few without considering the damage caused by 'megalomaniac leaders who have become convinced that powerful, visionary leadership is helpful, healthy and wise' (2013: 7), whereas I am critical of transformational leadership as it bears little resemblance to my lived experience. Unlike

Tourish, I am not looking to prevent the excesses of the megalomaniacal few – they will always emerge – rather I am looking to encourage the *moderate many* to engage in a more reality congruent exploration of organising, leading and leadership development. For leaders, this entails paying attention to what we find ourselves actually doing and how things are, rather than worrying about what we think we ought to be doing and how we would like things to be. And for leaders of leadership development, it means supporting participants to enhance their capacities for sense-making, reflexivity and practical judgement rather than promoting abstract ideas and ideals of leadership and organisation that bear little relation to our quotidian experience.

If there is an emancipatory intent on my part, then it is to free us from the fantasy of the heroic leader who single-handedly controls corporate futures. I contend that this would not only benefit the majority of leaders, the people they manage and the communities they serve, but it would also encourage the exploration of different perspectives, thus breaking the hegemony of the orthodox and reducing the potential for leadership development programmes (intentionally or otherwise) to continue to be little more than what Schein (1961) describes as a form of 'coercive persuasion', or more colourfully, as brain-washing (see Chapter 3). This involves reappraising the thinking, methods, tools and techniques that are integral to our practice with a view to ensuring that the process of sense-making before, during and after such interventions is congruent with our experience and the day-to-day realities of the participants and/or the people with whom we work (see Chapter 6).

To do this, we need to take our experience seriously, a process that I demonstrate throughout this book by drawing on reflective narratives from my own practice and those of others who have been taking a complexity approach to their work in Germany, Denmark, North America and the UK. There is nothing intrinsically wrong with the tools, techniques and methods explored in the following chapters (although there are some notable exceptions), but I do argue that how practical they are in helping managers to go about their day-to-day activities, in a way that is useful both to them and to those around them, depends on the approach, focus of attention and quality of the attendant and ongoing sense-making. This involves staying with the experience as far as possible and avoiding the false certainty offered by abstract and instrumental models and frameworks (see Chapter 3).

The tools and techniques that I have chosen to explore are:

- coaching, psychometrics and 360° feedback;
- forum theatre;
- experiential exercises;
- Action Learning Sets.

How to make the most of this book

If your predilection is to dip in and out of books, to quickly find the topic you are interested in and disregard the rest, then you might be pleased to know that Chapters 4, 5, 6 and 7 can be read independently and non-sequentially. However, I would also recommend that at some point you take the time to read Chapters 1, 2 and 3, as they provide an in depth insight into the complexity approach that informs the practice/ways of working explored in the(se) later chapters.

In Chapter 1, I explore the history of management and management education as a means of understanding how we have come to think about leadership and leadership development, organisation and organisation development. I set out why writing this book is so important to me, and why reading it will (hopefully) be important to you.

In Chapter 2, I compare my current sense-making of leadership with some recent developments in management/leadership research, establish a working definition for the specific form of leadership that I explore in this book and share how this influences the way in which we might usefully approach leadership development.

In Chapter 3, I establish a working definition for organisation as complex responsive processes of relating, the implications of this for leadership and organisation development, explore what sense-making, reflexivity and practical judgement look like in practice and share how these capabilities might help leaders of leadership development to avoid their programmes and interventions from becoming little more than a form of coercive persuasion (Schein, 1961).

The succeeding chapters generally start with a reflective narrative from my experience: that is, a reflection on an incident that provided me with some insight into the difference between how I am working with the leadership development technique, intervention, perspective under review and how it is more usually taken up in mainstream thinking/practice. And then following a brief, but often overlooked, exploration of the history/origins of the technique, intervention, perspective under review, I compare and contrast the complexity approach that I am taking with how it is more usually taken up on conventional programmes, illustrated with examples from my current practice and/or a vignette from a colleague/ friend who is also taking a complexity approach in their work.

In Chapter 4, I explore coaching and the use of psychometrics in leadership development. I make the case for more discursive (Stacey, 2012) and relational (de Haan, 2011) forms of coaching/mentoring, in contrast to the instrumental and solutions-focused approaches found on most conventional leadership development programmes. I also compare and contrast the traditional use of psychometrics and 360°/multi-rater feedback in coaching conversations with the complexity approach. On conventional programmes, psychometrics/360° feedback tools are used to develop self-awareness, or an understanding of people based on 'individual-centred psychologies' (Stacey and Mowles, 2016: 47). The complexity approach understands people to be 'fundamentally interdependent' (ibid.); if psychometrics/ 360° feedback tools are used at all, it is with a view to developing an awareness of self in relationship to others. I also compare and contrast conventional and complexity approaches to power and the shadow side of leadership and organisation.

In Chapter 5, I turn my attention to the use of drama, actors, improvisation and forum theatre (Boal, 1979) on leadership development programmes. I also compare and contrast conventional understandings of communication, conflict and creativity with a view from the perspective of complex responsive processes of relating.

In Chapter 6, I take a look at experiential exercises; including simulations and (live) case studies. I suggest that there are some salient lessons to be learned from these experiences, but they are often not those claimed by the organisations and consultancies promoting such activities; ranging from ropes courses to voyages at sea. The lessons that are often ignored in such interventions are the opportunities to hone the capacities for sense-making, reflexivity and practical judgement. I also look at how one might deepen the learning from such activities through the writing of reflective narrative accounts of experience.

In Chapter 7, I explore the Action Learning (Set) process (Revans, 1980). I contend that there are more similarities than differences between Revans' original philosophy and a complexity approach to group work, particularly when compared to Critical Action Learning (Brook *et al.*, 2015). I also explore how group analytic ways of thinking/working can be useful for understanding group dynamics and explore the parallels between managing and the group analytic concept of dynamic administration.

In Chapter 8, I reflect upon what writing this book has meant to me and I identify what is generalisable for others from what has gone before. I offer rules of thumb, rather than recipes, for what it means for us (as managers, students and practitioners) to take a complexity approach to leadership (development) and to enhance our capacities for sense-making, reflexivity and practical judgement.

So, read on. Keep an open mind, remain in 'search mode' and remember the caveats outlined above. Compare and contrast what you find on the following pages with your own day-to-day experience(s) and if you find something that resonates and you would like to take the conversation further, then please get in touch with me. I would love to hear what sense you are making of what you find here.

Kevin Flinn, St Albans, July 2017

Notes

1 For instance, 99 per cent of businesses in the UK are small and medium-sized enterprises (Ward and Rhodes, 2014).
2 Systems dynamics, for example, takes a non-linear view of complex systems (see Chapter 3).
3 I highlight Collins (*et al.*) because his publications span the best part of the two decades in which the many business scandals and crises experienced by Western economies seemingly forced some mainstream authors to reappraise their thinking and because the title of the 2011 book, written with Hansen, implies that he/they takes uncertainty/complexity seriously.
4 When I took the job as Head of Leadership and Organisational Development at UH, in 2007, I had no knowledge of Ralph Stacey or the perspective of complex responsive

processes of relating. It was a chance meeting with Ralph (see Flinn, 2011) that led to this discovery, hence my use of the term 'stumbled'.

5 For a more comprehensive definition of 'broadly critical', see Flinn and Mowles (2014).

References

Alvesson, M., Blom, M. and Sveningsson, S. (2017) *Reflexive Leadership: Organising in an Imperfect World*. London: Sage.

Barker, M. (2013) *Rewriting the Rules: An Integrative Guide to Love, Sex and Relationships*. Hove: Routledge.

Boal, A. (1979) *Theatre of the Oppressed*. London: Pluto Press.

Brook, C., Pedler, M., Abbott, C. and Burgoyne, J. (2016) 'On stopping doing those things that are not getting us to where we want to be: Unlearning, wicked problems and critical action learning'. *Human Relations*, 69(2): 369–389.

Collins, J. C. (2001) *Good to Great: Why Some Companies Make the Leap… and Others Don't*. London: Random House.

Collins, J. C. (2009) *How the Mighty Fall: And Why Some Companies Never Give In*. London: Random House.

Collins, J. C. and Collins, J. (2006) *Good to Great and the Social Sectors*. London: Random House.

Collins, J. C. and Hansen, M. T. (2011) *Great by Choice: Uncertainty, Chaos and Luck – Why Some Thrive Despite Them All*. London: Random House.

Collins, J. C. and Lazier, W. C. (1992) *Beyond Entrepreneurship: Turning Your Business into an Enduring Great Company*. Upper Saddle River, NJ: Prentice Hall Direct.

Collins, J. C. and Porras, J. I. (1994) *Built to Last: Successful Habits of Visionary Companies*. London: Random House.

Czarniawska, B. (2014) *A Theory of Organizing* (2nd edn). Cheltenham: Edward Elgar Publishing.

de Haan, E. (2005) 'A new vintage: Old wine maturing in new bottles (coaching)'. *Training Journal*, 20(3): 20–24.

de Haan, E. (2011) *Relational Coaching: Journeys towards Mastering One-to-One Learning*. Oxford: John Wiley & Sons.

Flinn, K. P. (2011) *Making Sense of Leadership Development: Reflections on My Role as a Leader of Leadership Development Interventions*. Unpublished thesis.

Flinn, K. and Mowles, C. (2014) *A Complexity Approach to Leadership Development: Developing Practical Judgement*. Leadership Foundation for Higher Education stimulus paper.

Foulkes, S. H. (1984) *Therapeutic Group Analysis*. London: Karnac Books.

Griffin, D. (2002) T*he Emergence of Leadership: Linking Self-organisation and Ethics*. London: Routledge.

Kellerman, B. (2012) *The End of Leadership*. New York: Harper Collins.

Mowles, C. (2011) *Rethinking Management: Radical Insights from the Complexity Sciences*. London: Gower.

Pfeffer, J. (2015) *Leadership BS: Fixing Workplaces and Careers One Truth at a Time*. New York: Harper Collins.

Revans, R. (1980) *Action Learning: New Techniques for Managers*. London: Blond and Briggs.

Schein, E. H. (1961) *Coercive Persuasion*. New York: Norton.

Shaw, P. (2002) *Changing Conversations in Organizations: A Complexity Approach to Change*. London: Routledge.

Smith, D. (2001) *Norbert Elias and Modern Social Theory*. London: Sage.

Stacey, R. D. (2001) *Complex Responsive Processes in Organizations: Learning and Knowledge Creation*. Abingdon: Routledge.

Stacey, R. D. (2012) *Tools and Techniques of Leadership and Management: Meeting the Challenge of Complexity*. London: Routledge.

Stacey, R. D. and Mowles, C. (2016) *Strategic Management and Organisational Dynamics: The Challenge of Complexity to Ways of Thinking about Organisations* (7th edn). Harlow: Pearson.

Stacey, R. D., Griffin, D. and Shaw, P. (2000) *Complexity and Management: Fad or Radical Challenge to Systems Thinking?* Abingdon: Routledge.

Tourish, D. (2013) *The Dark Side of Transformational Leadership: A Critical Perspective*. Hove: Routledge.

Ward, M. and Rhodes, C. (2014) *Small Businesses and the UK Economy*. Parliamentary Briefing Paper.

Welsh, I. (2016) 'What I have learned', *Esquire* (April). Available at: www.esquire.co.uk/culture/books/news/a9742/irvine-welsh-what-ive-learned/

Wilson, S., Jackson, B. and Proctor-Thomson, S. (2018) *Revitalising Leadership: Putting Theory and Practice into Context*. Abingdon: Routledge.

1

LEADERSHIP, MANAGEMENT AND ENTREPRENEURSHIP

Leadership, management and entrepreneurship

> I don't believe just 'cos ideas are tenacious it means they're worthy.
>
> *Tim Minchin (2009)*

It would seem to be standard practice, in Chapter 1 of leadership development books, for the author to outline his or her current understanding of leadership and leadership development, as well as offering some thoughts on organising and organisations – the contexts in which leadership and leadership development emerge and are played out. Here, however, you will have to wait until Chapter 2 because at this point I feel that it is more important to explore the historical roots of how we have come to think about these phenomena. In this chapter, then, I trace the social and political development of the dominant discourse on organising/organisations, leadership/management, and leadership/management education. My flouting of convention is not a ruse to signal that this is not a standard book on leadership development; rather, and more importantly, it is an invitation to stop and consider how dominant ways of thinking and acting have become taken for granted across all sectors. I unquestioningly advocated this selfsame praxis during my early career as a manager, and throughout my first decade as a management developer. It is a view of the world that I have come to seriously question and challenge – hence the writing of this book.

As outlined in the Introduction (see Caveat 4), entire books (research careers) have been dedicated to some of the themes to which I am only able to allocate a chapter (or part thereof) to here. Consequently, in this and the chapters to follow, I will focus on thinking and research that has helped me to better understand what I find myself doing as a leader of leadership development interventions. I privilege perspectives that inform my sense-making, and are congruent with my day-to-day reality and the lived experience(s) of the participants with whom I work. In my experience such perspectives are afforded little, if any, consideration in mainstream literature and in conventional leadership development programmes.

Over the last forty years, across the UK and many other Western economies, 'managerialist conceptions of leadership, leadership development, and organisation have come to dominate thinking, education and organisational practice' (Flinn and Mowles, 2014: 4). Managerialism is based on the belief that all aspects of organisational life can and should be controlled according to rational plans, procedures, structures and systems of monitoring, designed to achieve the objectives set by a CEO, or equivalent, and/or a small group of executive leaders who, it is deemed, bring something special to the table that 'ordinary' managers can't. This perspective 'has become a naturalised part of the organisational *habitus*[1] across the private, public, mutual and charitable sectors' (ibid.: 4, emphasis in the original). Habitus (Bourdieu, 1990; Elias, 1991) is a descriptor for the ways of thinking and working which we unwittingly replicate whether we find them useful or not, hardly stopping to acknowledge, let alone reflect upon, alternative approaches.

In ignoring the historical development of how we have come to think in this way, mainstream discourse covers over and perpetuates the illusion that conventional/managerialist notions of leadership, leadership development and organisation are universally accepted ideas, rather than contested and contestable ideologies, albeit incredibly tenacious ones. And, to paraphrase the quotation from singer/comedian/composer Tim Minchin that opens this chapter, taken from his excellent song, 'White Wine in the Sun' (ibid. 2009), tenacity is no guarantee of worthiness.

Where did all the managers go?

> For many writers and practitioners management has been superseded by leadership. Management is deemed to have failed and leadership is seen to hold out the pledge of helping achieve that success which management had earlier promised ... Management is now to leadership what administration used to be to management – a necessary but not sufficient function in the achievement of organizational success.
>
> *Jackie Ford and Nancy Harding (2011)*

When I took on my first training role almost two decades ago, the process of working with managers to develop their practice was known as management development. Over the years, management development has been superseded by leadership development. During this period I have worked in and with organisations in the mutual, private, charitable, and more latterly, public sectors in the UK and abroad, and I would say that two of the most noticeable differences between what was initially termed management development and what is now called leadership development are (i) the replacement of the word 'management' with 'leadership' in the programme titles, materials and marketing paraphernalia that promotes these activities; and (ii) the dramatic increase in the number of managers voluntarily attending such programmes.

In the dominant discourse, the leadership/management debate explores whether leadership and management are distinctive and separate activities. There is no questioning whether leaders/managers are best placed to run organisations in the first place: this is taken as given. Similarly, in mainstream and popular management literature, it is generally taken for granted that the purpose of organisations is to maximise profits, and that the optimum way to achieve this is through efficiency and standardisation – the twin pillars of managerialism (Shenhav, 1999[2]). However, when we take a look at the history of management and management education we see that there was nothing inevitable about (i) management's replacement of owner-entrepreneurs at the top of the organisational hierarchy (Khurana, 2007[3]); (ii) the seemingly universal acceptance of managerialist ways of working that have spread throughout Western, and some Eastern, economies since the end of the Second World War (Shenhav, 1999); or (iii) the setting apart of leadership as something distinct and superior to management (Zaleznik, 1977), which I contend is a rhetorical device to, amongst other things, justify the incredible asymmetry in pay and conditions between senior managers and the rest.

For managers enrolling on the programmes that I run, it is usually the very first time that they have explored how we have come to think about leadership and organisation, and acknowledge that it is just that – a way of thinking. For most participants, hierarchical structures and the vast asymmetry in influence (power) and remuneration between (senior) managers and the rest is just 'how things are' and, for some, 'how they should be'. In the remainder of this chapter, drawing on the thinking of Shenhav (1999); Djelic (1998); Harvey, (2005); Khurana (2007); Crouch, (2011); and Thomas et al. (2013), I draw attention to the fact that managers are a relatively modern organisational phenomenon and that their ascendancy to the top of the organisational hierarchy, the subsequent consolidation of this position, and the acceptance of the ever-widening gulf in pay between senior managers and the rest, was anything but inevitable. Moreover, the view, developed in business schools and elsewhere, of organisations as machine-like systems that can be manipulated at will by a small cadre of exceptional individuals who have something special that the rest of humanity do not have access to, is something that the complexity approach to leadership/leadership development that I explore in this book fundamentally refutes.

Where did managers come from in the first place?

As large-scale corporations expanded in late nineteenth-century America, and owner-entrepreneurs found it more and more difficult to manage the complex organisations that they had founded, a new group of employees started to emerge who not only challenged the foremen and supervisors for supremacy on the shop-floor, but also challenged the owner-entrepreneurs for control of the business itself

(Shenhav, 1999). To sustain this challenge, this new class of employees, called managers, embarked on a legitimisation project that looked to establish management as both a profession and a science, akin to medicine or law, and they were supported in this by the newly formed business schools (Khurana, 2007: 3). At the turn of the nineteenth century, this legitimisation project was bolstered during violent bouts of labour unrest in the US manufacturing industry. In contrast to the warring business owners and workers, the managers (mainly mechanical engineers) were able to present themselves as rational, neutral arbitrators working for the common good, and to promote their accumulated knowledge (based on mechanical engineering principles) as a rational, politically neutral 'science' of management (ideology) that would help business to maximise profitability through efficiency and the standardisation of organisational processes (systems) for the benefit of society (Shenhav, 1999).

Rising criticism of the legitimacy of such claims in the first half of the twentieth century – a typical example of which being the media backlash following the Stock Market Crash of 1929 – and political contestation over the ownership of the means of production were put aside as large-scale manufacturing's contribution to the war effort took precedence. Khurana argues that the Second World War 'generally softened Americans' historically suspicious attitudes towards large organisations and their management' (2007: 200). He continues:

> Americans were increasingly enchanted by claims that the same technologies that had won the war could now be used to strengthen society. As a result, large organizations came to be seen not only as tools by which certain immediate objectives could be achieved but also as the means by which problems like "social" and "political tensions" could be rectified.
>
> *(Ibid.)*

However, Harvey argues that irrespective of big business's new-found respectability, 'one condition of the post-war settlement in almost all countries was that the economic power of the upper classes be restrained and that labour be accorded a much larger share of the economic pie' (2005: 15). A form of what Harvey terms 'embedded liberalism' emerged across the USA and Europe where 'market processes and entrepreneurial and corporate activities were surrounded by a web of social and political constraints' (ibid.: 11). An unintended consequence of one of the US government's 'constraints' on business was the rise of the conglomerate – a form of organisation that, through mergers and acquisitions, combined a range of 'unrelated' businesses under a single company umbrella (Khurana, 2007: 208). Conglomerates emerged partly as a means of bypassing government regulations prohibiting the use of 'vertical or horizontal mergers' that would make it possible for an organisation to dominate a single industry, and partly as a way of increasing earnings per share, the measure that had become the stock market's 'key indicator of a firm's prospects' (ibid.: 208).

Khurana argues that the rise of the conglomerate where 'a single executive was often responsible for ten or twelve different businesses [meant that] concrete, industry or firm-specific knowledge and skills were devalued [replaced by] the newer more abstract tools and techniques of rational management [that] offered an approach to success that operated without regard to industry distinctions' (2007: 209). Management began to be characterised as a set of technical skills and knowledge that had a universality and transferability to all industries and sectors across the USA, and this new view of management and management 'science' (still largely based on mechanical engineering principles) steadily came to dominate US business school curricula. In turn, the USA's increasing influence on the post-war global economy, meant that it was not long before this perspective was exported to the Western world, with European organisations and business schools adopting US working and business education practices (Thomas *et al.*, 2013), albeit modified to take account of what Djelic (1998) describes as 'national peculiarities'.

Recovery and growth were strong in post-war Western economies. Indeed, during the 1950s the British Prime Minister, Harold Macmillan, told his Tory Party Conference audience that 'most of our people have never had it so good'. By the end of the 1960s 'embedded liberalism began to break down, both internationally and domestically' (Harvey, 2005: 11), with unemployment and inflation surging, and growth falling. The economic downturn continued into the 1970s and company shareholders became jittery as share prices and dividends fell. The challenge that the management elite faced in this period was that they were charged with being stagnant, bureaucratic technocrats, who were not willing to make the tough decisions necessary to maintain profitability, and who had been churned out by business schools which were more interested in producing competent administrators rather than charismatic, visionary leaders (Khurana, 2007).

The subsequent search for a remedy resulted in economic commentators and neoliberal economists scapegoating bureaucratic management. Jensen and Meckling (1976) advocated the explicit introduction of the principles of agency theory, arguing that if self-interest is the best motivator, then the way to encourage executive managers to drive shareholder value is to link their remuneration to the share price. (Crouch argues that like 'many neoclassical economists, Jensen was perplexed by the rise of corporate social responsibility. [That is] the voluntary acceptance by firms of obligations to customers, workers and, in particular the wider community' (2011: 105)). Shareholders agree and respond accordingly, incentivising executive managers to drive the value of the share price and dividends upwards, by linking senior management remuneration and bonuses to these measures. Khurana identifies this shift as the point at which the professionalisation project initiated by the early business schools, the first being Wharton in 1881, is abandoned:

[T]he logic of professionalism that underlay the university-based business school in its formative phase was replaced first by a managerialist logic that emphasized professional knowledge rather than professional ideals, and ultimately by a market logic that, taken to its conclusion, subverts the logic of professionalism altogether.

(2007: 7)

Depending on your political persuasion, the economic crises of the 1970s called for either more state intervention or less. This entailed adoption of the interventionist economic principles of John Maynard Keynes or an abandonment of them and a move towards the 'free market principles of neo-classical economics', that is, the neoliberal economic ideas advocated by, among others, Friedrich von Hayek (ibid.: 20). Crouch argues that:

> Keynesianism's crisis led to its collapse rather than to adjustments being made to it, not because there was something fundamentally wrong with its ideas, but because the classes in whose interests it primarily operated, the manual workers of western industrial society, were in historical decline and losing their social power. In contrast, the forces that gain most from neoliberalism – global corporations, particularly in the financial sector – maintain their importance more or less unchallenged.

(2011: 1)

In 1977, Zaleznik, in what is considered to be a seminal article, draws a distinction between managers and leaders. He argues that leaders bring inspiration, vision and human passion, which in turn drives corporate success, while managers organise to make these things happen. Business schools, stung by criticisms that they contributed to the decline in economic fortunes, began to echo this split, using it as part justification for the diverging fortunes of senior managers and the rest. During the 1980s business schools repackaged their offerings and started to court leaders rather than managers. They turned their attention to developing leaders,[4] rather than managers or administrators, thus consolidating the distinction between managers and leaders and providing some credibility/justification for the burgeoning gulf in salary differentials that developed between CEOs/senior managers, middle managers and employees. Between 1970 and 2000 the pay differentials between senior management and the lowest-paid staff in US organisations increased from 20x to almost 400x (Mishel and Davis, 2014). Leaders began to be portrayed as special individuals who could and did single-handedly shape and control corporate futures.

Consultants and corporate trainers followed the business school lead, replacing management development with leadership development and promising to develop the 'new' leadership capabilities that managers were deemed to be lacking. Plans became strategies, aspirations became visions, purpose became mission, and norms became values and cultures. Interestingly, as Stacey points out, although it is 'very highly paid executives at the top of any organization who are the ones really charged with the vision for the organization and the ones really supposed to change the culture', they are seldom the ones who attend leadership development programmes and thus lay claim to the title of leader; instead, 'it is usually large numbers of middle managers who go on them' (2010: 20).

This echoes my experience, and I would also add that the senior executives that do find their way onto the leadership development programmes that I run are well versed in the rhetoric of vision, values and culture change. However, this is not what they find challenging on a day-to-day basis. As mentioned in the introduction, the challenges that I invariably find senior executives wanting to explore are the same challenges faced by junior and middle managers; namely, how to rub along with the small circle of colleagues they most regularly interact with, while navigating their way through the day-to-day politics of organisational life. Consequently, this book is concerned with leadership development activities that can help participants to develop capabilities that will help them to do just that – activities that support the development of the capacities for sense-making, reflexivity and practical judgement (see Chapter 3).

Where have all of the entrepreneurs gone?

At the start of the project to legitimise and professionalise managers and management (Khurana, 2007), there were three identifiable sets of protagonists – managers, workers and owner-entrepreneurs. Before I bring this brief history of the social and political development of the dominant discourse on management, leadership and organisation up to the present day, I want to briefly consider what happened to the owner-entrepreneurs. Czarniawska-Joerges and Wolff (1991) describe three executive roles that occur in the 'theatre' of the organisation – managers, leaders and entrepreneurs. They argue that all three roles will always be part of the cast, but the decision over which of these three 'archetypes' will be called upon to take centre stage will depend on the 'fears and hopes of those who create organisations by their daily performance'. For Czarniawska and Wolff:

> Leadership is seen as symbolic performance, expressing the hope of control over destiny, management as the activity introducing order by coordinating flows of things and people towards collective action, and entrepreneurship as the making of entire new worlds.
>
> *(Ibid.: 529)*

The inclusion by Czarniawska-Joerges and Wolff of this third archetype, the entrepreneur, in addition to that of leader and manager is interesting.[5] At the start of what Khurana describes as the professionalisation project, when managers first stake their claim to be recognised as the people best placed to run organisations, the other key claimants were the owner-entrepreneurs and the workers themselves. As outlined above, during violent bouts of labour unrest in the US manufacturing industry, towards the end of the nineteenth century, managers presented themselves as rational, neutral arbitrators working for the common good, in contrast to the owner-entrepreneurs and workers who they portrayed as groups acting out of

self-interest. In current mainstream accounts of leadership and leadership development, owner-entrepreneurs no longer figure prominently. It is not that they do
not exist, rather that there is little differentiation made between leaders who
establish and develop businesses and those that are parachuted in or promoted to a
leadership role having had little if any involvement in the setting up of the
enterprise.

I contend that the archetype of the entrepreneur has been conflated with that of
leader in mainstream literature. Although we still class business owners as entrepreneurs, it is not a term that we generally use to describe senior (executive)
managers. However, as outlined above, the differentiation between managers and
leaders that occurred in the 1970s and 1980s characterised managers as those who,
in Czarniawska-Joerges and Wolff's terms, introduce order, while leaders are not
only portrayed as the controllers of destiny, but also as the makers of new worlds.
This is a view of leadership that continued to pervade the dominant discourse in
the 1990s and early 2000s. And so to the near-present.

As outlined in the introduction, the endless stream of scandals, crises and catastrophes, not least among them the banking crisis of 2008, encouraged (shamed?)
some mainstream academic and popular management authors to question their
view of leadership and the approaches to leadership development that they have
been advocating (Kellerman, 2012; Pfeffer, 2015). Some even go so far as to accept
that leaders, however powerful they may appear, do not control corporate destinies.
The argument now proffered by these authors is that the command and control
approaches that were appropriate in the industrial age, are no longer fit for purpose
in the new complex, global, knowledge-based, technological era.

However, rather than letting go of individualistic views of leadership and the
illusory, cause and effect certainties of systems thinking, some mainstream authors
merely recast them in the language of shared/distributed/relational leadership and/
or uncertainty/complexity (see Chapter 2). As I argue in the introduction this is
not so much old wine in new bottles, but rather the original wine, in the original
bottles, with the addition of some new words on the labels. Multitudinous business
failures, closures, crises, scandals, bailouts, etc., seem to have done little to dispel
the mainstream myth. Take the title of Ashley Vance's 2015 New York Times
bestselling biography of PayPal founder, Elon Musk, for instance – *Elon Musk: How
the Billionaire CEO of SpaceX and Tesla Is Shaping Our Future*. So, why might these
tenacious ideas still be considered worthy?

Speaking on Kirsty Young's Radio 4 programme, *Desert Island Discs*, in 2013,
Daniel Kahneman relates this anecdote from his early career as a psychologist
attached to the Israeli Army:

KAHNEMAN: It was something we had inherited from the British Army, actually. It
was a way to assess candidates for officer training. And there was a field test
which involved taking a group of people and tell them to do something with a
telephone pole, like pass an obstacle with all sorts of constraints, while we the
psychologists on the side take notes. And what was very striking to me was

that you could actually see the personalities; you knew what their true nature was like. And then every month we would get feedback from the Officer Training School and they would tell us how well we were doing, whether we could predict who would be a good cadet and who would not. And the answer was always the same; we couldn't. We had no idea what they were going to do. But what was truly remarkable was, you know, this was the Army, so we would hear on Friday that our work is useless, but Sunday morning there would be a new batch of recruits, we'd take them to the obstacle course and the statistics had absolutely no effect in reducing our confidence in our ability to see the true nature of people. And I called it the illusion of validity. That is, we felt we were valid, although we knew we were not.

YOUNG: Can you give me examples of more situations where you could employ that phrase and say that's what's happening there?

KAHNEMAN: The illusion of validity is really everywhere, you can see something very similar to it in the financial world where you have people who really know in principle that you cannot do better than the market but who somehow feel that they can do better than the market. You know, they are not hypocrites, they are not lying to anyone, they truly feel that they can do something that they know cannot be done.

I contend that the tenacity of the myth of the heroic leader in mainstream discourse, in spite of all of the evidence to the contrary, is a prime example of the illusion of validity (Kahneman, 2011: 209). Several years ago I conducted a Leadership Experience Group (LEG) (Flinn and Mowles, 2014) for a six-strong group of senior managers during a period in which their organisation, like many in the sector at that time, had hit some financial difficulties, brought about by unforeseen and unforeseeable external circumstances. During the first LEG session held after the financial situation was made known, conversation turned to what the Executive Team should or shouldn't, could or couldn't have done to avoid the situation, and a member of the group commented, 'They don't seem to know what they are doing, up there'. The majority of the group, seasoned senior managers, were quite sanguine, with several commenting that the CEO and the 'top team' could not be expected to foresee the future: 'You couldn't expect them to know that this would happen', 'I don't know what I'm doing from one day to the next; so I don't expect them to either', 'They're just muddling through like the rest of us'. However, the comment about not knowing 'what they are doing' got one member of the group quite animated, and he responded that 'I need to believe that they do know what they are doing. Even though rationally I know that it is impossible for them to foresee the future, I need to believe that they can.'

The myth of the autonomous (heroic) leader persists because some senior executives are happy to keep up the pretence that things are more predictable than they actually are, as this helps to justify, to both themselves and the workforces they manage, the colossal asymmetries in pay and influence that they benefit from. And some workers accept this illusion as it relieves the uncertainty and anxiety that might otherwise be provoked by acknowledging that no one knows what the future holds. This delusion has a usefulness, something that Alvesson and Spicer (2016) refer to as 'functional stupidity'; which goes some way to explaining its tenacity.

What am I saying, and why is this important?

What I am saying

Drawing on the works of Shenhav (1999); Djelic (1998); Harvey, (2005); Khurana (2007); Crouch, (2011); and Thomas et al. (2013) I contend that there is nothing natural or inevitable about the current way we organise ourselves in work settings. Leadership, management and the ideology of managerialism are not givens, they are something that we co-create on a daily basis. The emergence of managers as those best placed to run organisations, and reap (what are now) very lucrative rewards, has its origins in the struggles between this emerging class of employees, owner-entrepreneurs and workers in nineteenth-century America. Managers sought legitimacy by promoting themselves as neutral administrators who were motivated to pursue organisational efficiency for the good of society rather than for their own self-interest (Shenhav, 1999). These claims are supported by the establishment of the first business schools in the 1880s, which looked to build the credibility of the new management 'class' by working to establish management as a science and managers as professional pillars of the community, akin to doctors or lawyers. The knowledge base for this new 'science' relies heavily on the scientific management (mechanical engineering) principles developed by Frederick W. Taylor (2011). These claims did not go uncontested at the time, but the critical contribution that large-scale manufacturing operations made during the First and, more crucially, the Second World War, sees such challenges marginalised.

The success of US manufacturing during the Second World War captures the attention of European nations that were hitherto dismissive of US management (Shenhav, 1999) and business school practices (Thomas et al., 2013). Post-war investment in US business schools by the Ford and Carnegie Foundations consolidates the development of management as a technical science, concentrating funding on research that is 'quantitative and statistically reliable' (Khurana, 2007: 220), and the corresponding textbooks and business school curricula developed in this period are slowly but surely adopted by French, German, and British institutions (Thomas et al., 2013). The 'ideological assumption that human and non-human entities are interchangeable and can be equally subjected to engineering manipulation' (Shenhav, 1999: 197) becomes part of the dominant discourse. Management is seen as a technical skill that is transferable, leading to the rise of the general manager and the spread of managerialism across organisations, industries, sectors and continents – a view that continues to be propagated in mainstream literature right up to the present day.

The economic crises of the 1970s and growing competition from Japan during the 1980s signal a backlash against technocratic and bureaucratic managers and a call for their replacement by visionary leaders. This differentiation is made manifest in the remuneration of executive leaders. From the 1980s onwards executive salaries increase astronomically and bonus payments include share options as an incentive to senior managers to drive profits and thus increase the value of shareholder holdings and dividends. Business schools, management consultancies and corporate training functions alike catch the leadership bug, and management development is replaced by leadership development even though the vast amount of attendees are junior and middle managers whose chances of influencing the operations of the businesses in which they work are marginal.

The many corporate scandals, crises and catastrophes that come to light during the late twentieth and early twenty-first centuries see commentators questioning the morality of the corporate leaders that only a few years previously were being lauded, and in some cases honoured, for their business acumen. Additionally, acceptance that the world (of work) has moved on sees some mainstream thinkers like Jim Collins (Collins and Hansen, 2011) calling for a new leadership for the new complex, global, knowledge-based, technological age. However, rather than taking complexity seriously, as I do in the pages that follow, mainstream authors talk of simplifying and/or managing complexity (Morieux and Tollman, 2014).

Why this is important

First, it is important because a review of the history of management and management education puts the leadership/management debate into the appropriate cultural and social context. Prior to the 1970s the terms 'manager' and 'leader' were used interchangeably to describe people who found themselves in charge of organisations. The economic downturn of the 1970s alarmed company shareholders, and the subsequent search for solutions saw economic commentators and neoclassical/neoliberal economists scapegoating bureaucratic management. Jensen and Meckling (1976) adduce agency theory to argue that self-interest is the best motivator; consequently, if one wants to encourage senior managers to drive shareholder value, then the best way to do this is to link their remuneration to the share price. Board members respond accordingly and refocus management on driving the value of the share price and dividends by linking senior management remuneration and bonuses to these measures.

Around the same time, Zaleznik (1977) draws a distinction between managers and leaders, and this distinction is cited as part-justification for the burgeoning gulf in salary differentials that developed between executives, middle managers and employees. Business schools, stung by criticism that they had contributed to the economic downturn by concentrating on developing bureaucratic managers rather than visionary leaders changed tack. Consultants and corporate trainers followed suit, replacing management development with leadership development and promising to develop the leadership capabilities that managers were deemed to be lacking. What were once referred to as plans are now called strategic plans; aspirations morphed into visions; raison d'être has been replaced by purpose/ mission; and patterns of activity are talked about as cultures, shaped by core values. Leaders, formerly managers, now assume the positions once occupied by the owner-entrepreneurs. Consequently, these nouveaux owner-entrepreneurs are allowed to tinker with organisations as if they were personal possessions and plunder them for huge rewards, even though they played no part in setting up or developing these businesses.

This way of thinking has become part of the (organisational) habitus, that is, a taken-for-granted way of thinking about leadership and organisation that goes uncontested in mainstream discourse, thus rendering opaque the intense political and ethical implications of the managerialist and neoliberal ideologies on which the dominant discourse is based. Conventional explanations of leadership and organisation thus (wittingly or unwittingly, consciously or unconsciously) cover over the shadow side of organisational life. Leadership and management are seen as neutral activities for the common good, and the often cruel and potentially destructive aspects of organisational life are glossed over or ignored.

Second, this is important because in mainstream discourse organisations have come to be seen as systems that are envisioned, designed and manipulated by powerful leaders who instrumentally apply the scientific management principles of standardisation and efficiency to bring about certain and predictable outcomes aimed at the maximisation of profits. Of course, organisations can be greatly influenced by powerful leaders, and standardisation and efficiency projects do contribute to profitability, but there is nothing inevitable, predictable or certain about such outcomes. For each business leader claiming such instrumental success, there is another who pursues these courses of action only to find that despite all their efforts, sales drop, profits decline, share prices fall and bankruptcy ensues.

Furthermore, the inadequacy of rational, linear, instrumental systems perspectives in accounting for our lived experience has witnessed a surge of interest in complexity perspectives. Notions like VUCA (Volatility, Uncertainty, Complexity and Ambiguity) (Lawrence, 2013) are now commonplace in the mainstream, and there is even a growing acceptance that many of the situations that we find ourselves in as managers are paradoxical (Bolden et al., 2016). However, although some mainstream thinkers now bandy about terms like uncertainty and complexity (Collins and Hansen., 2011) they offer nothing new. In contrast, the complexity perspective that I draw on, and corresponding complexity approach that I explore here, proffers a very different understanding of uncertainty, complexity, ambiguity and paradox and what this might mean, then, for our practice as leaders and leadership developers.

Third, this is important because it is useful to remind ourselves that the original professionalisation project that business schools initiated at the end of the nineteenth century acknowledged leadership-management as a social, relational and interdependent phenomenon where one size didn't fit all, and the development of character and notions of stewardship were at least as important as the pursuit of technical capabilities. However, as Shenhav (1999) argues, the early twentieth-century 'project of standardisation and systemization … blurred the distinction between the social and the technical' which in turn allowed managers and business schools to 'expand the province of mechanical engineering to additional terrains' (ibid.: 196–197). Over the last forty years managerialism has swept through the private, public and charitable sectors. In recent times the scandals and crises that have come to light have catalysed the call, at least in some quarters, for more accountable leadership, a return to the ideas and ideals of stewardship (Khurana, 2007), and an acknowledgement that leadership is a social, relational and interdependent phenomenon (Shenhav, 1999).

Czarniawska-Joerges and Wolff's (1991) characterisation of leadership as performance – something transient that emerges between the actor and the audience rather than something that exists outside of the theatre – is useful in this regard. Here, leadership is seen as a socially constructed phenomenon rather than a reified 'it'. Similarly, Czarniawska-Joerges and Wolff's understanding of organisation, that is, something that we create in 'daily performance' echoes the understanding proffered by the perspective of complex responsive processes of relating, which understands organisation as the patterning of day-to-day interactions (complex responsive processes) between people (of relating). This perspective has radical implications for our understanding of organisations and hence the role and influence of leader-managers. I introduce and explore this perspective further in Chapter 3.

And third, this is important because positioning mainstream thinking in the appropriate historical, cultural and social context illustrates the timeless importance of sense-making, reflexivity and practical judgment; the capacities that I am supporting leaders to develop and that I explore in more detail in Chapter 3 and throughout this book. Khurana argues that standardisation and the adoption of mechanical engineering principles attempted to ground business instruction in science rather than the 'experience, improvisation and "rules of thumb"' that were previously given credence (2007: 59). Managers all too often enrol on leadership development programmes looking for recipes, prescriptions, hints and tips for what they should be doing as leaders. In the chapters that follow, I proffer a radically different approach to leadership/management development; a way of working that encourages participants to i) take their everyday experience seriously, ii) notice and think about how they are thinking and iii) enhance their capacities for practical judgement, that is, their ability to improvise in the moment and work with rules of thumb rather than recipes, something that leader-managers seemingly used to value.

Notes

1 Norbert Elias (1991) describes habitus as our taken-for-granted tendencies to act in particular ways. This might otherwise be described as 'second nature'.
2 Yehouda Shenhav's book is entitled *Manufacturing Rationality: The Engineering Foundations of the Managerial Revolution* (1999). In it he explores the rise of managers and management, and more particularly the colonisation of management by engineers and of organisational processes by 'manufacturing rationality'. It is a compelling read, brought to life by his

deep dive into articles published in US engineering journals in the late nineteenth and early twentieth century.

3 Rakesh Khurana's book is entitled *From Higher Aims to Hired Hands: The Social Transformation of American Business Schools and the Unfulfilled Promise of Management as a Profession* (2007). In it he traces both the rise of the manager and the history and development of business schools from their inception in the 1880s up to the present day. Khurana's thesis is compelling, assiduously researched, and all the more credible given that he is a Harvard Business School professor. It is well worth a read.

4 The business school at which I work being no exception: the MBA module that I teach is called Leadership and Change, even though the majority of students are junior and middle managers, not the senior managers and CEOs that much of the mainstream leadership literature is aimed at.

5 Like Khurana (2007), Czarniawska-Joerges and Wolff take a historical perspective. However, they identify three archetypes – leader, manager and entrepreneur – rather than the two that Khurana explores – leader and manager. Czarniawska-Joerges and Wolff argue that in the 1920s the fashion was for entrepreneurs, the makers of new worlds; however, following the stock market crash of 1929, the need for hope led to leaders being in vogue, and following the political crisis of the Second World War, the coordination needed to get things moving in the peace witnessed the rise of managers. I suggest that in the leadership/management debate the roles of entrepreneur and leader have become conflated.

References

Alvesson M. (2013). *The Triumph of Emptiness*. Oxford: Oxford University Press.

Alvesson, M., Blom, M. and Sveningsson, S. (2017) *Reflexive Leadership: Organising in an Imperfect World*. London: Sage.

Alvesson, M. and Jonsson, A. (2016) 'The bumpy road to exercising leadership: Fragmentations in meaning and practice'. *Leadership*, 0(0): 1–18.

Alvesson, M. and Karreman, D. (2016) 'Intellectual failure and ideological success in leadership studies: The case of transformational leadership'. *Journal of Management Inquiry*, 25(2): 139–152.

Alvesson, M. and Spicer, A. (2016) *The Stupidity Paradox: The Power and Pitfalls of Functional Stupidity at Work*. London: Profile Books.

Bolden, R., Witzel, M. and Linacre, N. (2016) *Leadership Paradoxes: Rethinking Leadership for an Uncertain World*. New York: Routledge.

Bourdieu, P. (1990) *The Logic of Practice*. Cambridge: Polity Press.

Collins, J. and Hansen, M. T. (2011). *Great by Choice: Uncertainty, Chaos and Luck – Why Some Thrive Despite Them All*. London: Random House.

Crouch, C. (2011) *The Strange Non-death of Neo-liberalism*. Cambridge: Polity.

Czarniawska-Joerges, B. and Wolff, R., (1991) 'Leaders, managers, entrepreneurs on and off the organizational stage'. *Organization Studies*, 12(4): 529–546.

de Haan, E. (2014) *The Leadership Shadow: How to Recognise and Avoid Hubris, Derailment and Overdrive*. London: Kogan Page.

Djelic, M. L. (1998) *Exporting the American Model: The Post-war Transformation of European Business*. Oxford: Oxford University Press.

Elias, N. (1991) *The Society of Individuals*. Oxford: Blackwell.

Flinn, K. (2011) *Making Sense of Leadership Development: Reflections on my Role as a Leader of Leadership Development Interventions*. Unpublished thesis.

Flinn, K. and Mowles, C. (2014) *A Complexity Approach to Leadership Development: Developing Practical Judgement*. Leadership Foundation for Higher Education stimulus paper.

Ford, J. and Harding, N. (2011) 'The impossibility of the "true self" of authentic leadership'. *Leadership*, 7(4): 463–479.

Griffin, D. (2002) *The Emergence of Leadership: Linking Self-organisation and Ethics*. London: Routledge.

Harvey, D. (2005) *A Brief History of Neoliberalism*. Oxford: Oxford University Press.

Jensen, M. C. and Meckling, W. H. (1976) 'Theory of the firm: managerial behavior, agency costs and ownership structure'. *Journal of Financial Economics*, 3(4): 305–360.

Jones, C. B. (2011) *Behind the Dream: The Making of the Speech that Transformed a Nation*. New York: Palgrave Macmillan.

Kahneman, D. (2013) *Desert Island Discs*, BBC Radio 4. Available at www.bbc.co.uk/p rogrammes/b0381l2v

Kahneman, D. (2011). *Thinking, Fast and Slow*. London: Penguin.

Kellerman, B. (2012) *The End of Leadership*. New York: Harper Business.

Khurana, R. (2007) *From Higher Aims to Hired Hands*. Oxford: Princeton University Press.

Lawrence, K. (2013) 'Developing leaders in a VUCA environment'. *UNC Executive Development*: 1–15.

Learmonth, M. (2005) 'Doing things with words: The case of "management" and "administration". *Public Administration*. 83(3): 617–637.

Learmonth, M. and Morrell, K. (2016) 'Is critical leadership studies "critical"?' *Leadership*. 0(0): 1–15.

Mead, G. H. (1934) *Mind, Self and Society from the Standpoint of a Social Behaviourist*. Chicago, IL: University of Chicago Press.

Minchin, T. (2009) *White Wine in the Sun*.

Mishel, L. and Davis, A. (2014) 'CEO pay continues to rise as typical workers are paid less'. *Issue Brief*. 380.

Morieux, Y. and Tollman, P. (2014) *Six Simple Rules: How to Manage Complexity without Getting Complicated*. Boston, MA: Harvard Business Review Press.

Mowles, C. (2015) *Managing in Uncertainty: Complexity and the Paradoxes of Everyday Organizational Life*. Hove: Routledge.

Mowles, C. (2011) *Rethinking Management: Radical Insights from the Complexity Sciences*. London: Gower.

Pfeffer, J. (2015) *Leadership BS: Fixing Workplaces and Careers One Truth at a Time*. New York: HarperCollins.

Pfeffer, J. (2016) 'Why the assholes are winning: money trumps all'. *Journal of Management Studies*, 53(4): 663–669.

Schein, E. H. (1961) *Coercive Persuasion*. New York: Norton.

Shaw, P. (2002) *Changing Conversations in Organizations: A Complexity Approach to Change*, London: Routledge.

Shenhav, Y. (1999) *Manufacturing Rationality: The Engineering Foundations of the Managerial Revolution*. Oxford: Oxford University Press.

Stacey, R. (2010) *Complexity and Organizational Reality: Uncertainty and the Need to Rethink Management after the Collapse of Investment Capitalism*. London: Routledge.

Taylor, F. W. (1947) *Scientific Management*. London: Harper and Row.

Thomas, H., Lorange, P. and Jagdish, S. (2013) *The Business School in the Twenty-First Century: Emergent Challenges and New Business Models*. Cambridge: Cambridge University Press.

Vance, A. (2015) *Elon Musk: How the Billionaire CEO of SpaceX and Tesla Is Shaping Our Future*. London: Random House.

Zaleznik, A. (1977) 'Managers and leaders: Are they different?' *Harvard Business Review*, 70 (2): 126–135.

2

RETHINKING LEADERSHIP

Doubt and disillusionment

> In essence certainty is necessarily dogmatic, whereas doubt has an important ethical value ... certainty's 'I know' easily leads to blindness ... Doubt, on the other hand, leads to openness, to other ways of acting and new understandings of the world.
>
> *Brinkmann (2017)*

In this chapter, I make good my promise to share with you the sense that I am currently making of leadership and the implications that this has for my own practice in relation to leadership development. I say currently because my praxis has shifted dramatically in recent years, and it will no doubt develop further in the years to come. This is not a confession of indecisiveness or a lack of conviction on my part, it is an acknowledgment that my current way of thinking is no more than that, a way of thinking: a good enough truth for me, for now. My sense-making of leadership is an ongoing, emergent amalgamation of the lived experience and reflexive research that I have been, am being, and will be exposed to/engaged in over the course of my working lifetime. However, I would not want to downplay the anxiety-provoking and identity-threatening struggle that accompanied the seismic shift in thinking/practice that I experienced, a movement of thought cata-lysed by radical doubt and disillusionment with the mainstream perspectives, tools and techniques of leadership and organisation with which I had been working in my role as a developer of managers/leaders (Flinn, 2011).

My disillusionment with mainstream conceptions, models, frameworks and recipes for leadership and organisation stemmed from the fact that they neither reflected nor adequately explained my lived experience and that of the majority of managers with whom I worked as a management/leadership developer, coach and lecturer. In my search for a more useful and reality congruent understanding, I found a perspective – the complexity approach that I share in this book – that continues to have a profound influence on my praxis: an ongoing process of thinking/acting catalysed by doubt and sustained by reflexive curiosity. I highlight doubt and disillusionment because similar emotional responses seem to be creeping into mainstream academic and popular management literature, as illustrated by the gentle tilt I took at Jim Collins in Chapter 1. Recently, authors such as Barbara Kellerman (2012) and Jeffrey Pfeffer (2015) have vented their disillusionment with leaders and leadership, and expressed doubts as to the usefulness of conventional leadership education, a position, they readily admit, that they and their contemporaries in the 'leadership industry' played no small part in co-creating.

Kellerman, Professor of Public Leadership at Harvard University's John F. Kennedy School of Government, in her 2012 book, *The End of Leadership*, declares that leaders and leadership development are in disrepute, and goes on to explain why, after over thirty years spent working in 'various leadership centres, institutes, and associations', she was compelled to write a book that 'bites the hand' that feeds her:

> The reason is that I am uneasy, increasingly so, about leadership in the twenty-first century and the gap between the teaching of leadership and the practice of leadership ... [is that] notwithstanding the enormous sums of money and time that have been poured into trying to teach people how to lead, over its roughly forty-year history the leadership industry has not in any major, meaningful, measurable way improved the human condition.
>
> *(Ibid.: 1–2)*

And Pfeffer, Professor of Organization Behaviour at Stanford University, building on Kellerman (2012), goes one step further to share the following insight in his book, *Leadership BS: Fixing Workplaces and Careers One Truth at a Time*:

> It is not just that all efforts to develop better leaders, decades of such effort notwithstanding, have failed to make things appreciably better. I realized that much of what was and is going on, although sometimes inadvertently and unintentionally, makes things much worse.
>
> *(2015: 5)*

The doubt and disillusionment that Collins and Hansen (2011), Kellerman (2012) and Pfeffer (2015) express is seemingly provoked by what they see as the abject failure of leadership and the leadership industry, characterised by the many business failures (Collins and Hansen) and scandals (Kellerman and Pfeffer) that emerged during the first decades of the twenty-first century (seemingly differentiated from the regular, pedestrian cycles of corporate bankruptcy and corruption by, in this instance, the banking crisis of 2008). However, I find little evidence of the reflexive curiosity required to challenge their current thinking. Doubt stimulates, in all four authors, a desire to rethink leadership and leadership development. They each challenge what Kellerman describes as the variance between 'teaching' and 'practice' (2012: 1), and champion the need to find a radically different approach. However, their respective searches reveal minimal engagement with perspectives that challenge mainstream thinking and the assumptions that continue to inform their sense-making in respect of leadership and organisation.

For example, in *Great by Choice: Uncertainty, Chaos and Luck – Why Some Thrive despite Them All* (Collins and Hansen, 2011), a book about how to 'thrive in [uncertainty and] chaos' (ibid.: 1), Collins and Hansen make no reference to either chaos theory or the complexity sciences (the sciences of uncertainty). Instead, they employ Collins' usual research method of identifying companies that he feels exhibit the characteristics he is looking for – in this case, 'spectacular performance' in 'unstable environments' that have beaten their 'industry index by at least 10 times' (the '10Xers') – with a view to identifying traits that are generalisable and transferable to other companies/settings. This results not only in another recipe (albeit, this time around, with an acknowledgement that its employment will not guarantee success), but also the following (surprising) defence of the prescriptions offered in Collins' previous books:

> As we conducted our 10X research, we simultaneously tested the concepts from the previous work, considering whether any of the key concepts from those works ceased to apply in highly uncertain and chaotic environments. The earlier concepts held up, and we are confident that the concepts from all four studies increase the odds of building a great company.
>
> *(Ibid.: 182)*

In *The End of Leadership*, Kellerman traces the history of how we have come to think about leading and leadership, and challenges the individualistic conceptions of leadership that continue to dominate mainstream discourse:

> Leading in America has never been easy. But it is now more difficult than ever – not only because we have too many *bad leaders,* but because we have too many *bad followers* … many of us are too timid, too alienated, and/or, too disorganized to speak up and speak out, making it easy for corporate leaders to do what they *want* – to do what's best for them and their bank accounts. Whatever it is that ails us, in other words, is not only about those at the top falling down on the job, but also about those in the middle and at the bottom falling down on theirs.
>
> *(2012: 124; emphasis in the original)*

She calls for more democratic forms of leadership, where 'learning about followership and learning how to follow' are as important as 'learning to lead and manage' and advocates for the development of 'contextual intelligence' over-generalised, one-size-fits-all prescriptions (ibid.: 94). Yet, in calling for less 'leader centric' conceptions of organisation and increased 'contextual intelligence' (ibid.:

199), Kellerman refers neither to social or relational perspectives on leadership (development), nor to any of the extensive literature relating to sensemaking (Weick, 2001).

And although Pfeffer, in *Leadership BS*, is highly critical of management, there is little exploration of the extensive cadre of critical perspectives on the subject, not least the extensive CMS literature. He starts out by treading similar territory to Kellerman, berating CEOs who 'took their companies over a cliff' only to leave with 'enormous severance packages' (2015: 20), before coming to a very different conclusion. Rather than pinning his hopes on the emergence of more democratic forms of leadership, and inciting followers to stop colluding with their unscrupulous superiors, as Kellerman does, Pfeffer advises his readers to take care of themselves and be guided by self-interest:

> Furthermore, the pursuit of individual self-interest might be ... good not just for you but also generally beneficial for the social systems including the work organizations in which you live.
>
> *(Ibid.)*

As outlined in the Introduction, I am painfully aware (particularly so at present) that authors cannot hope to read everything available on a given topic or subject. Given this constraint, it may appear a little disingenuous of me to point the finger at Collins and Hansen, Kellerman and Pfeffer for not engaging with (or if they did, not finding space for) thinking that proffers a different understanding of what they/ we are experiencing. However, I think it fair to say that having expressed doubts over conventional approaches to leadership and leadership development, one might expect to find them engaging with some alternative disciplines, approaches and research. The doubt expressed by this quartet contains little of the 'openness' that Brinkmann argues 'leads to other ways of acting and new understandings of the world' (2017: 53). Reflexive curiosity involves holding up one's current thinking/ practice/sense-making for scrutiny and comparing and contrasting it with one's lived experience and the lived experience and thinking/practice/sense-making of others, including those working from different perspectives and disciplines from oneself. In the remainder of this chapter, I hold up my current thinking/practice/ sense-making for scrutiny by engaging with some of the more recent developments in leadership research, and comparing and contrasting them with my lived experience and that of the leader-managers with whom I work. In choosing perspectives that offer a more ordinary, everyday understanding of leadership and organisation than that found in the dominant discourse, I hope to introduce you to thinking and approaches that get little or no exposure in conventional leadership discourse and development programmes.

One of the most helpful and most challenging lessons from the complexity sciences is that the patterns that emerge in interaction cannot be thought about as if they were separate from the patterns of interaction in which they emerge. Consequently, if one accepts that organisation is merely a term used to describe the global patterning that emerges in the patterning of many local interactions, and that phenomena such as leadership also emerge in these local/global patterns of inter-action, then attempting to separate leadership from the patterns of interaction in which it emerges does not make sense. I'll say more about this in Chapter 3, where I outline in more detail the perspective of complex responsive processes of relating. What this means for now is that the splitting of leadership and organisation, below, is merely a literary device, a conceit to aid comprehension. It is also worth reiter-ating at this point that I remain in search mode (Smith, 2001). That is, although I hope that what I say is plausible, I am not trying to persuade you to my way of thinking, rather I am inviting you to rethink, question and make sense of your own way of thinking as I make sense of mine.

Rethinking leadership

Before challenging my current understanding of leadership, that draws on the per-spective of complex responsive processes of relating (i.e. the complexity approach of the book's title), I need to share this understanding with you. To do this, let's take a look at an event that will be familiar to most of you: Dr Martin Luther King Jr's famous 'I have a dream' speech, and compare and contrast a conventional understanding of the man and this speech with my current stance. If you have heard the speech, take a few minutes to reflect upon the following questions relating to it. How long did it last? What was the context in which it was made? How would you describe King's delivery, and what, if anything, does this tell us about Martin Luther King Jr (MLK) as a leader? If you haven't heard the speech, and you have the opportunity (and the technology available) to watch it now, then it is readily available on YouTube (www.youtube.com/watch?v=I47Y6VHc3Ms).

The speech was delivered at the end of the March on Washington for Jobs and Freedom, attended by some 250,000 people in August 1963. It was made on the steps of the Lincoln Memorial at the culmination of a series of post-march activities that included musical sets from Bob Dylan and Joan Baez, and speeches by each of the leaders of the other Civil Rights groups in attendance. King's speech was just over sixteen minutes long and the 'I have a dream' section comes about two-thirds of the way in. From a mainstream perspective, one that views (leadership and) management as a natural science, a science of certainty, King's speech might be described as the predictable act of a charismatic and heroic individual who had a personal vision of the future and used his skilled oratory to galvanise a group of followers to 'buy into' his dream. It was a predictable, planned, linear process, that was systematically executed to perfection. Here leadership is viewed as an indivi-dualistic endeavour, with King transmitting his message to the expectant crowd who, in turn, enthusiastically receive, acknowledge and accept it.

However, if we take another view of this episode …

In his account of the speech, *Behind the Dream: The Making of the Speech that Transformed a Nation*, a member of Martin Luther King Jr's legal team, Clarence B. Jones, claims that the 'I have a dream' section of the speech was improvised on the spur of the moment, prompted in part by King's friend, the gospel singer Mahalia Jackson (Jones and Connelly, 2012). Jones reports that up until the point where King launches into his 'I have a dream' refrain, some eleven minutes into the speech, he had stuck to his script. Jones and Connelly reflect:

> Martin … paused … this alone was nothing unusual. The hesitations and breaks were all part of his oratory process, the rhythms he mastered at the pulpit. Yet in that split second of silence, something historic and unexpected happened. Into that breach, Mahalia Jackson shouted to him from the speakers and organisers stand. She called out, "Tell 'em about the 'Dream', Martin, tell 'em about the 'Dream'!" Not many people heard her. But I did. And so did Martin … Observing this from my perch, I knew he'd just put himself into Mahalia's hands, given himself over to the spirit of the moment. That is something a speaker simply cannot know typing away in the quiet hotel suite. It has to be felt, right there at the lectern. But by then of course, for most orators, it's too late. Not for Martin Luther King Jr., though.
>
> *(Ibid.: 107–108)*

From the perspective of complex responsive processes or relating, drawing on the complexity sciences – the sciences of uncertainty – King's speech might be described as the simultaneously predictable and unpredictable patterning of the interdependent actions of many people, whereby all are influencing while simultaneously being influenced. The speech is predictable in that it was written down, typed, and annotated in advance of the day, and unpredictable in that the most famous passage was not planned but improvised on the spur of the moment, and although spontaneous, this wasn't the first time that King had shared 'his' dream. From a complexity perspective, meaning is not the pre-planned, predictable linear process described by sender-receiver models of communication (Shannon *et al.*, 1949), rather it is co-created in non-linear, iterative patterns of gesture and response (Mead, 1934), whereby the gesture and response cannot be separated from each other, or indeed from the history of gestures and responses that preceded them (Mead's understanding of communication is explored more fully in Chapter 5).

In the complexity approach that I am taking, leadership is understood to be a social and relational phenomenon not located within an individual but within the interdependent interplay of many people's intentions/actions. King is simultaneously influencing, and being influenced by, the crowd. And how 'his' gesture plays out will depend on how it is taken up in local interaction (Stacey and Mowles, 2016). That is, people will make sense of what King is saying in the simultaneous interplay of their own private dialogue and the dialogue(s) that they engage in with the small number of people with whom they will interact at the event, and with the small number of people with whom they subsequently share their experience after the event. These conversations will be influenced by all the other conversations that those involved engage in, again, in local interaction, which will also reflect all of the other multitudinous responses that they encounter in newspapers and on the TV, radio, etc. in the weeks, months, years ahead. And, of course, one's response might also be influenced by whether one had experienced and/or witnessed discrimination first hand.

Drawing on the perspective of complex responsive processes, I am arguing that the leadership capacities that King exhibits are (i) sense-making, the capacity for recognising the patterns of interaction that groups of interdependent people are caught up in and articulating an understanding (and/or next step) that resonates with others and brings them into communion (and it is through this process of mutual recognition that leadership emerges. That is, in recognising themselves in what King is saying, the crowd simultaneously recognise King as leader); (ii) reflexivity, the capacity to become more detached in one's involvement in order to notice what is currently happening (the patterns of thinking/doing that are emerging and how you are influencing and being influenced by them) with a view to questioning whether this is useful to you and those around you; and (iii) practical judgement, the capacity to decide what is needed in the moment, and if one realises that something novel is needed, to have the courage to change tack. And these capacities are not separate; rather, they are interdependent. It would be impossible to say where one started and the others ended.

That's my current understanding of leadership, and it is a great deal to take in, particularly if one has only ever been exposed to mainstream conceptions of leading and leadership. In Chapter 3, along with the more comprehensive introduction to the perspective of complex responsive processes of relating that I promised earlier, I will provide a more expansive explication of sense-making, reflexivity and practical judgement, but for now, I want to model the reflexive curiosity that I am advocating and start by revisiting the question that researchers, teachers, students and participant-leader-managers on leadership development programmes continue to grapple with: leadership/management – same or different?

Leadership/management – same or different?

My usual response to this question is that leadership and management are one and the same – intertwined (Flinn, 2011; Flinn and Mowles, 2014). In part, they have been artfully separated in the dominant discourse to legitimise the large salary differentials that executives enjoy (see Chapter 1). However, the tenacity of the classic notion that leaders are somehow different from managers (Kotter, 2008), the pocket of mainstream soul searching (Kellerman, 2012; Pfeffer, 2015) that has accompanied the many business failures and scandals that have surfaced since the works of Shenhav (1999) and Khurana (2007) were first published, the establishment of a distinct branch of CMS called Critical Leadership Studies (CLS) (Crawford *et al.*, 1997) and the recent emergence of a number of practice-based perspectives of management/leadership – a practice theory of management (Tengblad, 2012) and Leadership-as-Practice (L-A-P) (Raelin, 2016) – prompt me to take a fresh look at this question/debate.

I approach this question/debate from three angles. First, under the heading 'Can one be a leader without followers?' I explore leadership and leading as a social rather than an individualistic phenomenon, a view that takes account of 'followers' or, how I would more accurately describe them, other people. Second, I consider what it is that leaders actually find themselves doing when leading in organisational settings. And finally, I explore leadership as something that is co-created and dynamic rather than fixed, something that is discovered in practice and not to be confused with abstract models, theories and accounts that one finds in mainstream textbooks, popular management literature and business (auto)biographies.

Can one be a leader without followers?

In mainstream and popular leadership literature, lots of space is given to exploring leaders and leadership, but very little to the exploration of followers/followership (Kellerman, 2012; Blom and Alvesson, 2015). Similarly, in the business schools and corporate training rooms that I work in, consideration of *others* by programme participants invariably revolves around questions such as 'How do I get X to do Y?', 'How do I get my team/department/organisation to "buy in" to the new working practice/structure/strategy?', 'What can I do to bring about a change of culture in this place?', 'What can I do to overcome resistance to change?', etc. When I attend such programmes as a participating leader-manager, there is very little, if any, questioning of whether what is being requested of X is reasonable, or whether the new working practice/structure/strategy, or the change of culture is necessary, sensible or realistic. Getting people to 'buy in' (i.e. getting the other party or parties to see things your way) is often (mis)understood as a form of consultation, rather than being more accurately described as a form of coercive persuasion (Schein, 1961). On these conventional development programmes, whatever course of action the leader-manager decides to take is obviously the right course of action, and following the taking of said action, any subsequent variance between intention and outcome is rationalised away – 'X didn't do Y'; 'There wasn't "buy in"'.[1]

I chose the Martin Luther King Jr speech in order to highlight the differences between mainstream thought and the complexity approach that I find more reality congruent, because all too often when participants on leadership development programmes are invited to discuss leadership and leaders who they admire they pick out figures such as King and Nelson Mandela. I find comparisons between what Mandela might have found himself doing, and what we as leader-managers in organisations find ourselves doing, problematic for many reasons, but for the moment I want to concentrate on the one aspect of this type of comparison that provokes most dissonance for me. The difference that is most often overlooked in such discussions is that there is a high degree of voluntarism in the recognition of King and Mandela as leaders, whereas generally, as leader-managers, we are not chosen, not by our teams at any rate. We are appointed, usually by senior managers in the organisational hierarchy. Employees don't usually get to choose their leader-managers.

This raises the question: is it useful to think of managers as leaders, when employees have limited choice as to whether to follow or not?

Of course, the answer to this question depends on one's working definition of leadership. For those mainstream thinkers who see management and leadership as separate roles (Zaleznik, 1977; Kotter, 2008), leaders set direction, align people, and provide motivation. This characterisation of leadership involves what Alvesson *et al.* describe as 'efforts to influence others within an asymmetrical relation, mainly through meanings, cognitions, and ideas, not through administration or instructions for specific behaviours', which the authors define as management (2016: 3). For Blom and Alvesson, leadership differs from formal authority (management) as it leaves potential followers with a choice:

> Formal hierarchy may lead to compliance, and senior positions and leadership tend to overlap, but … leadership captures something different from formal positions and interactions. You may accept and comply with the manager's formal mandate, but when it comes to management of meaning (values, ideas, beliefs, understandings) subordinates can more or less choose if they take a follower position or not.
>
> *(2015: 270).*

Furthermore, they argue that the invitation to take up a 'follower position' is not so much politely declined, as actively resisted (ibid.). They problematise mainstream texts on leadership that proceed from the assumption that employees 'need or desire followership', to argue that employees are much more likely to 'avoid and minimize leadership/followership relations in a bid to protect their autonomy and identity' (ibid.: 267). They argue that there are potential 'upsides' of following, which they note as 'inclusion, support, direction, meaning [and the] reduction of uncertainty and anxiety' (ibid.). However, they also discovered that even where these upsides were present, people still resisted the 'downsides', that is, the negative impact of leadership on their identity and autonomy, irrespective of whether the leader was deemed to be competent or not (ibid.).

Blom and Alvesson suggest that the talking up of the importance of leadership, that now characterises much of the dominant discourse, may well paradoxically have hastened the demise of followership, whereby 'the reinforcement of ambitions and fantasies of aspiring leaders may lead to a shortage of aspiring followers' (2015: 279). They contend that any thoughts of replacing management with leadership, the task that I was commissioned to undertake by my manager when I joined the University of Hertfordshire (Flinn, 2011), can only be achieved rhetorically as most organisational settings 'still involve significant subordination to management, including allocation of work tasks, requests to comply with corporate bureaucracy, implementing corporate strategies and fulfilling specific objectives and evaluating work performances' (Blom and Alvesson, 2015: 275). They accept that hierarchy, management and leadership are all necessary parts of organisational life, but they conclude that the significance of leadership in organisations might be diminishing because when 'people see themselves more as 'non-followers' (e.g. professionals, peers, co-workers) … there will be "less leadership"' (ibid.: 277).

What resonates with me about Blom and Alvesson's research is that the people in their study, rather than crying out for leadership, sought to avoid and minimise it, not only as a constraint on their freedom, but also as a challenge to their sense of self. In my professional and personal experience, for all the mainstream discourse about the importance of purpose, vision, mission, values and culture, most people just get on with their day-to-day work paying little, if any, attention to such distractions (Flinn, 2011). We tend to accomplish whatever it is that we accomplish in the workplace through working with the small group(s) of people with whom we interact daily, in what can be described as local interaction(s) (Stacey and Mowles, 2016). In my experience, the artefacts that senior managers produce, which are incidentally also developed in local interaction(s) with small groups of people – strategy documents, Key Performance Indicators, visions/missions, and values – have very little direct influence on the day-to-day activities of the majority of employees, or indeed on the day-to-day activities of the senior managers who produced them in the first place.

Blom and Alvesson's finding that most employees neither 'expect their manager (or senior colleague) to define the right values, beliefs and meanings for them' nor to provide 'support and development' (2015: 268), has particular relevance to the sector in which I currently spend most of my time, the UK Higher Education (HE) sector. In HE, comparing the task of managing academics to 'herding cats' has become a cliché, as has the notion that academic members of staff have little affiliation to the institutions that pay their salaries. Academic fealty, it is argued, is paid to the school, the discipline, or a smaller subset thereof. Richard Bolden et al.'s (2012) study of UK HE institutions suggests that academic staff not only avoid the identity and autonomy constraints, the 'downsides' of leadership that Blom and Alvesson (2015) identify, but they also look elsewhere for the 'upsides' of inclusion, support, direction and meaning.

The academic staff that Bolden et al. surveyed reported that they looked to 'colleagues', 'former colleagues' and their 'PhD supervisors' for this support rather than formal leaders in their institutions (2012: 18). Here 'formal' denotes those in positions of authority. That is, leaders who have been appointed, usually by other leaders, to take up a position in the organisational hierarchy in which they have line-management responsibility for (authority over) others. This would also include those people who may not have formal line-management responsibility/authority but who have been placed in a position that provides them with a degree of disciplinary power by proxy. Informal denotes those leaders who have no formal position of authority, but who are able to articulate or exhibit a way of thinking/working/being that others follow; in complexity terms, there is a shift in the patterning of interactions whereby people recognise themselves in what one of the group is saying/doing, and in recognising themselves they recognise what the other is doing as (an act of) leader(ship).

In my experience, informal leaders, like the ones identified in Bolden *et al.*'s study, often gain influence precisely because they are not part of the establishment. And this highlights another aspect of leadership and organisation that often goes unexplored, or at least under-explored, in the mainstream and that is the dynamics of power and how they play out in patterns of inclusion and exclusion[2] (Elias, 1939). I will explore in more detail the complexity perspective on power in the Chapter 5, but for now it is enough to say that the power chances of the 'established' (those in positions of authority) are usually more resilient than those of the 'outsiders' (Elias and Scotson, 1994), that is, the informal leaders (those without any formal position of authority). Consequently, if one adopts the distinction that Alvesson and Jonsson make between leading and managing, then the unqualified use of the term 'leader' for those in positions of authority is not useful as the majority of actions taken by those in formal positions in the organisational hierarchy are concerned with 'administration or instructions for specific behaviours' (managing), rather than 'efforts to influence others ... through meanings, cognitions, and ideas' (leading) (2016: 3). This distinction problematises mainstream definitions of leadership which mistakenly label all gestures of the powerful as (acts of) leadership.

I still find the splitting of (acts of) leadership and (acts of) management problematic, but I am going to ignore this for now, as differentiating between 'acts of leadership' and 'acts of management' facilitates the articulation of something from my experience of working with MBA students over the last six years. One of the activities that we task students with each year is to work in groups to undertake a project in the community. For the students, experienced middle and senior managers who are studying part-time for their MBAs while working, this often involves engaging with local charities. The pressures of work, family life and overlapping deadlines for MBA assignments, means that the task of contacting and arranging something with a charity/community group often falls to the group member that has the time and/or inclination. Following the event, the students reflect on the project and identify what, if anything, is generalisable from their experience to their day-to-day practice. In these reflections, students often characterise the person who made the initial contact with the charity/community project as the group leader. During debriefs I or one of my teaching team colleagues, invariably find ourselves asking whether the activities that this person undertook are best described as acts of leadership or acts of coordination.

So far, in answer to the question 'Can one be a leader without followers?' I am arguing that (i) mainstream conceptions of what constitutes leading and leadership take little account of followership, and doing so problematises simplistic definitions that categorise those in positions of authority as leaders; (ii) leading and leadership are not the exclusive preserve of those in positions of authority; and (iii) not all (many) of the common place, regular activities of those in authority should be classed as (acts of) leadership. This leads to the second theme of the 'What's the difference between leadership and management?' debate, and that is, as managers in organisations, what is it that we actually find ourselves doing on a daily basis, and how does this compare with mainstream and popular management conceptions of what leaders should or ought to be doing?

What do leaders actually find themselves doing when leading in organisational settings?

One of the most significant changes to my practice as a result of taking a complexity approach to leadership development is to encourage the managers with whom I work to take our day-to-day experience seriously. This means making sense of what is actually happening in our quotidian interactions with a view to questioning whether what we are doing together is useful to us and to those around us. My modus operandi as a leadership developer, prior to embarking on the DMan, found me sharing an idealised view of what constituted effective leadership (the organisation's competency framework, the latest leadership theory/ framework, etc.), inviting participants to measure themselves against this with a view to identifying the gap between current practice and the idealised view, and then supporting them with the development of an action plan to close the 'gap'. This is a reductive description of my former practice, and I am not suggesting that there was no merit whatsoever in what I was doing. Indeed, as a young manager I attended such programmes, and I do not recall dismissing them out of hand. However, what I do recall is the anxiety provoked by not being able to replicate the espoused theories in practice, which leaves me questioning how useful my former conventional approach to leadership development was for participants in supporting their day-to-day activities as leader-managers.

I mention this, because my former normative approach to leadership development is still very much in evidence across the leadership industry. Indeed, Pfeffer contends that:

> The leadership industry is so obsessively focused on the normative – what leaders should do and how things ought to be – that it has largely ignored asking the fundamental question of what is actually true and going on and why. Unless and until leaders are measured for what they really do and for actual workplace conditions, and until these leaders are held accountable for improving both their own behaviour and, as a consequence, workplace outcomes, nothing will change.
>
> *(2015: 23)*

As argued above, if Pfeffer had looked further than mainstream leadership discourse, he may well have engaged with some of the thinking from CMS scholars. CMS is an umbrella term that covers a wide range of disciplines and researchers, who were challenging mainstream conceptions of leadership, leadership development and organisation long before CMS came to be recognised as a distinct school of thought in the 1990s (Willmott, 1992). As outlined in the Introduction, after decades of working at the margins, ideas from CMS are finding their way onto leadership development programmes, as developers and participants acknowledge the shadow side of organisational life that is underexplored in mainstream textbooks and popular management literature.[3] CMS scholars have a long history of challenging the normative.

Mats Alvesson, independently and in collaboration with various colleagues, has for many years been researching whether the leadership claims of managers in organisations are supported by what they actually find themselves doing in practice (Alvesson and Sveningsson, 2003a, 2003b; Alvesson, 2013; Alvesson and Spicer, 2011; Alvesson and Karreman, 2016). Some of his more recent research finds him revisiting this territory, but rather than simply comparing and contrasting how managers account for what they are doing with what happens in practice, Alvesson and Jonsson explore the influence that the current leadership discourse (contained in 'books ... courses and other educational settings'), along with organisational expectations (policies, values, ambition), and one's own 'personality and self-image' (2016: 15) might be having on what it is that managers do.

To do this they follow Kim, a middle manager in a large, international manufacturing organisation, as she carries out her day-to-day responsibilities. Although Kim describes her leadership style as participative with a strong emphasis on coaching, Alvesson *et al.* discover little evidence of this. Instead, they find Kim dealing with issues based on 'spontaneous readings of the situation, without much sign of careful reflection or an integrated, coherent idea or framework guiding an overall leadership ambition' (2016: 14). This view of leading/managing as an improvisatory activity echoes my own research findings (Flinn, 2011), as does their experience of finding 'very little leadership in any distinct meaning (where the followers are transformed or managed in terms of meaning, or where some other systematic influence agenda is expressed) ... the actions are more administrative or operational' (Alvesson and Jonsson, 2016: 14).

As outlined above, for all the talk of leadership, the managers with whom I work on leadership development programmes are more concerned with performance management, workload and budgeting issues than they are with visions, values or strategic plans, irrespective of their seniority. Indeed, following exposure to abstract theories of leadership that prescribe what they ought to be doing as leaders, managers frequently second-guess their own practices and try to match their experience to the models (see Chapter 3). One of the cornerstones of the complexity approach to leadership development is helping participants to avoid getting caught up in idealised and reductive prescriptions that bear little resemblance to the complex reality of their working lives (Flinn and Mowles, 2014). This is also something that Alvesson and Jonsson hope that their study will contribute to:

> Thus, in practical terms, our study contributes toward helping managers, in particular middle managers, whose task or ideal is to "lead" others, by raising awareness of the conflicting ideas and problems, and so liberate them from the ideals and role models that look fine in management books but that few may

be able to live up to. Much leadership talk about patterns, ideals, styles, clear ideas, and coherence may prevent managers and others from clear insights of managerial practice and put unnecessary burdens on managers to produce leadership as prescribed.

(2016: 16)

They call for 'more in-depth studies of individual cases where questions such as the possible (in)consistency in behavior and the possible influence are studied in practice', arguing that 'there is a shortage of ambitious case studies of typical managers, in which context, content, and behavior are taken seriously' (ibid.: 2–3). My initial response on reading this statement was 'Well it depends where you look!' For many years Tony Watson has researched how 'people in managerial work shape their personal identities and their working lives – at the same time as being shaped by the world around them' (Watson and Harris, 1999: vii). Meanwhile, Stefan Tengblad and Ola Edvin Vie provide a useful overview of the many 'classic, mature and recent' studies of 'management in practice' that have been carried out over the last sixty years across North America, the UK, Scandinavia, Germany and the Netherlands (Tengblad, 2012).

Tengblad also calls for more reality congruent research into leadership and organisation:

> There is an urgent need to establish a strong research tradition based on the realities of managerial work – for example, the realities of information and work overload, complexity, uncertainty, performance pressure, surprises, unintended consequences, and irreconcilable expectations, to say nothing of the emotional demands of work.

(2012: 7)

He and his colleagues are working 'towards a practice theory of management' in which the focus of attention is on 'how management is performed in everyday work practices by countless numbers of managers all over the world' (ibid.: 5), in contrast to mainstream concepts of how it ought to be done. For Tengblad, this 'shifts the attention from formal management techniques to rules-of-thumb and behavioural patterns' (ibid.).

Joseph Raelin (2016) has edited a volume of research entitled *Leadership-as-Practice*. Raelin describes this as 'a new movement in leadership research and practice destined to shake the foundations of the very meaning of leadership in the worlds of both theory and application' (ibid.: 1). This new movement conceives of 'leadership as occurring as a practice rather than residing in the traits or behaviours of particular individual's', that is, 'leadership as a social, material, and jointly accomplished process' (ibid.: 3). Raelin contends that L-A-P 'resonates with a number of closely related traditions such as collective, shared, distributed, and relational leadership', but argues that, unlike these perspectives, L-A-P does not characterise leadership as a 'role-driven, entitative influence relationship' (ibid.: 4), that is, L-A-P researchers understand leadership as a complex phenomenon that goes beyond leader/follower relations.

Both of these perspectives, a practice theory of management (Tengblad, 2012) and L-A-P (Raelin, 2016) resonate with the complexity approach to leadership and leadership development that I am advocating here. My approach is informed by the perspective of complex responsive processes of relating that I first encountered during my doctoral studies at UH. For over twenty-five years the complexity research group at UH has been encouraging leaders, as practitioner-researchers, to take what they do in their ordinary, everyday interactions seriously. On the DMan, managers are encouraged to put 'people and what they are doing at work at the heart of their enquiry: how they talk to one another, how they are bound up in relationships of power, how they make judgements which express ideology' (Mowles, 2015). The narratives that I share in this book, as well as vignettes from DMan colleagues, give a flavour of this, and I would argue that they are made all the more powerful as these are not third party observations, but first-hand accounts of practice that have been iteratively deepened through engagement with and challenge by doctoral supervisors and learning community colleagues during the three-year course of study.

I agree with Alvesson and Jonsson (2016) that narratives of leadership are often not substantiated in/by practice, and I also concur with Blom and Alvesson's (2015) observation that sometimes leadership is not only unnecessary, but also avidly resisted. However, I would also argue that some accounts of leadership/ management *are* a fair representation of practice (see the vignettes contained in this book and the accounts documented in the work of Tengblad (2012) and Raelin (2016)), and Blom and Alvesson's observations represent only one side of the coin. In other words, although I agree that the talking up of leadership might have contributed unexpectedly to a decline in the number of people who are willing to follow (Blom and Alvesson, 2015), I also contend that it has led simultaneously to a demand from workers for managers to step into the space that Alvesson *et al.* refer to as leadership (Alvesson and Jonsson, 2016). Thus, as more and more managers refer to themselves as leaders it should come as little surprise that workers retort with, 'OK, show us some leadership!'

Ever since the Hawthorne Studies[4] in the 1920s, and the subsequent rise of the human relations theory/movement, managers at all levels are expected to make 'efforts to influence others … through meanings, cognitions, and ideas' (Alvesson and Jonsson, 2016: 3). And as much as we might resist leadership, there are times when we expect our line managers to make sense of the context in which we find ourselves and proffer next steps. For example, during (a) the introduction of new projects, initiatives or ways of working; (b) times of uncertainty, and/or periods of major upheaval and change, we look (with hope or barely disguised *Schadenfreude*) to our manager-leaders, the ones who are paid more than us, to provide us with direction, support and motivation; and (c) during the interview process for a management role, could any candidate interview for the job and hope to be appointed without declaring the passion they have for leading, their vision for the future, and the changes they will make in order to maintain or return the team/department/organisation to the top of the ratings/rankings/stock market?

So far, in answer to the question 'What do we actually find ourselves doing when leading in organisational settings?' I argue that (i) mainstream conceptions of what we think managers are and/or ought to be doing are often not substantiated in practice, and although there are accounts and perspectives that offer a more reality congruent understanding of praxis, they are given little space in orthodox literature; (ii) the talking up of leadership has paradoxically increased resistance and raised expectations at the same time; and (iii) if, for argument's sake, we define leadership as 'efforts to influence others within an asymmetrical relation, mainly through meanings, cognitions, and ideas, not through administration or instructions for specific behaviours', which Alvesson and Jonsson define as management (2016: 3), then I contend that every manager with whom I am currently working is expected to do both. Of course, how such gestures are taken up is not within the gift of the individual, and this points to the third and final theme arising from the Martin Luther King Jr narrative, which I want to consider here, and that is leadership as a socially constructed phenomenon, something that arises in interaction rather than being a reified 'it'.

Leadership as a phenomenon that is co-created in practice

I noted above that the practice theory of management (Tengblad, 2012) and L-A-P (Raelin, 2016) perspectives have a great deal of resonance with the complexity approach that I am offering and exploring in this book. For Sveningsson *et al.*, the idea of leadership existing outside of the relationships in which it emerges and is sustained is ludicrous:

> The exercise of leadership in splendid isolation is meaningless. Leadership by definition exists between people, therefore, it is an expression of a mutual relationship … Leadership does not emanate a priori because someone in an organisation is assigned the leadership role.
>
> *(Tengblad, 2012: 79)*

Drawing on the work of Shamir (2007), Sveningsson *et al.* argue that all involved are:

> co-makers of the leadership relationships that evolve, [they] connect and define one another, mutually and relationally. Individuals become leaders when one or several people accept the importance of their directions/ideas and are influenced by them. The leader who is influenced by someone else's conceptions and interpretations is being led. The leader then becomes a follower.
>
> *(Sveningsson et al, 2012: 79)*

For Raelin, L-A-P 'depicts immanent collective action emerging from mutual, discursive, sometimes recurring and sometimes evolving patterns in the moment and over time among those engaged in practice' (2016: 3). For Raelin, 'leadership is not dependent on any one person to mobilise action on behalf of everybody else. The effort is intrinsically collective' (ibid.: 4). Echoing Sveningsson *et al.*'s (2012) view of leadership, Raelin argues that those who emerge as leaders (the 'meaning makers' in his terms) 'may be serving in managerial roles, but anyone within the team can be responsible provided they have astute awareness of the perspectives, reasoning patterns, and narratives of others' (2016: 4). For Raelin, this view challenges authors who focus on 'the dyadic relationship between leaders and followers', such as Kellerman (2012) in *The End of Leadership* (Raelin, 2016: 216).[5]

In *Reflexive Leadership: Organising in an Imperfect World*, Alvesson *et al.* acknowledge 'the social, relational and processual character of leadership' (2017: 8). For them, this 'involves both leaders and followers engaged in mutual interaction based on the influencing of meaning and understanding. It goes beyond a static attention to the individual leader and his/her ideas, convictions and personal psychology' (ibid.).

> This view of leadership is based on voluntary compliance. People position themselves as followers based not on legal requirements or out of fear of negative sanctions, but because leadership acts provide some meaningful as well as practical, emotionally and morally convincing direction. In this way leadership forms the basis for motivation since it provides some sensible idea or purpose in terms of performing specific work tasks.
>
> *(Ibid.: 8–9)*

They further argue that leadership is but one of a set of six practices that constitute how we get things done in organisational settings. They identify the other five 'alternatives and supplements to leadership' as:

- management
- exercise of (coercive) power
- peer influencing (via networks)
- group work, and
- autonomy (self-management).

(Ibid.: 17)

However, they are also at pains to proffer the caveat that they 'of course recognise the many ambiguous cases where the six positions are mixed' (ibid.). They call for the adoption of 'reflexive leadership, which means that people – senior and junior – think carefully about how to organize work and how to use both leadership and other ways of organizing to make workplaces function well' (ibid.: 2–3).

So far, under the heading 'Leadership as a phenomenon that is co-created in practice' I argue that leadership is something that is co-created in interaction, and is not only open to those who find themselves in formal positions of authority. This view resonates with the understanding of leadership that I shared in the Martin Luther King Jr narrative above. Drawing on the thinking of Stacey and Mowles (2016), I view leadership as a social and relational phenomenon that is neither confined to those in formal positions in the organisational hierarchy nor only available to extraordinary individuals in possession of special attributes that others do not have (as the dominant discourse would have us believe). A person is recognised as a leader when others recognise themselves in what that person is saying and/or doing, and in recognising themselves they come to recognise that person as a leader. Leadership emerges in interaction. It is co-created in social processes of mutual recognition.

I agree with Alvesson *et al.*'s thesis that leading/leadership is only one of the phenomena that arise when human beings come together to get things done in organisational (and other) settings and that leadership is not only open to those in formal positions of authority. And the identification of the types of activity that supplement leadership may have helped my MBA students to account for what happened during their community project in a more nuanced way than categorising almost every act as an act of leadership (see above). However, the overarching inference that senior and junior workers might get to choose 'how to use both leadership and other ways of organising to make workplaces function well' (Alvesson *et al.*, 2017: 2–3), does not make sense to me. The six practices that Alvesson *et al.* (2017) identify and Raelin's (2016) notions of collective, shared, distributed, and relationa forms of leadership are useful as descriptors of some of the phenomena that emerge in the patterning of human interaction that we call organisation, but as concepts that can be instrumentally introduced, encouraged and/or controlled at will, less so.

This brings us back to the argument that I made early on in this chapter: if one accepts that organisation is merely a term used to describe the global patterns of interaction that emerge in the interplay of many local patterns of interaction, and that phenomena such as leadership also emerge in these local/global patterns of interaction, then attempting to separate leadership from the patterns of interaction in which it emerges does not make sense. And I would argue that this is the main difference between Alvesson *et al.*'s reflexive leadership, Raelin's L-A-P, Tengblad and colleagues' practice theory of management and the complexity approach that I am offering here. These three perspectives seem to[6] be working from the premise that we can choose the form of pattern our interactions take and/or step in and out of them to manipulate them at will, whereas I argue that we cannot do so. We are forming while simultaneously being formed by the patterns of interaction we are caught up in, and we can influence but we cannot control. Moreover, the individuals involved in these local patterns of interaction will not necessarily agree with the descriptor that might be offered for the pattern they are involved in. One person's 'management' might be another's 'exercise of (coercive) power'. I will expand on this in the next chapter.

Leadership: towards a working definition

Although revisiting my thinking and engaging with some recent developments in leadership research has not fundamentally shifted the sense that I am making of leadership, it has really helped me to clarify my thinking and I hope that it has given you a chance to reflect on yours. The first point of clarification concerns the form of leadership and thus leadership development that I am focusing on in this book. The vast majority of people who attend the leadership development programmes that I am involved in are line managers, that is, they occupy formal positions of authority in the organisational hierarchy.[7] Consequently, I am concentrating on leadership and leadership development as it pertains to line managers, that is, leader-managers in formal positions of authority. That is not to say that what follows will not be relevant and/or useful to those who find themselves having to lead (and/or support the development of those who lead) without or beyond authority, but I feel it is important to clarify the focus. Leader-managers are called upon to both cajole and coerce, and although one might anticipate that at this point in the twenty-first century this might privilege influence over insistence, both are necessary. The idea that leadership development can somehow be separated from management development does not make sense to me.

Second, drawing on Alvesson (2013); Alvesson and Sveningsson (2003a, 2003b); Alvesson and Karreman (2016); Alvesson and Jonsson (2016); Blom and Alvesson (2015); Bolden et al. (2012); and Czarniawska-Joerges and Wolff (1991), even though one might occupy a formal position of authority in the corporate hierarchy, this does not necessarily mean that one will come to be recognised as a leader. The constraints on autonomy and sense of self that come with being 'invited to follow', allied to the growing rhetoric that we are all leaders now, fuels follower resistance and might go some way to explaining why academic colleagues look to informal leaders as their first port of call for support rather than their line managers (Bolden et al., 2012). However, I also contend that the talking up of leadership cuts both ways, with team members expecting their line managers to play up to the archetypes outlined in Chapter 1 – manager (co-ordinator), leader (bringer of hope) and entrepreneur (maker of new worlds) (Czarniawska-Joerges and Wolff, 1991).

Third, leadership is something that co-created in interaction. We do not get to choose what form leadership takes, as this emerges in the patterns of interaction that constitute organisation. Thus, any talk of introducing, unleashing or encouraging collective, shared, distributed, and relational (Raelin, 2016) forms of leadership becomes problematic. Nor do we get to choose which form of organising we would like to 'use' in order to 'function well' (Alvesson et al., 2017). Similarly, if one accepts that leadership is a social and relational phenomenon, then one cannot choose to be a participative, collaborative, transformational or authentic leader. As descriptors of patterns that one might notice in organisational settings, such categorisations might be useful, but as concepts that can be instrumentally fashioned they are less so. Suggestions of this type confirm for me the difficulties that arise when one artificially tries to separate out a phenomenon like leadership from the patterns of interaction in which it emerges. This is something I will pick up in the next chapter where I will establish a working definition for organisation from the perspective of complex responsive processes of relating.

Leadership: a working definition

I see leadership as making sense of the social context in which one finds oneself and then articulating an understanding/next step in which people recognise themselves and in so doing come to recognise one as leader. And I see management as coping with the context and the intended and unintended consequences of working from the new understanding and/or taking that next step into the unknown. However, one cannot separate leadership and management, as it is in the process of coping that one makes sense of the context and comes to form the understanding and/or next step that is articulated and recognised as leading/leadership. They are both sides of the same coin.

Do I think I've nailed it? No! Every definition of leadership is open to challenge and contestation. An emergent social phenomenon like leadership will always be difficult to pin down, but this does not mean that we should stop inquiring into it. Indeed, we should ensure that we never cease to reflect on the part we play in it, either as leaders or as active or passive followers, consumers or victims. We should always be involved in the reflexive exploration of the question, 'Who are we, and what are we doing together?' And is what we are doing together useful (legal, ethical, moral and sustainable) for us and for those around us (colleagues, co-workers and the wider community). What implications does this have for me as a leader of leadership development? Am I involved in leadership or management development? Both? Is leadership about enabling or constraining? Both, and at the same time (see Chapter 7). There is no model, framework or recipe for leadership beyond developing the capacities for sense-making, reflexivity and practical judgement and in the chapters that follow I explore what it means to take a complexity approach to leadership development.

Notes

1   When I find myself in these spaces, the thing that strikes me most is how little room is given for doubt and reflexive curiosity – the capacities that catalysed and facilitated the dramatic shift in my thinking and practice that began over a decade ago.

2   Informal leaders are often subsequently and/or consequently called upon to take up formal roles in the organisational hierarchy. The rationalisation for this course of action sometimes falls into the 'keep your enemies close' category, but more usually occurs because informal leaders are articulating something that others recognise and are attracted to, including those making recruitment decisions. Of course, appointments to formal

positions shifts the power dynamic, which may in turn lead to the 'follower resistance' that Blom *et al.* (2015) talk of, as the previously 'informal' leader becomes part of the management Establishment.

3 On the programmes that I am involved in, for instance, one might find Dennis Tourish exploring *The Dark Side of Transformational Leadership* (2013), and/or Erik de Haan cautioning participants to guard against *The Leadership Shadow: [that is] How to Recognize and Avoid Derailment, Hubris and Overdrive* (de Haan *et al.*, 2014).

4 The Hawthorne Studies were psychological experiments carried out to test the effect that small changes to the working environment (i.e. lighting) have on the productivity of factory workers.

5 Raelin refers to Kellerman because her article appears in the same edition of the journal that this article is published in (see Raelin, 2017).

6 I say 'seem to' as the L-A-P anthology contains a broad church of thinking and thinkers, as does the practice theory of management volume, and to a lesser extent (at least in terms of the number of contributors), Alvesson *et al.*'s 2017 book. I need to engage more closely with all three texts and look at some more of the individual contributors' most recent research publications. This is something that I look forward to.

7 And of the small number of leaders that do find their way onto the programmes that I lead, who are not in formal positions of authority, the vast majority express the wish that they were. For these colleagues, the perception is that it is easier to get things done 'through administration or instructions for specific behaviours' rather than through the negotiation of 'meanings, cognitions, and ideas' (Alvesson and Jonsson, 2016: 3).

References

Alvesson M. (2013) *The Triumph of Emptiness*. Oxford: Oxford University Press.

Alvesson, M., Blom, M. and Sveningsson, S. (2017) *Reflexive Leadership: Organising in an Imperfect World*. London: Sage.

Alvesson, M. and Jonsson, A. (2016). 'The bumpy road to exercising leadership: Fragmentations in meaning and practice'. *Leadership*, 0(0): 1–18.

Alvesson, M. and Karreman, D. (2016) 'Intellectual failure and ideological success in leadership studies: The case of transformational leadership'. *Journal of Management Inquiry*, 25 (2): 139–152.

Alvesson, M. and Spicer, A. (2016) *The Stupidity Paradox: The Power and Pitfalls of Functional Stupidity at Work*. London: Profile Books.

AlvessonM. andSpicer, A. (Eds) (2011) *Metaphors We Lead By: Understanding Leadership the Real World*. London: Routledge.

Alvesson, M. and Sveningsson, S. (2003a) 'The great disappearing act: difficulties in doing "leadership"', *Leadership Quarterly*, 14: 359–381.

Alvesson, M. and Sveningsson, S. (2003b) 'Managers doing leadership: The extraordinization of the mundane'. *Human Relations*, 56: 1435–1459.

Blom, M. and Alvesson, M. (2015) 'Less followership, less leadership? An inquiry into the basic but seemingly forgotten downsides of leadership'. *M@n@gement*. 18(3): 266–282.

Bolden, R., Witzel, M. and Linacre, N. (2016) *Leadership Paradoxes. Rethinking Leadership for an Uncertain World*. New York: Routledge.

Bolden, R., Gosling, J., O'Brien, A., Peters, K., Ryan, M. K., Haslam, S. A., Longsworth, L., Davidovic, A. and Winklemann, K. (2012) *Academic Leadership: Changing Conceptions, Identities and Experiences in UK Higher Education*. Leadership Foundation for Higher Education Stimulus Paper.

Brinkmann, S. (2017) *Stand Firm: Resisting the Self-Improvement Craze*. Cambridge: Polity Press.

Collins, J. and Hansen, M. T. (2011) *Great by Choice: Uncertainty, Chaos and Luck – Why Some Thrive despite Them All*. London: Random House.

Crawford, M., Kydd, L. and Riches, C. (Eds) (1997) *Critical Leadership Studies*. Buckingham: Open University Press.

Czarniawska-Joerges, B. and Wolff, R. (1991) 'Leaders, managers, entrepreneurs on and off the organizational stage'. *Organization Studies*, 12(4): 529–546.

de Haan, E. and Kasozi, A. (2014) *The Leadership Shadow: How to Recognize and Avoid Derailment, Hubris and Overdrive*. London: Kogan Page.

Elias, N. (1939) *The Civilizing Process*. Oxford: Blackwell.

Elias, N. and Scotson, J. L. (1994) *The Established and the Outsiders*. London: Sage.

Flinn, K. (2011) *Making Sense of Leadership Development: Reflections on my Role as a Leader of Leadership Development Interventions*. Unpublished thesis.

Flinn, K. and Mowles, C. (2014) *A Complexity Approach to Leadership Development: Developing Practical Judgement*. Leadership Foundation for Higher Education stimulus paper.

Ford, J. and Harding, N. (2011) 'The impossibility of the "true self" of authentic leadership'. *Leadership*, 7(4): 463–479.

Griffin, D. (2002) *The Emergence of Leadership: Linking Self-Organisation and Ethics*. London: Routledge.

Jones, C. B. and Connelly, S. (2012) *Behind the Dream: The Making of the Speech that Transformed a Nation*. New York: Macmillan.

Kellerman, B. (2012) *The End of Leadership*. New York: Harper Business.

Kotter, J. P. (2008) *Force for Change: How Leadership Differs from Management*. New York: Simon and Schuster.

Khurana, R. (2007) *From Higher Aims to Hired Hands*. Oxford: Princeton University Press.

Mead, G. H. (1934) *Mind, Self, and Society*. Chicago, IL: University of Chicago Press.

Mowles, C. (2015) *Managing in Uncertainty: Complexity and the Paradoxes of Everyday Organizational Life*. London: Routledge.

Pfeffer, J. (2015) *Leadership BS: Fixing Workplaces and Careers One Truth at a Time*. London: HarperCollins.

Raelin, J. A. (Ed.) (2016) *Leadership-As-Practice: Theory and Application*. London: Routledge.

Raelin, J. A. (2017) 'Leadership-as-practice: Theory and application – an editor's reflection'. *Leadership, 13*(2): 215–221.

Schein, E. H. (1961) *Coercive Persuasion*. New York: Norton.

Shamir, B. (2007) From Passive Recipients to Active Co-producers: Followers' Role in the Leadership Process. In B. Shamir. R. Pillai, M. Bligh and M. Uhl-Bien (Eds) *Follower-centred Perspectives on Leadership. A Tribute to the Memory of James R. Meindl*. Greenwich, CT: Information Age Publishing.

Shannon, C. E. and Weaver, W. (1949) *The Mathematical Theory of Communication*. Urbana, Il: University of Illinois Press.

Shaw, P. (2002) *Changing Conversations in Organizations: A Complexity Approach to Change*. London: Routledge.

Shenhav, Y. (1999) *Manufacturing Rationality: The Engineering Foundations of the Managerial Revolution*. Oxford: Oxford University Press.

Smith, D. (2001) *Norbert Elias and Modern Social Theory*. London: Sage.

Stacey, R. (2010) *Complexity and Organizational Reality: Uncertainty and the Need to Rethink Management after the Collapse of Investment Capitalism*. London: Routledge.

Stacey, R. D. and Mowles, C. (2016) *Strategic Management and Organisational Dynamics: The Challenge of Complexity to Ways of Thinking about Organisations* (7th edn). Harlow: Pearson.

Sveningsson, S., Alvehus, J. and Alvesson, M. (2012) Managerial Leadership: Identities, Processes, and Interactions. In S. Tengblad (Ed.) *The Work of Managers: Towards a Practice Theory of Management*. Oxford: Oxford University Press.

Tengblad, S. (Ed.) (2012) *The Work of Managers: Towards a Practice Theory of Management*. Oxford: Oxford University Press.

Tourish, D. (2013) *The Dark Side of Transformational Leadership: A Critical Perspective*. Hove, Routledge.

Watson, T. J. (2001) *In Search of Management: Culture, Chaos and Control in Managerial Work*. Andover: Cengage Learning (EMEA).

Watson, T. and Harris, P. (1999) *The Emergent Manager*. London: Sage.

Weick, K. E. (2001) *Making Sense of Organization*. Oxford: Blackwell Publishing.

Willmott, H. (Ed) (1992) *Critical Management Studies*. London: Sage.

Zaleznik, A. (1977) Managers and leaders: are they different? *Harvard Business Review*, 70(2): 126–135.

3

RETHINKING LEADERSHIP DEVELOPMENT

In search of certainty

> The idea that we live life in a straight line, like a story, seems to me to be increasingly absurd and, more than anything, a kind of intellectual convenience. I feel that the events in our lives are like a series of bells being struck and the vibrations spread outwards, affecting everything, our present, and our futures, of course, but our past as well. Everything is changing and vibrating and in flux.
>
> *Nick Cave (2017)*

It's Friday afternoon, and I have been working with a group of managers on a programme entitled Making Sense of Leading (MSOL) since 9.00 am. The programme consists of a series of mainly one-day workshops exploring leadership in an experiential and broadly critical way.[1] We are eight days into the twelve-day programme and today we are 'Making Sense of Leading … Change'. Seven out of the usual group of ten members are present, and in addition, we have been joined for the day by a participant from a previous cohort, Paul, who has completed the whole programme bar this session as he was unavailable when his group took part in this particular workshop six months ago.

During this morning's Community Meeting[2] discussion turned to the heightened activity we are all facing at the start of a new academic year. Students arrived on campus two weeks ago and the challenges of inducting thousands of new and returning students figured in the reflections of all eight participants (three academic colleagues and five from professional services) in one way or another. The general discussion soon turned to the particular, and participants focused on UH's time-tabling system. The system was introduced last year and it would be fair to say that for the vast majority of staff and students the change did not go as smoothly as everybody might have liked. Indeed, the difficulties were such that the Vice Chancellor apologised publicly for the 'teething troubles'.

Group discussion generated three key reasons for what was perceived as 'poor change management'. Reason one, the university allotted nine months to implement a system that it had taken other institutions three years to introduce. Reason two, the 'off the shelf' system chosen could not accommodate the idiosyncratic variables (human and technical) that were previously managed manually by people (timetablers) talking to other people (teaching staff and students) and negotiating a way forward that made sense for the vast majority of all involved. And reason three, 'senior management' had either misread the very vocal dissent of large numbers of staff as 'noise' that would abate once the system was up and running or they were not aware of the operational realities until it was too late. The group reported that twelve months on the situation had not improved, but colleagues had become adept at finding the 'workarounds' needed to address the system's many inadequacies.

During the discussion I intervened to problematise the oversimplistic game of 'If only they'd ...' that several of the participants had got caught up in.

I let the use of the generalised term 'they' go and asked the group to consider how something like this might come about, given the fact that some of the consequences of introducing the new system seemed to be both unintended and unwanted by everyone involved. I suggested that in these circumstances, it might be difficult for 'they/them' to discern the difference between the 'noise' of initial anxiety and 'alarm bells' that presage imminent disaster. The group agreed that this was difficult, and several recalled episodes where 'this can never be done' soon morphed into reflections along the lines of 'why didn't we do this years ago?' Several participants shared examples of changes that they had been (or were still) involved in. They problematised idealistic cause and effect notions of change management and offered a far messier account of what they found themselves doing in these situations. One of the participants said that in his experience, when tough decisions had to be made, political considerations often outweighed common sense. Paul commented that since completing MSOL he is less anxious. He told the group that he pays more attention to what might be going on around him, and does not feel that he can be, or indeed has to be, in control of this. The Community Meeting ended after the allotted hour had passed.

Later on in the morning we engaged in an experiential activity, an exercise that I was introduced to some years ago as 'All Change', but I have also seen it referred to as 'Managing and Being Managed' and there are no doubt other titles for it. Briefly, the exercise entails splitting the participants into an On Site group and a Central group. Given the numbers available I put six participants into the On Site group, leaving two to make up the Central group. The exercise calls for the groups to be geographically separated, so I escorted the Central group to a nearby room and provided them with a hard copy of the brief:

'All Change'

Central brief

You are the Central group

Brief

You have 40 minutes to achieve the task outlined below. You must comply with the rules and you are responsible for the completion of the task.

Task

You need to move the On Site group members from their present positions to their new positions but only by making the permitted moves.

The On Site group members are already in their starting positions.

Your task is to move the people who are on the right-hand side of the X facing left, to the left-hand side of the X still facing left and in their original sequence. And vice versa.

Rules

1. Only one person at a time from your group may liaise with the On Site group.
2. The remainder of the Central group must stay in this room.
3. The On Site group has been instructed to do nothing without your specific approval.
4. This brief must stay in this room.
5. There are only two permitted moves: (i) an On Site group member may move forward into an empty space, so long as the empty space is immediately in front of them; and (ii) an On Site group member may move forward and around one person if that person is facing him or her, and there is an empty space immediately behind that person.
6. No member of the On Site group can turn round, everyone must remain facing forward at all times.
7. Only one person may move at a time.
8. Success is defined as being a continuous mistake-free process from start to finish.

I returned to the main room and invited the members of the On Site group to take up the starting positions that I set out on the floor earlier this morning before anyone arrived. I handed one of the group a hard copy of the On Site brief and instructed them to share it with the others:

'All Change'

On Site brief

You are the On Site group

Brief

- You are currently situated in your starting positions.
- You are required to remain in your allotted positions unless otherwise instructed by the Central group.
- You are required to remain in this room for the duration of the exercise.
- Communication with the other room is not permitted.
- Any failure to observe these rules will mean that you have failed the task.
- You may wish to discuss how you would like to work together.

Some background to the exercise might be useful at this point. The Central group are allowed to engage with the On Site group at any time they like, but in all of my years of using this exercise no Central group has ever been in a hurry to do so. There tends to be a 10- or 15-minute (often longer) hiatus during which the Central group make sense of the brief and, more often than not, they start to solve the problem without involving or having any contact with the On Site group. The On Site group, for their part, tend to comply with the brief and resist the temptation to converse with the Central group. During this period On Site and Central group members are apt to speculate and fantasise about the task and the motives of the other group. On Site groups tend to view themselves as subordinate to the Central groups, and even when the terms 'On Site' and 'Central' are used, in preference to 'staff' and 'managers', these organisational archetypes soon take precedence. The discussions following the exercise usually serve to deepen the problematisation of linear models of change as well as the inadequacies of mainstream conceptions of communication, and today was no exception. Following the exercise, we spent a good deal of time reflecting on those aspects of the exercise that are analogous to our lived experience, further problematising idealistic conceptions of how change happens.

It is now the afternoon session. The participants have been working in three small groups (two threes and a pair) to prepare a short teach-back presentation on their chosen mainstream theory of change. Paul's small group chose Kotter's eight-step process for leading change (Kotter, 1996), and they have decided to present first. Paul steps up to the front of the room to present on behalf of his group. Following the conversations that we engaged in this morning, I anticipate a description of Kotter's steps, followed by either a comprehensive critique of the model, or at least a firm challenge when compared with real-life change processes that Paul has experienced. Instead, Paul walks the audience through a 'change' that he has recently experienced with his team. He tells us that he sees a great deal of resonance between this model and his lived experience. In implementing the change he tells us that he did indeed create a sense of urgency (Kotter's Step 1) by taking his team on an away day to discuss the change. He then identified his guiding coalition (Kotter's Step 2); created his vision (Kotter's Step 3); communicated this vision at a follow-up away day (Kotter's Step 4); and so on. Paul proceeds to walk us through all eight of Kotter's steps articulating how they 'perfectly describe' what he and the team experienced.

When asked by one of the participants whether this was something new for the team, Paul says, 'No, not really'. Paul tells the group that the 'change' was an open day for prospective students. This was something that he and the team had been involved in many times previously, but it was a bigger event than usual and had been requested at relatively short notice. Another way of looking at this, then, is that Paul's team was asked at short notice to put on, what was for them, a fairly routine event, albeit on a scale that they had not experienced before. This 'change' called for more planning (away day) and more support and encouragement (what Paul described as 'vision and communicating that vision') from Paul than was usual, as a relief against the team's anxiety provoked by the extra responsibility (bigger event than usual) and workload (less time than they would usually have to organise) involved.

So what sense do I make of this?

Chris Rodgers' 'Management in Five Acts' framework (see Figure 3.1) illustrates how removed and abstract the models that we find ourselves referring and deferring to on conventional leadership development programmes are from our day-to-day experience.

Act 1 provides a reality congruent explanation of what we find ourselves doing each day in organisational (indeed, all) settings, that is, 'acting *forwards*, moment-by-moment, into a continuously emerging and unknowable future', and for Rodgers, '*hopefully doing this with purpose, courage and skill*'. Acts 2, 3 and 4 outline the increasingly abstract 'acts' that might follow as we account for what we are doing to others (Act 2), how conventional researchers generalise these accounts into theories of practice (Act 3), and how 'mainstream consultants, writers and policy makers' package them as best practice prescriptions for what we all ought to be doing to move from a 'dysfunctional/unhealthy current state' to a 'transformed/healthy future state' (Act 4). But as Rodgers points out in Act 5, 'we continue to do *the only thing* that we (and everyone else) can *actually do in practice*' and that is 'acting *forwards*, moment-by-moment, into a continuously emerging and unknowable future'.

The fact that Paul was able to retrospectively 'fit' what he and his colleagues found themselves doing into the Kotter model came as no surprise. As human beings, we have become adept at this form of post-rationalisation. Indeed, when participants on leadership development programmes encounter mainstream models and frameworks for the first time they often claim that they have been taking this very approach for years, but didn't have a label for it, and now they have. The two aspects of Paul's presentation that did surprise me were (i) how quickly the

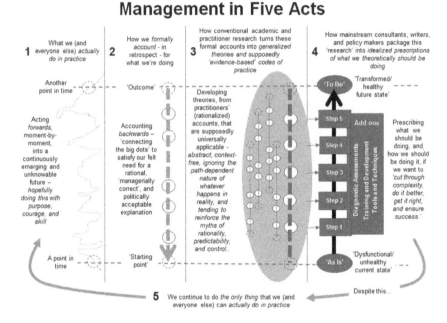

FIGURE 3.1 'Management in Five Acts'
Source: Chris Rodgers.

ordinary everyday activities that he and his team were involved in got lost in abstract conceptions of 'visionary leadership' and 'transformational change'; and (ii) the absence of any critique. Kotter's model is a typical example of the idealised, linear, cause and effect recipes for change that we had been problematising in the morning, yet not two hours later, Paul (a graduate of MSOL and a very vocal critic of idealised models of leadership and change earlier that day in the Community Meeting) finds himself advocating this model as a near-perfect description of what he and his team experienced.

This reflective narrative was triggered by what Patricia Shaw describes as a 'vivid moment of experience' (2010). Shaw describes such moments act as a 'common reference that you can point to, explore together, come to an understanding and sense-making together; which really has meaning for people in their everyday activity' (ibid.). In addition to giving an insight into my experience/practice, my reflections on this incident also serve as an illustration of the type of reflective narrative that:

i my colleagues and I encourage student-practitioners (managers) on the MBA programme at Hertfordshire Business School to write as a starting point for their sense-making and reflexivity in relation to their own practice with a view to catalysing the ongoing development of their capacities for practical judgement;

ii   I encourage those managers (student-practitioners) completing the accreditation for MSOL at UH to write for all of the the same reasons (albeit with a much smaller word count than that afforded to the MBA students – see Chapter 6).

iii   you will find in the chapters that follow as a means of highlighting the themes and elements of practice that I am pointing to and as a catalyst for reflexive curiosity – both mine and yours.

Taking experience seriously

What if there is no alternative to a situation where information is all over the place and where meaning can only be made by many different people making sense together in many different groupings and conversations? What if this is the most effective way of developing knowledge when the future is so unpredictable?

(Stacey et al.*, 2000)*

There are many themes and questions arising in the above narrative, but the ones that I want to explore in this chapter are (i) the tenacity of mainstream conceptions of leadership and organisation in the face of our experience to the contrary; (ii) the need to avoid the potential for leadership development programmes to become little more than what Edgar Schein (1961) describes as processes of coercive persuasion/brainwashing; (iii) organising and leading as complex responsive processes of relating; and (iv) the importance of the capacities of sense-making, reflexivity and practical judgement.

The tenacity of mainstream conceptions of leadership and organisation

A superficial reading of Rodgers' framework might suggest that he is arguing that Acts 2, 3 and 4 have no real influence on us as 'we continue (Act 5) to do *the only thing* that we (and everyone else) can *actually do in practice*' and that is (Act 1), to act '*forwards*, moment-by-moment, into a continuously emerging and unknowable future' (see Figure 3.1, emphasis in the original).[3] However, it is my contention that although the prescriptive models and theories found in mainstream literature and adduced on conventional leadership development programmes, like the Kotter model that Paul presented in the narrative above, are poor representations of what actually occurs in reality, they do have the potential to influence what happens. Chris Grey and Jana Costas contend that although things like company accounts, annual reports, organisation charts and the like are merely 'representations of organizations, not organizations themselves ... one cannot claim that the organisation and its representations are 'truly separate' as the 'various representations of organization also construct organization' (Grey and Costas in Czarniawska (2016: 136).

As outlined in Chapter 1, conventional conceptions of leadership and organisation, and the models, frameworks and prescriptions that accompany them, are tenacious fixtures in the organisational *habitus*. The deceptive certainty (illusion of validity – Kahneman, 2011, 2013) that they provide is seductive, not least because of the high expectations that are now placed on leaders, exacerbated by the 'talking up of leadership' (Blom and Alvesson, 2015) that has occurred in recent years, as discussed in Chapter 2. Like Paul, many of the managers that I work with try to make the 'ought' (Act 4 in Rodgers' framework above) their reality. This diverts attention away from what they actually find themselves doing with others and blinds them to the ongoing emergent patterns of human interaction (the operational realities) that they are participating in, which in turn diminishes the potential for acting into them in more useful, creative and spontaneous ways. What this means is that rather than making sense of what is actually happening and negotiating a way of going on together that resonates with those involved, extra effort is expended trying to implement, say, Step 3 of the chosen model, rather than working with what is actually going on and 'developing knowledge [that might be more helpful] when the future is so unpredictable' (Stacey *et al.*, 2000).

Patricia Shaw, one of the pioneers of the perspective of complex responsive processes of relating, along with Ralph Stacey and Doug Griffin argues that this ability to articulate what might actually be going on is lacking in the leader-managers who she works with. In her experience:

> Leaders are good at explanation, and they are very poor at description. They fail to be able to give detailed, telling, resonating, descriptive accounts of what happens and how it happens. They are too quick to move to wanting to find cause and effect, and too simplistic linear connections between events. They lack a kind of descriptive, reflective capacity to inquire into the way circumstances happen and change.
>
> *(Shaw, 2010)*

Taking complexity seriously involves noticing what might be right in front of our noses, hidden in plain sight. In this sense one could argue that taking a complexity approach entails looking to make the invisible (more) visible. As illustrated by the narrative above, mainstream models and prescriptions appeal to the managerialist ideology that has become an invisible element in the organisational habitus; invisible to the extent that even in the act of acknowledging that there is something wrong with this picture, we can find ourselves painting the same landscape over and over again. That is, we find it difficult to shake off this way of thinking even in the process of critiquing it. The simultaneous co-existence of these opposing perspectives is a paradox that goes some way to explaining why participants like Paul find themselves advocating models that are at odds with their lived experience and mainstream authors, like Collins and Hansen (2011), see no contradiction in acknowledging the complexity and ambiguity of (organisational) life at the same time as identifying the steps that their readers need to take in order to bring about certainty and predictability.

Using the Nick Cave quotation that opens this chapter as a jumping-off point, I contend that mainstream conceptions of organisation and leadership are 'an intellectual convenience' that keeps us from having to describe the 'flux' of our day-to-day experience. Stacey (2012) argues that abstractions of this nature serve a number of functions. First, they are used as rhetorical devices to persuade. Having worked for a consultancy that based its approach to change management engagements on the Kotter model, I can certainly vouch for this. Second, they can be used as a defence against the anxiety of not knowing. During turbulent times the belief that you, or whosoever you are looking to for guidance, has a roadmap for the future can be comforting, however illusory this might prove to be. Indeed, Hirschhorn (1995) drawing on Winnicott (1965) argues that abstract models are 'transitional objects' that allow managers to avoid the day-to-day anxiety of dealing with their own emotions by hiding behind tools and techniques, thus masking 'the real dilemmas of managing' (Hirschhorn, 1995: 119). I contend that the false certainty that Collins and Hansen (2011) are offering falls into this category. And third, Stacey (2012) argues that abstractions such as this can be used as a technique of 'disciplinary power', that is, as a tool for monitoring and control, which in the case of the Kotter model might involve checking that leader-managers have followed all of the eight steps effectively.

Working in the flux of our day-to-day experience involves letting go of the intellectual convenience of conventional conceptions of leadership and organisation and working with what 'is' rather than how mainstream authors contend it 'ought' to be, as well as paying attention to what we actually find ourselves doing as we go about the ordinary everyday activities that constitute work. This means taking our experience seriously. It entails thinking differently. It implies working differently. For me, this involves taking a complexity approach to leadership and organisation, leadership and organisation development. In the remainder of this book, I want to share with you what this looks like in my thinking/practice. As I have been at pains to point out in these early chapters, I am not looking to convince you of my view but rather I am encouraging you to take a reflexive look at your own. Why is this important?

Well, for leaders of leadership development it is important to take a reflexive turn in order to guard against the potential for the programmes and interventions that they lead to become little more that a form of coercive persuasion (Schein, 1961) or corporate brainwashing. The encouragement of participants on leadership development programmes to reflect on practice is ubiquitous, yet the quality and focus of this activity is often superficial and instrumental. Below, I explore reflexivity as a means of encouraging participants to question the basic assumptions and ways of thinking/doing to become (more) aware of organisational routines, social objects (Mead, 1934) and games (Elias, 1970; Crozier and Friedberg, 1980; Bourdieu, 1990) that they, and those around them, are all caught up in.

Leadership development as coercive persuasion/corrective training

Schein coined the phrase 'coercive persuasion' to describe development interventions designed to bring about attitudinal change (Schein, 1989: 426). He compared the induction and development of managers with the induction and development of novice nuns in convent schools, and the 'thought reform' of political prisoners during the Korean War (ibid.: 426–427). Schein contends that the management development programmes that come closest to coercive persuasion are those that 'remove the participant for some length of time from his normal routine ... thus providing a kind of moratorium during which he can take stock of himself and determine where he is going and where he wants to go' (ibid.: 433). He argues that the 'brainwashing' techniques employed during such moratoria include:

1. Prevention from leaving the learning experience.
2. Intense interpersonal and psychological pressure to destabilize sense of self and current beliefs and values.
3. Learners are put into teams so that those at more advanced stages of moving to new culture can mentor those at less advanced stages.
4. The team is rewarded if all its members demonstrate that they have learned the collective values.
5. The new values ... are presented in many different forms.

(Schein, 1961)

Schein argues that we can be oblivious to the use of coercive techniques if we believe that what we are doing is in some way 'legitimate':

> [W]e cannot ignore that the same methods of learning, i.e. coercive persuasion or, colloquially, brainwashing, can be and are being used equally for goals that we deplore and goals that we accept. If we deplore the goals we condemn the methods, forgetting or denying that we are using the same methods in our organizations for goals that we consider legitimate.
>
> *(1999: 170)*

He goes on to argue that 'true "generative learning" based on learner freedom becomes, from this point of view, a concept that is itself culturally defined. To be encouraged to make choices and "live free" can be experienced as being just as coercive as to be encouraged to "conform" and "fit in" depending upon what is valued in a given cultural context' (ibid.: 171).

Stacey does not perceive corrective training as negative per se, arguing that 'complex modern organisations cannot function without the techniques of surveillance, hierarchical normalisation and corrective training' (2011: 18). However, he argues that 'when leadership theories and leadership development programmes focus attention on idealised and, thus, unrealistic theories ... the danger ... is that the techniques of disciplinary power are utilised in completely taken-for-granted ways which are not open to question or critical reflection. This makes it possible for the techniques to be taken up in increasingly extreme ways which produce counterproductive domination and block creativity and innovation' (ibid.).

Of course, even where the techniques of coercive persuasion and corrective training are intentionally employed, it does not guarantee that an actual change in attitudes, beliefs and behaviours will actually occur. Indeed, Stacey, drawing on Ofshe (2000), argues that although participants might 'show all the appearance of making the change in public ... in private they [may] display well developed skills of resistance ... The programmes do not really change the beliefs of many people but they do train them in the public display of willing acceptance' (Stacey, 2011: 9). Similarly, Schein (1961) found that the vast majority of political prisoners who seemed to have been 'converted' reverted to their old beliefs on return to their homeland.

The reason for introducing this concept here is to draw attention to the fact that the vast majority of corporate and business school leadership development programmes are steeped in managerialist ways of thinking (see Chapter 1) with no other perspectives on leadership and organisation being acknowledged, let alone explored and given serious consideration. I contend that not sharing critical and/or complexity views of leadership and organisation with participants on conventional programmes is a form of coercive persuasion. Similarly, on critical management and/or complexity-based leadership development programmes, not acknowledging and exploring conventional views leaves one open to the same accusation. In addition, such an omission might also leave participants exposed, that is, lacking the wisdom required to judge (practical judgement) when to challenge and when to play the game with a 'display of willing acceptance' (Stacey, 2011: 9).

So far, in this book I have revealed glimpses of the perspective that informs the complexity approach to leadership and organisation that I have been working with in my thinking/practice – the perspective of complex responsive processes of relating. This seems to be an appropriate point at which to explain and explore the key aspects of this perspective more fully.

Organising as complex responsive processes of relating

> You will not change the world tomorrow by thinking differently, but you may find that you have a more fruitful and interesting experience as a manager or as a teacher or adviser of managers.
>
> *Stacey and Mowles (2016)*

The following explication of the perspective of complex responsive processes of relating is my take on the thinking of Stacey *et al.* (2000); Stacey (2010, 2012); Griffin (2002); Shaw (2002); Mowles (2011, 2015) and Stacey and Mowles (2016). This thinking has most definitely helped to make my experience as a manager, teacher and adviser of managers more 'fruitful and interesting' (ibid.: 21). If my account of the perspective resonates with something that you have become aware of in your own thinking/practice, then I would encourage you to find the time to engage directly with the source material. A useful starting point? The titles above, the DMan theses that the vignettes in this book are taken from (see Chapters 4, 5 and 6) and/or any of the publications from the last fifteen years that are freely available.[4] And should you choose to do so, I am confident that your investment of time and effort will be more than adequately repaid.

When Ralph Stacey joined UH as a lecturer, some thirty-five years ago, he was tasked with teaching strategy on the MBA programme. Having completed a first degree in economics at the University of Witwatersrand in Johannesburg (for which he won prizes for his work in economic modelling), Stacey moved to the UK to complete a Masters and then a PhD in economic model building and forecasting using sophisticated statistical models at the London School of Economics (Mowles, 2017). He went on to hold a number of senior management roles in planning for major corporations and in strategy for a firm of stockbrokers in the City of London before joining UH in 1985 (ibid.).

During his years in industry Stacey came to recognise how bad we humans are at forecasting and how rational, linear, cause and effect approaches to organising offer little by way of explanation for the many surprises, both pleasant and unpleasant, that life in organisations seems to continually throw up.

Consequently, he became interested in what it is that we are all doing together in organisations when involved in activities like forecasting, and how, in spite of all of the rational planning methods contained in the academic textbooks that he was now expected to share with students on the MBA programme, we are continually surprised by what actually plays out. Thus, if the world we live in is inherently uncertain and unpredictable, and management science offers little beyond futile attempts (my words) to make it so, where do we go from here? For Stacey, who already had an interest in mathematical modelling and non-linear dynamics, the next step was to explore what the complexity sciences – the sciences of uncertainty – might have to offer.

In the computer modelling of non-linear (where cause doesn't lead to equal effect) phenomena like the human brain or weather patterns, unpredictable, yet coherent, population-wide patterns emerge in the interaction of thousands of agents (bits of computer code) in the absence of any blueprint, plan or guidance from any one or small number of 'super agents'. The patterns that emerge in these complex adaptive systems (CAS) are predictable and unpredictable at the same time. Each agent in a CAS model is connected to a small number of agents in the total population and each agent can only act/interact in accordance with the particular principles that govern them (that is, how they have been coded to act by the programmer). Through the interaction of agents, which CAS scientists call self-organisation, population-wide patterns emerge.

Stacey's early publications explore what it might mean to move from thinking about organisations as cybernetic systems (machines made up of parts that contribute to a whole that can be designed and manipulated at will), to an understanding of organisations as CAS (patterns of interaction between agents which are predictable and unpredictable at the same time, where global patterns emerge in processes of self-organisation that cannot be designed in advance or controlled at will). However, in collaboration with Doug Griffin and Patricia Shaw (Stacey's PhD students who joined him in setting up the DMan at UH), Stacey's thinking soon shifted. Unlike agents in a computer programme, humans have the capacity to become aware of the patterns that we are caught up in and articulate something of this. Additionally, although we are both enabled and constrained in our relations with others, we nevertheless have the potential to act spontaneously.

Stacey, Griffin and Shaw looked to the 'pragmatism of G. H. Mead (1934, 1938) and the process sociology of Norbert Elias (2000, 2001)' (Mowles, 2017) to explain their experience of trying to get things done with others in organisational settings. This point is worth reiterating and keeping in mind: Stacey, Griffin and Shaw were interested in understanding what they and the researcher-practitioners they worked with were experiencing in the everyday politics of life in organisations. They concluded that while CAS are, and continue to be, a useful source domain from which useful analogies can be drawn in order to make sense of what might be happening in work (and other) settings, these models are not directly attributable to organisations. Organisations are not CAS.

Indeed, this would also be a good point at which to abandon the literary device/conceit, employed in Chapter 2, namely splitting leadership from organisation. From a complexity perspective, the reification of organisation as something concrete and separate from the iterative processes of human communicative interaction that constitute organisation, does not make sense. Barbara Czarniawska, acknowledging the work of Shenhav (1999), argues that 'in the late 1960s, organization theorists changed the dominant meaning of the term *organization* so as to be able to import systems theory' (quoted in Robichaud and Cooren, 2013: 3; emphasis in the original). She argues for a distinction between organisation and the process of organising. She contends that one might categorise organisation as the artefacts – buildings, systems, policies and procedures, governance structures, etc. – and organising (Weick, 1979) as the social processes that construct the artefacts that help people to organise (Czarniawska, 2014). So, although we are more or less able to control the artefacts of organisation, we are not able to control the social processes of organising that created them in the first place. Thus we find managers making changes to organisation in the hope of controlling how we are organising (ibid.). This resonates with the complexity approach to organisation developed by Stacey and colleagues. Drawing on the natural sciences of complexity and the social sciences of pragmatist philosophy, process sociology and social psychology, they focus on the social processes of organising.

Organisation: a working definition

One could say that organisations are complex responsive processes of relating. However, this definition has a saying everything whilst saying nothing quality to it.

Let's explore this understanding of organisation a little further. From the perspective of complex responsive processes of relating, organisations can be more usefully (and accurately) understood as ongoing patterns of communicative interaction between interdependent human beings in which our identities (roles, personas, ways of being) are being shaped at the same time as we are shaping the identities of others in ongoing patterns of interaction. Patterns emerge as a consequence of the interplay of everyone's plans and intentions as they participate in the ongoing game of organisational life. Through the interplay of local patterns, global patterns emerge. What happens locally influences the global at the same time as what's happening globally constrains the local. That which emerges cannot be designed and/or controlled by any one or small group of individuals, irrespective of how much influence they may have. This patterning of interaction (the game) does not exist outside of our participation in (playing of) it. It is predictable and unpredictable at the same time. There is no equilibrium to be found or optimum state to be reached, patterns just lead to more patterns; no more no less.

A number of concepts arise in this view of organisation that are often ignored, misunderstood or dealt with differently in conventional, critical and alternative complexity perspectives, namely, (i) interdependence; (ii) local interaction and emergence; (iii) participation (in the game); and (iv) treatment of paradox (Stacey and Mowles, 2016).[5] I now briefly explain each of these concepts in turn, identify the implications for leadership and leadership development and point you to the relevant chapter in which these ideas are explored in more detail.

Interdependence

Interdependence involves more than simply acknowledging that as human beings we are reliant on each other. It means letting go of our conception of human beings as autonomous individuals. We cannot do whatever we want. We are enabled and constrained by, at the same time as enabling and constraining, each other. That is, we are interdependent. This fundamentally challenges mainstream perspectives of leadership based on individual psychology and leadership development interventions based on narrow conceptions of power and what it means to be self-aware. The implications of this radically different way of thinking for coaching, and the use and usefulness of psychometric tools and 360° feedback in leadership development programmes, are explored in Chapter 4.

Local interaction and emergence

Local interaction describes what in complexity science terms is known as self-organisation. Stacey and colleagues prefer local interaction to self-organisation because self-organisation is regularly misinterpreted by the managers they are working with to mean some form of free for all, where all do what they please. Local interaction points to the fact that even though we might be caught up in population-wide patterns of interaction that we describe as organisation, we only regularly interact with a very small number of that overall population – our team, the team of managers we get together with, and representatives from the groups we support and/or support us. Thus, interactions are local. Similarly, emergence is often taken to mean 'whatever will be, will be', and/or is viewed as some mysterious process that we have little influence over. However, for Stacey and colleagues, the exact opposite is true. Emergence is not something magical or mystical, instead it is a description of how the global patterns of human interaction – which we call organisations – emerge in the interplay of the intentions of all involved in many, many local interactions. And, as outlined above, we cannot simply do what we please (and if we could this would lead to chaos), but that does not mean that we do nothing and it certainly does not mean that we do not try to influence things in our favour.

Taking a complexity approach involves accepting that we cannot predetermine what happens in local interaction and therefore we cannot control what might emerge in the global patterning. It is not that we don't try to influence what we would like to see happen in the macro, through restructures, strategic plans, policy changes and the like, rather that we might understand such things as gestures that might influence but will not control what actually happens in the micro. We can influence and our influence might be great, but we cannot control. What plays out will depend on how such gestures are taken up (responded to) in local interaction. The implications for leadership and leadership development are that we might pay more attention to what we find ourselves doing with others in local communicative interaction (conversation), as well as exploring communication as ongoing processes of gesture and response (Mead, 1934), areas that will be explored in Chapter 5.

Participation in the game

One cannot separate oneself from the patterns of interaction that one is caught up in, and the patterns of interaction that we are caught up in are shaping us at the same time as we are shaping them. From this perspective, conceptions like adaptive leadership, where leaders can be on the balcony looking down at the dance (Heifetz and Linsky, 2002) do not make sense. There is no stepping outside of these patterns of interaction to see the 'big picture' before stepping back in to fix, shape or control the patterns that emerge. This does not mean that we cannot or should not speculate about what might be happening in the 'big picture', but we should not kid ourselves that speculations are any more than that. There is no stepping out of the dance. Instead of viewing leader-managers as objective observers, a complexity approach sees leader-managers as participative inquirers (Stacey and Mowles, 2016: 33). From this perspective, leadership development is about helping participants to develop the capacity for becoming more detached in their involvement in the game (Elias, 1970). In Chapter 6, I explore how team-building exercises, Outward Bound-type interventions, simulations and live case studies might be engaged with more fruitfully to encourage the development of this capability.

Paradox

In organisational life, we encounter many contradictions. We invite diversity and then ask those who effect difference only to do so in ways that we already feel comfortable with. We pursue alignment, so that everyone is 'on the same page' at the same time as encouraging creativity and innovation. From the perspective of complex responsive processes of relating, paradoxes like forming and being formed, the co-existence of the non-linearity and messiness of change, and the 'perfection' of the Kotter model for Paul, cannot be resolved. They can only be lived with and explored. In Chapter 7, I explore the use of Action Learning Sets in leadership development programmes and argue that there is much in Revans' (1980) original philosophy to support the exploration of paradox. However, this has been lost over the years with the Learning (in relation to the creation of new knowledge) and Set (in respect of exploring group dynamics) aspects of Action Learning Sets being played down and the focus being placed on the Action element, which often means ignoring, collapsing or adopting a 'this and then that' (first one side, then the other) approach to paradox.

The implications for leadership and leadership development

Working from the above definition of organisation, leadership is merely one of the many phenomena (patterns) that emerge in the local and population-wide patterns of human, social, communicative interaction that we call organisation. As outlined in Chapter 2, leadership is a social and relational phenomenon. That is, one does not get to choose whether one is recognised as a leader or not. Leadership, if it does emerge, is something that is co-created in social interaction. Consequently, it makes no sense to talk about one's leadership style or approach, whether authentic, distributed, transformational, authoritarian, etc., because how such a gesture is responded to by others is not within one's gift. As generic descriptors of intent, these concepts have limited utility; as recipes or roadmaps for how one might participate as a leader-manager in local interaction, they are fairly meaningless.

So, if taking a complexity approach to leadership development means neither encouraging participants to conform to a certain style of leadership nor advocating abstract conceptions of what mainstream researchers and authors think leaders ought to be learning/doing, what does it involve? In other words, what is it that I find myself doing as a leader of leadership development? Well, I am bound to say that there is no formula; leadership development programmes are also complex responsive processes of relating, and every programme is different. However, I do set out with a clear structure in mind and some specific ideas for what we might engage with as a learning community. So, what are the key themes that I point to and hope to explore in taking a complexity approach to leadership development?

First, *navigating the everyday politics of organisational life*. That is, becoming aware of the games we are caught up in, becoming more adept in the playing of them and keeping in mind that in the playing of them we are simultaneously played. Second, *awareness of the context(s) in which we find ourselves.* This involves paying attention to the patterns emerging in local (your team and the individuals/teams you and/or your team regularly interact with) and global (wider organisational, sector, societal) interaction and acting accordingly. Third, *awareness of self in relation to/with others and finding one's way in groups.* This entails working with affect and living with uncertainty and the anxiety that this provokes. Fourth, *acknowledging the shadow side of leading-managing.* That is, being aware of the potential for leaders to become idealised and/or for hubris to set in, leading to denigration (Stacey, 2012) and/or derailment (de Haan and Kasozi, 2014). Fifth, *exploring the importance of stewardship* and our responsibilities to the triple bottom line – people, planet, profit. Sixth, *creating spaces for reflective and reflexive inquiry* (Shaw, 2005). Patricia Shaw argues that 'our traditional understanding of control – of being able to trace simple chains of cause and effect, of re-engineering the form of our organizational activities – is proving illusory' (ibid.: 19). She contends that 'this is leading us to explain continuity and change as arising through intensive processes of joint inquiry amongst diverse participants. The focus is shifting from the design of outcomes to the design of, and participation in, inquiry processes' (ibid.). And finally, *enhancing the capacities* that help with all of the above, namely, *sense-making, reflexivity and practical judgement.*

Sense-making, reflexivity and practical judgement

As outlined earlier, there are topics that I will be covering in a chapter or part thereof that some authors have written multiple books about, and/or dedicated whole research careers to. The topics of sense-making, reflexivity and practical judgement most definitely fall into this category. However, in this case, although this is the only section that directly explores sense-making, reflexivity and practical judgement, in one way or another the whole book is dedicated to this concept. I say concept, rather than concepts, as I see sense-making, reflexivity and practical judgement as intertwined elements of the same process. That is, it would be impossible to say where one starts and the other(s) end(s). They are inseparable elements of the process that I referred to earlier as reflexive curiosity. As with leadership and organisation and leadership and management in earlier chapters, the splitting of sense-making, reflexivity and practical judgement here is purely a literary device to aid comprehension.

Sense-making

> To appreciate organizations and their environments as flows interrupted by constraints of one's own making, is to take oneself a little less seriously, to find a little more leverage in human affairs on a slightly smaller scale, and to have a little less hubris and a little more fun … In the last analysis, organizing is about fallible people who keep going.
>
> *(Karl E. Weick 2001: xi)*

Weick *et al.* (2005) summarise sensemaking as having a 'genesis in disruptive ambiguity'. For them, it begins with 'acts of noticing and bracketing ... a mixture of retrospect and prospect' with a 'reliance on presumptions to guide action'. It is a social and interdependent activity whereby:

> Answers to the question "what's the story?" emerge from retrospect, connections with past experience, and dialogue among people who act on behalf of larger social units. Answers to the question "now what?" emerge from presumptions about the future, articulation concurrent with action, and projects that become increasingly clear as they unfold.
>
> *(Ibid.: 413)*

Maitlis and Christianson view sensemaking as 'an activity that is central to organising', defining it as 'the process through which people work to understand issues or events that are novel, ambiguous, confusing, or in some other way violate expectations' and they argue that it is central to the 'key organizational processes of change, learning and creativity and innovation' (2014: 57). They also explore two more recent constructs that they feel contribute to an understanding of how sensemaking occurs in organisations: (i) sensegiving; and (ii) sensebreaking. They describe sensegiving as a process that is 'often studied in the context of how organizational leaders or managers strategically shape the sensemaking of organizational members through the use of symbols, images, and other influence techniques', although they also acknowledge that it is 'not simply a top-down process ... as those receiving sensegiving have their own interpretations and can actively resist efforts from leaders to influence strategic change' (ibid.: 67). And they describe sensebreaking as a process in which people are asked to 're-consider the sense that they have already made, to question their underlying assumptions, and to re-examine their course of action' (ibid.: 69). They argue that sensebreaking is 'often a prelude to sensegiving, in which leaders or organizations fill the meaning void created through sensebreaking with new meaning' (ibid.).

Maitlis and Christianson identify three things that trigger sensemaking in organisations:

1. environmental jolts and organizational crises;
2. threats to identity ... individual and group identity.
3. planned change interventions – sensebreaking and sensegiving by new leaders.

(2014: 71–75)

For Maitlis and Christianson, sensemaking is triggered by events or incidents where 'the meaning is ambiguous and/or the outcomes uncertain', that is, situations that 'interrupt people's ongoing flow, disrupting their understanding of the world and creating uncertainty about how to act' (ibid.: 70). However, they also argue that even when there are such 'discrepant cues', they may not trigger sensemaking 'if group norms or the organizational culture mitigate against it'. They offer examples from their research where 'people accommodate, explain away, or normalize discrepant cues' (ibid.). One of the reasons they give for this is that habitual routines often reduce mindfulness.

I would agree and I would also argue that the opposite occurs, where in the absence of discrepant cues some leaders will seek to trigger what might be described as sensebreaking and sensegiving as a means of stamping their authority, making their mark, or delivering on the promises made at interview to effect change, etc. However, as pointed out previously, they cannot control how such gestures are taken up by others. For example, I would describe my dissemination of Kotter's (1996) eight-step recipe for transformational change to participants on MSOL as a form of *sensesharing*. However, Paul's response to this gesture was to see it as the perfect framework through which to describe his experience. That is, what I offered as sensesharing was taken up as sensegiving.

Barbara Czarniawska (2014) differentiates between three types of logic that are used in sensemaking: the logic of practice; the logic of theory; and, drawing on Bourdieu's (1990) conception of officialization, the logic of representation. She describes the logic of practice as 'concrete (situated in time and space) … discursively incomplete … drawing as it does on a fragmentary understanding of "tacit knowledge" and expressed in narratives that are chronologically ordered' (Czarniawska, 2014: 11). The logic of theory is described as 'abstract', hiding 'its rhetorical accomplishments' behind 'claims to formal logic' and 'methodological criteria of truth' (ibid.). The logic of representation is also described as 'abstract … but often [uses] hypothetical concrete examples', 'rhetorically sophisticated', it uses 'stylized narratives' that borrow their 'legitimacy' from the logics of theory and practice' (ibid.).

Czarniawska argues that the 'current logic of representation demands a kind of imitation of the logic of theory, legitimated by the claim that it originated in the logic of practice. Difficult, but not impossible!' (2014: 11). This resonates with my experience of Paul's presentation of the Kotter model at the beginning of this chapter. Paul legitimated Kotter's framework by claiming that it was a perfect representation of what happened for him in practice. As noted above, the tenacity of mainstream models and theories is partly explained by the utility they offer as a defence against anxiety and as rhetorical devices to persuade. They offer what Kahneman (2013) describes as the illusion of validity.

The concept of sense-making that I am pointing to is a little more mundane than the sensemaking referred to by Weick *et al.*, Maitlis and Christianson, and Czarniawska, as it also proceeds in the absence of crisis, threats or planned change. This is one of the reasons why I feel it is necessary to differentiate between sense-making and sensemaking. Sense-making is paradoxically both an individual cognitive process and a social phenomenon at the same time. Sense-making is simultaneously retrospective and future-oriented as it emerges in the living present. Sense-making is both ongoing and episodic at the same time. That is, the sense-making process may well be punctuated by episodic crises, but it is also an ongoing process that doesn't and shouldn't just occur as the result of novelty. Unlike sensemaking, which is seen as something that is triggered by difference and/or disruption, sense-making (reflexivity and practical judgement) is something that we should initiate even as things seem to be going swimmingly.

Mead (1934) used the term 'social objects' to draw attention to the generalised tendencies of people to act in similar/familiar ways in similar/familiar situations. These similar ways/situations tend to generate habitual, repetitive and unconscious patterns of interaction. Mead argued that when social objects become idealised, i.e. stripped of all constraint and contestation, they are more aptly termed 'cult values'. For example, Mead (1932) argued that democracy is a cult value, as is treating others with respect. For Mead, if cult values are then applied without making any allowances for the specific circumstances one finds oneself in, then those taking such action form a cult that excludes all those that do not comply. I contend that managerialism, efficiency and standardisation have become cult values. Indeed, one of the reasons why leadership development programmes are experienced by participants as a form of coercive persuasion/corrective training is because of the requirement to unquestioningly accept such 'givens' and be seen to fit in.

Elias (1970), Crozier (1980) and Bourdieu (1990) variously refer to the generalised tendencies of groups to act in similar/familiar ways in similar/familiar circumstances as 'games'. For Elias (1970) becoming more detached in our involvement is a difficult but important capacity to develop in order to ensure that we do not get caught up in games (patterns of power relating) that are unhelpful or destructive. For Crozier and Friedberg, it is important to try to understand the 'power games which indirectly structure the strategies of the actors involved and [that] constrain freedom of choice' (1980: 6). Elias argues that it is 'difficult for players to comprehend that their inability to control the game derives from their mutual dependence and positioning as players, and from the tensions and conflicts inherent in [the] intertwining network' of the game (1972: 87).

Elias and Scotson (1994) also point out that calling the game into question can leave us open to the risk of being excluded. Bourdieu argues that although no individual player can control the game, they can increase their power chances by accumulating 'cultural capital' (1990: 125). All of these authors and concepts will be explored in more detail in Chapter 6. At this point, I am arguing that becoming more detached in our involvement and thinking about our thinking (reflexivity, see below) might lead to a novel understanding of those events that we currently consider routine, habitual or expected. Indeed, if one takes a complexity approach to sense-making, then no two interactions will ever be the same. They are predictably unpredictable. Consequently, one could argue that there is always the threat of disruption, even if this only occasionally materialises.

Reflexivity

If we practise detachment from our thoughts we learn to observe them as though we are taking a bird's eye view of our own thinking. When we do this, we might find that our thinking belongs to an older, and different, story to the one we are now living.

(Philippa Perry 2012)

Reflexivity is one of the concepts that participants find difficult to practice, and often struggle to differentiate from reflection. Stacey and Mowles describe reflexivity as 'being aware of the impact on how one thinks of both one's personal history and the history and traditions of thought of one's community' (2016: 36). Cunliffe and Jun argue that reflexivity is 'concerned with understanding the grounds of our thinking [which involves] engaging in the reflexive act of questioning the basis of our thinking, surfacing the taken for granted rules underlying organisational decisions, and examining critically our own practices and ways of relating with others' (2005: 227). And Alvesson and Spicer describe reflexivity by outlining what occurs when it is not present. They argue that:

> [one of the] telltale aspects of functional stupidity [is the] *absence of reflexivity* [which] happens when we stop asking questions about our assumptions. Put simply, it involves taking for granted what other people commonly think. We often fail to question dominant beliefs and expectations. We see rules, routines and norms as completely natural: they are just as things are.
>
> *(2016: 78; emphasis in the original)*

What I take from the above descriptions is that reflexivity involves becoming aware that our ways of thinking/acting are not natural, foundational truths, but ways of thinking/acting that have developed over time and have become part of the personal and collective understandings available to the communities in which we live and work. These ways of thinking/acting may well be 'just as things are' (Alvesson and Spicer, 2016: 78), but that does not mean that we cannot challenge them, particularly when they are no longer useful to us and/or those around us. Paul's description of the change model would have been readily accepted as a routine aspect of any of the conventional leadership development programmes that I have participated in as a manager. However, as facilitator, taking a complexity approach, Paul's description was what Shaw (2010) describes as a 'vivid moment of experience'. As outlined above, this is a 'moment of common reference that you can point to, explore together, come to an understanding and sense-making together that really has meaning for people in their everyday activity' (ibid.). That is, an opportunity for reflexivity – a chance to notice and think about how we are thinking. In the case of the narrative above, it is an opportunity to explore conventional, critical and complexity perspectives on change and compare and contrast these with our lived experience. As outlined in previous chapters, this raises doubts and, potentially, disillusionment. The decision required is whether and how you bring it to the attention of others, and this requires practical judgement.

Practical judgement

> I say make a mark, put a foot onto the path, see (and feel and think) how it
> lands; and then you can make a good guess about where to put the next foot.
>
> (Philippa Perry 2012)

There are many terms used for what I am referring to as practical judgement.
Aristotle used the term *phronesis*, which translates from the original Greek as pru-
dence or practical wisdom (Eikeland, 2006). I prefer the term *practical judgement*
(Hager 2000) over *practical wisdom* as this reminds me, and the managers with
whom I work, of the deliberative nature of phronesis, and the fact that we do not
and will not always get it right. Deliberation is a characteristic of Aristotle's original
conception that is often lost in (mis)interpretations of phronesis as some form of
sixth sense, intuition, magic or mystical touch. Hager, after Noel (1999), argues
that there are three main categories of phronesis as described in the literature:
(i) acting rationally; (ii) responding to the particulars of the context; and (iii) taking
into account the ethical implications of the courses of action that one is considering
(Hager, 2000: 282). When Hager wrote his piece, he felt that the available interpretations of Aristotelian phronesis fell short of capturing all three categories,
although he concedes that Dunne (1993) came close. I contend that Eikeland's
explication does contain all three of the categories identified by Noel (1999) and
more.

Eikeland argues that Aristotle saw phronesis as both an intellectual and an ethical
virtue; that is, one cannot be '(intellectually) prudent (phrónimoi) without being
(ethically) good' (2006: 20). Eikeland's definition of phronesis puts this ethical
dimension of phronesis front and centre:

> Phrónêsis does not try to manipulate, or merely persuade, but must present its
> own thinking and reasons for deciding and acting in certain ways as openly as
> possible to the mindful judgement of others, trying to show, and convince,
> making them see, but still respecting their autonomy ... Phrónêsis must take
> into consideration where the others are, emotionally, intellectually, and in
> their skills and attitudes, in trying to find the right thing to do, but it cannot
> use these circumstances manipulatively trying to set through some hidden
> agenda, without ruining itself qua phrónêsis. It must know how to deal with
> egotistical, strategic, manipulative behaviour in others without itself becoming
> like this, but also without simply being subdued by it and letting such behaviour
> prevail in others and in general.
>
> (Ibid.: 34–35)

Eikeland's definition resonates with Khurana's (2007) view of manager as steward
and Kellerman's (2012) caution to 'followers' to avoid colluding with the 'manipulative' behaviours of 'egotistical' senior executives. Eikeland's understanding of
Aristotle's conception of phronesis is rather more idealistic and individualistic than

my conception of practical judgement, but as an aspiration for how one might play into the role of leader-manager, I think it has merit. My claims for practical judgement are far more modest and involve the articulation of a next step into an unknown future that resonates with you and those around you. That is, having made sense of the context and/or situation in which we find ourselves and explored the thinking that influenced and/or is sustaining this current state, it is about identifying and articulating a next step in to the unknown in the knowledge that this will inevitably have intended and unintended consequences, some of which might not become apparent for some time. However, as pointed out above, this is not a three-step linear process, as practical judgement involves sense-making and reflexivity, while reflexivity involves sense-making and practical judgement, and so on.

Sense-making, reflexivity and practical judgement are descriptors for what we already do as leader-managers, whether we are conscious of it or not. I am arguing that what Paul and the rest of us find ourselves doing on a day-to-day basis is akin to Rodgers' Act 1 ('acting *forwards*, moment-by-moment, into a continuously emerging and unknowable future'), even if we find ourselves explaining what we are doing in the language of Act 4 ('*cut[ting] through complexity … and ensuring success*'). In Chapters 4, 5, 6 and 7, I take a look at a number of conventional leadership development interventions with a view to exploring how, in taking a complexity approach to leadership development, I am encouraging the development of the capacities of sense-making, reflexivity and practical judgement as a means of helping participants to navigate 'what is' rather than spending an inordinate amount of time worrying about how it 'ought to be'. To put it another way, as Weick would have it, 'to find a little more leverage in human affairs … to have a little less hubris and a little more fun' (2001: xi).

Notes

1 For a comprehensive description of 'Making Sense of Leading' (and a definition of 'broadly critical'), see Flinn and Mowles (2014).

2 The Community Meeting is an opportunity for the group, at the beginning of each workshop, to catch up, share what they have been thinking about since our last meeting, and discuss their experience and experiences of the theme for the day. The name and process of the Community Meeting is a variation of what I experienced on the DMan programme at UH; see Chapter 7 and Flinn and Mowles (2014).

3 I would also contend the depiction of the patterns of interaction that constitute Act 1. The squiggly line, depicting the 'acting forwards' from 'a point in time' to 'another point in time', seems to suggest some form of progress. From the perspective of complex responsive processes, patterns of interaction may be changing and time will be passing, but these patterns of interaction don't 'go' anywhere. This is merely another spatial metaphor.

4 Search on Google Scholar, and/or take a look at the following blogs: (i) Chris Mowles, available at https://reflexivepractice.wordpress.com and (ii) Complexity Management Centre, available at https://complexityandmanagement.wordpress.com

5 For a painstaking analysis of the similarities and differences in the way that interdependence, emergence, participation and paradox are taken up in conventional, critical

and alternative complexity perspectives, compared to how these four criteria are understood from the perspective of complex responsive processes of relating, see Stacey and Mowles (2016).

References

Alvesson, M., Blom, M. and Sveningsson, S. (2017) *Reflexive Leadership: Organising in an Imperfect World*. London: Sage.

Alvesson, M. and Spicer, A. (2016) *The Stupidity Paradox: The Power and Pitfalls of Functional Stupidity at Work*. London: Profile Books.

Blom, M. and Alvesson, M. (2015) 'Less followership, less leadership? An inquiry into the basic but seemingly forgotten downsides of leadership'. *M@n@gement*, 18(3): 266–282.

Bourdieu, P. (1977) *Outline of a Theory of Practice*, London: Cambridge University Press.

Bourdieu, P. (1990) *The Logic of Practice*. Cambridge: Polity Press.

Cave, N. (2017) Interview. *The Guardian*. Available at www.theguardian.com/music/2017/may/04/nick-cave-death-son-struggle-write-tragedy

Collins, J. and Hansen, M. T. (2011) *Great by Choice: Uncertainty, Chaos and Luck – Why Some Thrive despite Them All*. London: Random House.

Crozier, M. and Friedberg, E. (1980) *Actors and Systems: The Politics of Collective Action*. Chicago, IL: University of Chicago Press.

Cunliffe, A. L. and Jun, J. S. (2005) 'The need for reflexivity in public administration'. *Administration & Society*, 37(2): 225–242.

Czarniawska, B. (2013) In D. Robichaud and F. Cooren (Eds) *Organization and Organizing: Materiality, Agency and Discourse*. Abingdon: Routledge.

Czarniawska, B. (2014) *A Theory of Organizing* (2nd edn). Cheltenham: Edward Elgar Publishing.

Czarniawska, B. (Ed.) *A Research Agenda for Management and Organisation Studies*. Cheltenham: Edward Elgar.

de Haan, E. and Kasozi, A. (2014) *The Leadership Shadow: How to Recognize and Avoid Derailment, Hubris and Overdrive*. London: Kogan Page.

Dunne, J. (1993) *Back to the Rough Ground: 'Phronesis' and 'Techne' in Modern Philosophy and in Aristotle*. London: University of Notre Dame Press.

Eikeland, O. (2006) 'Phrónêsis, Aristotle, and Action Research'. *International Journal of Action Research*, 2(1): 5–53.

Eikeland, O. (2007) *The Ways of Aristotle: Aristotelian Phrónêsis, Aristotelian Philosophy, and Action Research*. Bern: Peter Lang.

Elias, N. (1956) 'Problems of involvement and detachment'. *British Journal of Sociology*, 7(3): 226–252.

Elias, N. (1970) *What Is Sociology*. London: Hutchinson.

Elias, N. (1991) *The Society of Individuals*. Oxford: Blackwell.

Elias, N. (2000) *The Civilizing Process: Sociogenetic and Psychogenetic Investigations*. Cambridge, MA: Blackwell.

Elias, N. (2001). *The Society of Individuals*. Trans. E. Jephcott, ed. M. Schröter. New York: Continuum International Publishing Group.

Elias, N. and Scotson, J. L. (1994) *The Established and the Outsiders*. London: Sage.

Flinn, K. and Mowles, C. (2014) *A Complexity Approach to Leadership Development: Developing Practical Judgement*. Leadership Foundation for Higher Education stimulus paper.

Grey, C. and Costas, J. (2016) Invisible Organizations: A Research Agenda. In B. Czarniawska (Ed.) *A Research Agenda for Management and Organisation Studies*. Cheltenham: Edward Elgar.

Griffin, D. (2002) *The Emergence of Leadership: Linking Self-Organisation and Ethics*. London: Routledge.

Hager, P. (2000) 'Know-how and workplace practical judgement'. *Journal of Philosophy of Education*, 34(2): 281–296.

Heifetz, R. A. and Linsky, M. (2002) *Leadership on the Line: Staying Alive through the Dangers of Leading*. Boston, MA: Harvard Business Review Press.

Hirschhorn, L. (1995) *The Workplace Within: The Psychodynamics of Organizational Life*. Cambridge, MA: MIT Press.

Kahneman, D. (2011). *Thinking, Fast and Slow*. London: Penguin.

Kahneman, D. (2013) Desert Island Discs. BBC Radio 4. Available at: www.bbc.co.uk/p rogrammes/b03811 2v

Kellerman, B. (2012) *The End of Leadership*. New York: Harper Business.

Khurana, R. (2007) *From Higher Aims to Hired Hands*. Oxford: Princeton University Press.

Kotter, J. P. (1996) *Leading Change*. Harvard, MA: Harvard Business Press.

Kotter, J. P. (2008) *Force for Change: How Leadership Differs from Management*. New York: Simon and Schuster.

Maitlis, S. and Christianson, M. (2014) 'Sense-making in organizations: Taking stock and moving forward'. *The Academy of Management Annals*, 8(1): 57–125.

Mead, G. H. (1932) 'Scientific method and the moral sciences'. *International Journal of Management Inquiry*, 11: 128–146.

Mead, G. H. (1934) *Mind, Self, and Society*. Chicago, IL: University of Chicago Press.

Mead, G. H. (1938) *The Philosophy of the Present*. Chicago, IL: Chicago University Press.

Mowles, C. (2011) *Rethinking Management: Radical Insights from the Complexity Sciences*. London: Gower.

Mowles, C. (2015) *Managing in Uncertainty: Complexity and the Paradoxes of Everyday Organizational Life*. London: Routledge.

Mowles, C. (2017) Ralph Stacey: Taking Experience Seriously. *The Palgrave Handbook of Organizational Change Thinkers*. London: Palgrave Macmillan.

Noel, J. (1999) 'On the varieties of phronesis'. *Educational Philosophy and Theory*, 31(3): 273–289.

Ofshe, R. (2000) Coercive Persuasion and Attitude Change. In E. Borgatta and R. Montgomery (Eds) *Encyclopaedia of Sociology*, Vol. 1. New York: Macmillan.

Perry, P. (2012) *How to Stay Sane*. London: Pan Macmillan.

Raelin, J. A. (Ed.) (2016) *Leadership-as-Practice: Theory and Application*. London: Routledge.

Revans, R. (1980) *Action Learning: New Techniques for Managers*. London: Blond and Briggs.

Schein, E. H. (1961) *Coercive Persuasion*, New York: Norton.

Schein, E. H. (1989) In H. J. Levitt, L. R. Pondy and D. M. Boje (Eds) *Readings in Managerial Psychology* (4th edn). Chicago, IL: Chicago University Press.

Schein, E. H. (1999) 'Empowerment, coercive persuasion, and organizational learning: Do they connect?' *The Learning Organization*, 6(4): 163–172.

Schein, E. H. (2006) 'From brainwashing to organizational therapy: A conceptual and empirical journey in search of 'systemic' health and a general model of change dynamics. A drama in five acts'. *Organization Studies*, 27(2): 287–301.

Shaw, P. (2002) *Changing Conversations in Organizations: A Complexity Approach to Change*. London: Routledge.

Shaw, P. (2005) 'Conversational inquiry as an approach to organisation development'. *Journal of Innovative Management*, Autumn: 9–22.

Shaw, P. (2010) Be the Change Conference, Copenhagen Business School. Available at: https://cast.cbs.dk/media/Udvikling+af+dialog+i+organisationer/1_7190wb9m

Shenhav, Y. (1999) *Manufacturing Rationality: The Engineering Foundations of the Managerial Revolution*. Oxford: Oxford University Press.

Stacey, R. D. (2010) *Complexity and Organizational Reality: Uncertainty and the Need to Rethink Management after the Collapse of Investment Capitalism*. London: Routledge.

Stacey, R. D. (2011) *Leadership as the Agency of Disciplinary Power*. Unpublished chapter.

Stacey, R. D. (2012) *Tools and Techniques of Leadership and Management: Meeting the Challenge of Complexity*. London: Routledge.

Stacey, R. D., Griffin, D. and Shaw, P. (2000) *Complexity and Management: Fad or Radical Challenge to Systems Thinking?* Abingdon: Routledge.

Stacey, R. D. and Mowles, C. (2016) *Strategic Management and Organisational Dynamics: The Challenge of Complexity to Ways of Thinking about Organisations* (7th edn). Harlow: Pearson.

Tengblad, S. (Ed.) (2012) *The Work of Managers: Towards a Practice Theory of Management*. Oxford: Oxford University Press.

Weick, K. E. (1979) *The Social Psychology of Organizing* (2nd edn). London: McGraw-Hill.

Weick, K. E. (2001) *Making Sense of Organization*. Oxford: Blackwell Publishing.

Weick, K. E., Sutcliffe, K. M. and Obstfeld, D. (2005) 'Organizing and the process of sensemaking'. *Organization Science*, 16(4): 409–421.

Winnicot, D. W. (1965) *The Maturational Processes and the Facilitating Environment*. London: Hogarth Press.

4

COACHING, PSYCHOMETRICS AND 360° FEEDBACK

Introduction

> If 'leadership' is constituted as nothing more than a project of rendering the self more perfect so as to enable career advancement, shaping the self in ways that align to whatever approach or style constitutes the latest leadership fad, then something so self-absorbed in its focus likely offers little in terms of advancing collective well-being.
>
> *(Wilson et al. 2018)*

The replacement of the word 'leadership' with 'coaching' in the quotation above would be a fair description of what in my experience has become the prevailing approach to coaching taken on conventional leadership development programmes. In this chapter, I compare and contrast this stance with the complexity approach to coaching that my colleagues and I have been taking at UH. I also reflect on the use and usefulness of psychometric tools in general, and 360° feedback questionnaires in particular, and proffer a radically different perspective on power to that found in mainstream and popular management (text)books. However, before getting into all of that, I want to share a reflective narrative account of the incident that provoked me to reflect upon this area of my practice.

A collusion of coaches?

I attended an event not so long ago where the topic under discussion was the situations in which it is appropriate for a coach to challenge a coachee. The majority of the audience were practising coaches – some experienced, some new. It was an interactive session involving a mixture of presentations, and small group and whole group discussion. The speaker also used role play and simulation to illustrate some of the situations discussed and called on members of the fifteen-strong audience to join her at the front of the room to act out the scenes that she and/or we wanted to explore. Towards the end of the session, the question of what to do if a team member is unwilling to be coached was raised. Having decided that this scenario would be a useful scene to see played out, the speaker asked me to play the role of the manager and the person sitting next to me to play the role of the reluctant team member.

I dutifully stood up to perform my role and the speaker asked me to explain to 'my team member' what needed to change. I fell easily, albeit uncomfortably, into the character I was invited to portray, and found myself describing how this team member had struggled to transition to the new way of working that the organisation had adopted some six months previously. The speaker then invited me to join her and the team member in a three-way simulated conversation in which the speaker played the coach. I was asked to describe the worst-case scenario, that is, what would happen if this member of staff was unable to make the transition that I had described. I said that ultimately it would mean a change of job, or a change of organisation. My part done, I was invited by the speaker to return to my seat in the audience. The speaker went on to coach the team member. She probed the reasons for the team member's 'resistance' and challenged her reluctance to work with a coach.

Following the simulation, I felt embarrassed, extremely uncomfortable and a little angry.

Throughout the simulation, three things simultaneously vied for my attention as I tried to make sense of what was happening. First, I was concerned that those audience members who I did not know (or indeed did, as several of my colleagues were in attendance) would see my portrayal of the manager as an insight into my practice. However, I quickly rationalised that if this was the case, I could live with it. Second, I was uncomfortable with my and, to a lesser degree, the group's seeming acceptance of the necessity or indeed usefulness of inviting a coach/third party into this scenario, particularly as some form of mediator between manager and team member. And, third, I was a little angry that I and the group, again to a lesser extent, had tacitly agreed to the labelling of the team member as 'resistant to change' and her reluctance to work with a coach as something pathological that needed to be cured. However, as I did not want to be discourteous to the speaker, a guest invited by a colleague who I also did not want to risk embarrassing, I stayed silent. Indeed, in keeping with the theme of the event, I colluded when I could have challenged.

This (vivid moment of) experience (Shaw, 2010) is a useful example of how unexpectedly brushing up against another's praxis immediately leaves you confronted with your own.

Coaching (and mentoring): a brief history

Garvey *et al.* provide a brief and useful history of mentoring and coaching in the second edition of their book, *Coaching and Mentoring: Theory and Practice* (2014). They argue that the 'use of [the] words "coaching" and "mentoring" [has] subtly altered over time to become more or less interchangeable' (ibid.: 11). They concur that references to mentoring can be found in the writings of Plato, Socrates, Aristotle and Homer, and go on to track how this concept was picked up by Fenelon and Caraccioli in seventeenth- and eighteenth-century France and built on by Honoria in three volumes (volumes 1 and 2 appeared in 1793 and volume 3 in 1796) of *The Female Mentor* (ibid.: 14–19).

However, the authors are less convinced that the term 'coaching' might similarly be traced back to Ancient Greece and Socratic dialogue (de Haan, 2008) arguing that such claims are 'speculative and associative' (Garvey *et al.*, 2014: 19). They contend that the first actual reference to coaching appears in Thomas Thackeray's novel *Pendennis*, published in 1849, where the term is used to describe the mechanism offered to university students to support 'academic attainment' (ibid.: 21). By 1867 the scope had broadened to include the development of boating and rowing skills (ibid.). Garvey *et al.* argue that in the early accounts of mentoring the purpose is 'to assist the learner to integrate as a fully functioning person within the society they inhabit'; whereas the purpose of coaching, as depicted in early writings, is to 'improve performance and attainment' (ibid.: 24). The one thing that descriptions of each process have in common is that both the coach and the mentor are identified as being 'skilled, more experienced or more knowledgeable person[s]' (ibid.: 24–27). They conclude that the differentiation that was once clear has become blurred over time to the point where 'coaching and mentoring are essentially similar in nature' (ibid.: 32).

The three leadership development textbooks that frequent the reading lists of UK business school programmes are written by Dalton (2010); Gold *et al.* (2010); and Carmichael *et al.* (2011). As outlined in the Introduction, in such textbooks, depth is understandably sacrificed for breadth. Carmichael *et al.* dedicate just three pages of their almost 400-page book to the subject of coaching. They draw on a number of sources, including the Chartered Institute of Personnel and Development, to note that the use of coaching in organisations spans the spectrum of performance improvement, through dealing with personal challenges, to helping people adjust psychologically to changes they might be experiencing (ibid.: 228–230). Meanwhile, Dalton dedicates five pages of his 500-page book to coaching, mentoring, counselling and sponsoring. He also sees coaching, mentoring and counselling overlapping along a spectrum, with coaching ('senior person, usually with authority, helps a junior person become more effective') at one end, mentoring ('an experienced person providing guidance, encouragement, feedback and support to a learner') in the middle, and counselling ('where the mentor … becomes heavily involved in the identity, self-esteem and personal growth issues of the protegé') at the other end (2010: 206–211). Gold *et al.* (2010: 235–255) invest some twenty pages of the available 400 in the discussion of coaching and mentoring. This includes a substantial section exploring how to 'develop a culture that supports coaching' across an organisation. They argue that it is important to distinguish coaching, which they define as a guided activity aimed at solving a problem, from counselling and therapy (ibid.: 237).

Simon Western argues that coaching in organisations emerged from career counselling and employee assistance programmes and focused on 'the wounded self', that is, 'the employee who was broken, stressed and underperforming' (2012: 5). However, he contends that its popularity only really grew when coaching went 'beyond the healing of a "wounded self"' to offer 'positive and action oriented interventions' that focused on the 'celebrated self' as promoted by 'positive psychology and the happiness industry' (ibid.). This new focus promised 'change, transformation, self-discovery, higher productivity [and] improved performance in work … and in life more generally' (ibid.).

The traditional use of coaching on leadership development programmes involves the participants working directly with a coach in order to identify and support their personal development. In other words, the coach will work with the coachee to identify the gap between where he or she is now and where he or she wants (or others think he or she ought) to be, generate options to close the gap, and then devise an action plan to (supposedly) make this happen. The framework that is most often used to describe this process on conventional leadership development programmes is John Whitmore's (2002) GROW (Goal, Reality, Options, What Next/Now/Will you do?) model. The GROW model is referenced by both Gold *et al.* (2010) and Carmichael *et al.* (2011) in their discussions of coaching, with Gold *et al.* arguing that 'this view of coaching is so well known and popular that it is churlish to even attempt to provide criticism' (2010: 241). This is quite a telling comment!

One of the main reasons why I felt compelled to write this book is to challenge the unthinking acceptance of the mainstream discourse that pervades conventional textbooks, leadership development programmes and business school curricula alike. There is nothing intrinsically wrong with coaching models, frameworks and perspectives like GROW (Whitmore, 2002), they have their place and can be useful in helping a coachee to identify and develop the technical capabilities required for his or her role. However, working in this way can also become highly abstract, with the coach and coachee caught up in individualistic fantasies of how things *ought to be* (Act 4 of Rodgers' 'Management in Five Acts', see Chapter 3), leading to the type of self-absorbed view of leadership that Wilson *et al.* (2018) caution against in the quotation that opens this chapter. The approach to coaching that my colleagues and I have been taking at UH is to support leader-managers to develop an awareness of self in (direct) and with (indirect) relation to others (the interdependent, social patterns of interaction that we find ourselves caught up in) with a view to enhancing the capacities of sense-making, reflexivity and practical judgement required to work with *what is* (Act 1).

Coaching (and mentoring) at UH: a brief history

Leading Through Coaching (LTC) is a leadership development programme that was introduced at UH about five years ago. It began life as a response to requests from participants of MSOL for some form of follow-up programme. This initially led to Responding to the Challenges of Leading (RCL), a programme consisting of four half-day sessions held four times a year, at which half of each session was spent as a whole group (Community Meeting) and the other half working in pairs in partnered conversation. The focus on conversation and relationship revived my interest in a discipline that takes conversation and relationship seriously, namely, coaching. I began looking for colleagues at the university who were involved in coaching and found Sally Graham. Sally was studying for a Masters in Executive Coaching at Ashridge Business School and the relational approach that Ashridge take was of interest to me, not least because it draws on the perspective of complex responsive processes of relating and group analysis – perspectives/methodologies that had become very important to me in my practice.

I asked Sally to pull something together for the participants on RCL, as an opportunity to engage with the discipline of coaching as a means of enhancing their capacities as leader-managers for conversation and relationship. That is, something that would support leader-managers to develop their awareness of self in relation to/with others and to develop the capability to open up conversations in both one-to-one and group situations. LTC was the result. On the programme participants do coach each other, but not with a view to fixing the coachee or improving his or her performance per se, rather with a view to supporting them to (i) make sense of the contexts in which they find themselves; (ii) take a reflexive look at the thinking that is sustaining the way things are; and (iii) exercise practical judgement in articulating a next step that might resonate with those involved. At this point, we had no thoughts or grand plan as to where this might lead beyond helping the participants with whom I was working to explore conversation and relationship in depth.

Of course, once you invite others into the conversation, all involved are influenced by, whilst they are simultaneously influencing, each other as well as influencing and being influenced by what then transpires. The ongoing interplay of intentions of all involved (me, Sally, the colleagues she invited to support her with LTC, the programme participants, the managers and senior managers with whom we had to negotiate the necessary time and budget) contributed to emergence of an accredited programme where participants would agree to coach/mentor colleagues on MSOL and, on graduation, become part of a pool of coaches available to anyone in the organisation who voluntarily requests such support. The programme is aimed at people who manage/lead others. Colleagues who are more interested in becoming coaches are directed to the coaching programmes/qualifications offered by the business school. We set out to enhance the capacity of LTC participants to become adept at rubbing along with others and, by and large, this is what we have managed to do. However, it would be fair to say that the unintended consequences – building a cadre of managers who are able to act as coaches and opening up spaces for conversational approaches to leadership and organisation – have been a welcome bonus.

Since Sally retired, my colleagues (Helen and Jill) and I have run the programme and we continue to draw on coaching as a means of helping leader-managers to become adept at conversation and relationship and to understand and work with affect – their own and that of those they interact with. The capabilities that we are looking to develop on LTC – noticing, questioning, listening, summarising, recognising the patterns of interaction we are caught up in, acknowledging emotions, living with uncertainty/anxiety and having an awareness of psychodynamic/ unconscious processes like projection, transference and counter-transference (Thornton, 2016) – support the enhancement of the capacities for sense-making, reflexivity and practical judgement. And it is these capacities that we would encourage participants to utilise in order to answer the question, 'What, if anything, from the discipline of coaching is useful to your thinking/practice as a leader-manager?'

In his book, *Stand Firm: Resisting the Self-Improvement Craze*, Svend Brinkmann, Professor of Psychology at Aalborg University in Denmark, argues that coaching has become a 'key psychological tool in a culture that revolves around the self' (2017: 75). He takes issue with coaching that looks to convince the coachee that they can find the answer to all of life's problems within, arguing that frequently they can't. Brinkmann recommends sacking your coach and turning instead to the people we once looked to for such support – friends. He advises us to pursue interventions/activities/ways of thinking that 'discourage over-reliance on your inner self and encourage a more rounded world view' (ibid.: 14); a complexity approach to coaching/mentoring attempts to do just that. In contrast to most traditional leadership development programmes, taking a complexity approach means engaging with coaching as a means of developing an awareness of self in and with relation to others, not as an end in itself but rather as an adjunct to developing the capacities for sense-making, reflexivity and practical judgement.

Coaching as a form of work therapy

Stacey contends that coaching 'as a form of mentoring … could be a very important technique with regard to the exercise of practical judgement' (2012: 7). He makes a distinction between the 'instrumentally rational, step-following forms of coaching' and 'more discursive and exploratory forms … understood as a kind of work therapy' (ibid.). Cox in Palmer and McDowall (2010) compares and contrasts the differences between coaching and therapy across four dimensions: objective, level of interpretation, depth of relationship, and time limit. Table 4.1 below, is my rather reductive and polarised depiction of Cox's more nuanced discussion (see Cox in Palmer and McDowall, 2010: 160–163), but I have found this to be a useful way of helping managers on LTC to acquaint themselves with the philosophy of the programme and the complexity approach to coaching/conversation.

TABLE 4.1 The difference between therapy and coaching

	Therapy	*Coaching*
Objective	Psychological change	Improved performance
Interpretation	High ('analytic')	Low (face value)
Relationship	Deep	Superficial
Time limit	Open	Fixed

Source: adapted from Cox in Palmer and McDowall (2010).

The approach to coaching taken on LTC lies somewhere between these two poles. Borrowing Stacey's concept of 'work therapy' (2012: 109), the amended table now looks something like this (see Table 4.2 below):

TABLE 4.2 The difference between therapy, coaching as a form of work therapy and coaching

	Therapy	*Coaching as a form of work therapy*	*Coaching*
Objective	Psychological change	Negotiable	Improved performance
Interpretation	High ('analytic')	Negotiable	Low (face value)
Relationship	Deep	Negotiable	Superficial
Time limit	Open	Negotiable	Fixed

Source: adapted from Cox in Palmer and McDowall (2010).

What I take from Stacey's notion of work therapy is not that he is advocating therapy in the workplace, rather he is suggesting that more discursive coaching conversations, that is, conversations that explore the complexities of day-to-day experience and the strong emotions and anxieties that are often provoked as we try to get things done together, are more useful than conversations based on idealistic (and unrealistic) expectations of how leaders and organisations ought to be. Stacey argues that the 'coach's work in the development of more fluid and complex conversation involves curbing the widespread pattern in organizations where leaders and managers focus on the future and move immediately to planning and solving problems' (2012: 109). Stacey advocates staying with the uncertainty a little longer, opening up the conversation rather than closing it down. This resonates with the experience I share in the narrative above where the speaker/coach paid little attention to the present or past, focusing instead on how the coach might support the coachee to embrace the future by accepting the new ways of working that the coachee is being forced to adopt.

The opportunity that the managers on LTC provide for their coachees (participants on MSOL and colleagues at the university) falls into the 'coaching as a form of work therapy' category. To use Western's (2012) terminology, coaching conversations will neither focus on the 'celebrated self' nor on the 'wounded self', but rather will accept that they cannot be split. This means that conversations might well be experienced as being therapeutic, but they are not therapy. Indeed, it is important for coaches to be able to identify when lines become blurred and to recommend that a coachee seek the professional help of a trained and qualified therapist. In describing the approach to coaching taken on LTC as a form of work therapy, the point that I am looking to make is that from a complexity perspective, the (i) objective; (ii) degree of analysis; (iii) quality of relationship; and even (iv) the timing of the coaching cannot be planned in advance, these things can only be negotiated, and iteratively calibrated, one conversation at a time. Both parties then pay attention to what it is that they are doing together and are prepared to end the relationship should its continuation not be in the best interests of either party and/or develop beyond the psychological capability of the coach.

Stacey contends that a coach who 'follows rules and step-by-step procedures when working with leaders and managers is in fact using the tools and techniques of instrumental rationality' (2012: 109). He argues that this form of coaching might at best 'foster competence' but it will not help to 'develop proficiency and expertise' (ibid.). In using the terms competency, proficiency and expertise, Stacey is drawing on Flyvberg (2001), who draws on the work of the Dreyfus brothers who created a five-phase model of development – novice, advanced beginner, competent performer, proficient performer and expert (Dreyfus and Dreyfus, 1986). In one experiment, the brothers filmed six paramedics administering CPR (ibid.: Chapter 2). Five were trainees, and the sixth was a seasoned paramedic with a great deal of 'experience in life saving techniques' (ibid.: Chapter 1). The videos were then shown to groups of (i) experienced paramedics; (ii) trainee paramedics; and (iii) instructors. Each participant in the experiment was shown all six films before being asked which of the six paramedics they would choose to resuscitate them, if they were in need of CPR. Some 90 per cent of the experienced paramedics chose the experienced paramedic, while 50 per cent of the trainees also chose the experienced paramedic (ibid.: Chapter 2). However, the seasoned paramedic was only picked out by 30 per cent of the instructors.

If we think about what might be generalisable from this particular experiment, one might say that those instructors who did not choose the seasoned paramedic were looking for CPR to be done 'by the book' and may well have viewed the seasoned paramedic's exercise of practical judgement as 'sloppy' or 'unprofessional'. The experienced paramedic did not follow the procedure in a step-by-step fashion; instead they abandoned the rules to meet the needs of the patient. An interesting aside for me in this is the fact that the trainees identified the expert paramedic more consistently than did the instructors. Paramedics have access to an instruction manual on how to administer CPR; however, it is still necessary to adapt to the individual circumstances that one finds oneself in. For leader-managers, the mainstream recipes and formulas for how to navigate the complex responsive processes we are caught up in are illusory, so how many patients are we losing for the want of some practical judgement?

Similarly, the implications for coaching is that models, like GROW, will only be useful up to a point. They can help new coaches to put a foot on the ground in terms of developing their proficiency as a coach but when it comes to developing expertise they may constrain more than enable. To develop expertise, one may have to let go of models and frameworks and become comfortable working more discursively. In Stacey's opinion, 'coaches who work in a discursive way with groups of leaders and managers may help to widen and deepen communication in a group and so produce greater meaning. And this, Stacey argues, 'cannot be reduced to rules and procedures' (2012: 109). This perspective chimes with the relational coaching approach taken by Erik de Haan and colleagues at Ashridge Business School. De Haan is director of the Centre for Coaching at Ashridge and for him:

> In coaching, a number of different levels are present simultaneously. The focus is often not only on the technical or organisational issue raised, and on the ways of dealing with it, but also on the personal dynamic and emotional undercurrents at the root of such issues.
>
> *(2008: 9)*

De Haan argues that the 'professionalisation' and burgeoning research disciplines that have emerged around 'helping conversations' serve to amplify the impoverishment of modern workplaces where it is 'difficult … to conduct a conversation imbued with trust'. De Haan sees this as 'an indication of greater distance and coolness in interpersonal relationships' (ibid.: Preface). Mowles (2017) recognises the 'distrust of feelings' and the tendency to categorise overt displays of emotion in work settings as 'unprofessional'. Psychotherapist Susie Orbach is also struck by how often clients who have come to see her about personal issues end up focusing on 'work and the emotional and power relationships that exist there' (2008: 14). This often leaves them uneasy or irritated:

> It is as though despite work being really important, we shouldn't really get hot and bothered – or pleased and delighted – because work is not quite accepted as a legitimate site for what is considered emotionally important or valuable.
>
> *(Ibid.)*

For Orbach, work is not just 'something that is emotionally, intellectually and economically sustaining'. It is 'self-expressive, a critical identity marker, a source of self-worth, and a place in which interesting and challenging dilemmas get posed and more often than not, addressed in creative and original ways' (ibid.), while simultaneously being an arena in which emotions run high and destructive processes find expression (ibid.: 17). She reflects that 'we are never going to avoid being affected by the people we work with … They will influence, delight and disturb us ... So we need to know how to relate to that disturbance. We need to find a way of being curious about the uncomfortable aspects so that we are not immediately reactive in a negative manner' (ibid.: 16).

Although Orbach is writing from the perspective of somebody working in the helping professions, I contend that there are parallels for us as leader-managers, coaches and human beings. Orbach argues that the ability to 'make yourself available' to the needs of another and to enter that space 'with curiosity and interest rather than with a compelling personal agenda of your own needs' requires 'a level of emotional literacy towards oneself in which something less instrumental, proscriptive and more open and curious can occur'[1] (2008: 15). This resonates with the complexity approach to coaching that we take on LTC. In the narrative that opens this chapter, the speaker (as coach in the scenario), displays some of the thinking that Brinkmann cautions us to be wary of, that is, she implies that the coachee is the author of his or her own story – the trials as well as the triumphs. From this perspective, anyone finding themselves in a tight spot need not fret, as they have all the resources they need within them and it is the coach's job to help them to access these hidden resources to turn the situation around. In short, whatever happens is your own fault, but don't worry because you also have everything you need to put it right. The speaker (as coach) treats me and the other participant (as manager and team member, respectively) as *autonomous* individuals. From the speaker's point of view, the team member's (reluctant coachee's) 'resistance to change' is a choice that he or she is autonomously and independently making.

Taking a complexity approach means acknowledging that the team member and manager are *interdependent* individuals. From this perspective, the team member's (reluctant coachee's) response to change is something that has emerged in the social processes of interaction that he or she is caught up in. Consequently, I would be interested to explore what is happening between the team member, manager, other team members, colleagues in other teams and departments, customers, suppliers, other organisations, etc. and to look at the influence this is having on the team member's conceptions and response to the changes that have been introduced. I would also be interested to explore why the manager feels impelled to invite a coach to work with his or her 'reluctant' team member rather than talking with and negotiating a way forward that both could live with (see Chapter 5).

This incident also raised for me the question of ethics. Working with a coachee to consciously or unconsciously have them comply with the wishes of their manager, with or without the coachee's consent, is a form of coercion. Don't get me wrong – as I argue in Chapter 3, coercion is a necessary and legitimate feature of organisational life, but we need to be aware that when we portray coaching as a neutral development opportunity, we obscure the ethical implications of what we are doing. Coaching might be a useful way of supporting someone through a transition, but the choice to have it should remain with the coachee. During the brief whole group conversation that occurred after the simulation, themes of power, inclusion/exclusion, shame and ethics were not explored. It seemed as though coaching was unreservedly accepted by the group as an activity for the good. There was little, if any, acknowledgement of the shadow side of coaching. As Stacey points out 'It is important … not to idealise mentors and coaches. Mentors and coaches may well relate to those they mentor and coach in ways that are self-satisfying, domineering and manipulative (2012: 110).

Now I am not suggesting that offering coaching to somebody who is struggling to adapt to new ways of working is always 'self-satisfying, domineering and manipulative' but what I am arguing is that we should be alert to the fact that the meaning of such a gesture is not in the gift of the manager and/or the coach. The scenario above highlights the potential for coaching to become another form of coercive persuasion (Schein, 1961)/disciplinary power (Stacey, 2011). The speaker/coach in the above scenario did not question the ethics of what she was being asked to do and neither did we, the audience of experienced and new coaches. It would take a lot of courage to refuse coaching in this situation. Many a prospective coachee might be reluctant to talk to an outsider – someone brought in by their superior – but with his or her job on the line, how likely is it that he or she will (be able to) say 'no'?

The themes arising in the narrative include the potential for (i) dissent, that is, the questioning of new working arrangements/structures/policies/procedures, to be regarded as 'resistance to change' and pathologised as something to be cured (in this instance with the help of a coach); (ii) coaching to be experienced by coachees as a form of coercive persuasion/disciplinary power: (iii) coaches, particularly when employed by third parties, to become the agents of said coercive persuasion/disciplinary power; (iv) coaching to become what Mead (1934) describes as a cult value, that is a social object (see Chapter 3) stripped of all constraint, an activity *for the good* that is difficult to criticise; and finally (v) accepting that all things (that happen to us) can be explained by and reduced to individual psychologies/agency. I'll pick up on each of these themes as the chapter progresses, but at this point I want to take the opportunity to explore the conventional means through which the perspective of others is brought into the coaching process, and that is through the use of psychometrics.

Psychometrics

In management development the overriding tendency has been to limit the interpretation of complex group phenomena to psychological processes … Yet as Brown (1985) pointed out, 'it would be simple minded in the extreme to attribute the problems of race relations or worker-management relations to purely psychological processes'.

(Reynolds and Trehan 2003: 166)

[T]he figurations of interdependent human beings – cannot be explained if one studies human beings singly.

(Elias 1978)

On traditional leadership development programmes, psychometrics are used as a means of developing self-awareness in addition to self-reflection. If one takes a complexity approach to leadership development, an approach that understands leadership to be a social and relational phenomenon that is co-created in ongoing patterns of communicative interaction between people who are 'fundamentally interdependent' (Stacey and Mowles, 2016: 47), then the usefulness of the majority of psychometric and personality profiling tools, based as they are on 'individual-centred psychologies' (ibid.), is immediately problematised. During twenty years spent working in leadership development roles, I have become accredited in a (large) number of these tools[2] and as my collection of certificates increases, so my faith in the use and usefulness of such instruments decreases. It is neither my intention to critique each tool here nor my inclination to enter into any form of academic debate about the validity and/or reliability of these instruments, rather I want to share my experience of working with psychometric tools in general and to explore the use and usefulness of 360° (also known as multi-rater) feedback processes in particular.

In Chapter 3, I explored the function of abstract models and frameworks as rhetorical devices to (i) persuade; (ii) defend against the anxiety of not knowing (transitional objects); and (iii) discipline/correct. This goes some way to explaining my experience of psychometrics in general and 360° feedback in particular as a coachee/participant in coaching/leadership development programmes. Indeed, I contend that these instruments are more of a crutch for the coach/leadership developer as they are a useful resource for the coachee/participant. My experience of psychometrics as a participant on leadership development programmes echoes my experiences of them as a facilitator/coach. The majority of instruments that I have worked with, both as a facilitator/coach and as a participant on leadership development programmes, have been self-report. That is, participants are invited to complete a questionnaire containing questions such as 'what role do you take in ...', 'how do you prefer to ...', 'if given the choice between X and Y, what is your preference?' The resulting report then plays back what one's answers signify in relation to the particular framework or model that one has been invited to compare oneself with/to.

Depending on the tool, the resulting report usually provides some form of shorthand summary in the form of a set of letters, a number of colours, a role preference or two, a thumbnail sketch of one's work self, leadership style, etc. All reports come with a set of caveats and instructions on how to make the most of the information contained therein, but in my experience these are more often than not superseded by the following 'howevers':

1. However often the facilitator/coach cautions participants not to pigeonhole or reduce people to the said letters, colours, reductive profiles that the answers to the questions have produced in the report, they do.
2. However often the facilitator/consultant cautions participants not to second-guess where their managers/team members/colleagues might figure in

relation to the framework (given the fact that we do not have access to their profiles), they do.

3. However often the facilitator/coach cautions people not to get too bogged down in conversations about validity and/or reliability and/or the rigour of the research method(s) used in the development of the tool, they do. And,

4. However often *this* coach/facilitator cautioned himself not to become embroiled in conversations in which he ended up having to defend a tool that he himself considered dubious, he all too often did.

360° feedback

> [I]dentity has also come to be an important element of control in organiza-
> tions; many types of activity in today's organizations can be seen as attempts to
> control and regulate ideas and views about who we are and what we can do,
> such as cultural change programmes, feedback on management and leadership,
> leadership development, coaching and ideas about authentic leadership.
>
> *(Sveningsson and Alvesson 2016)*

One of the psychometric tools that looks to triangulate one's self-perceptions with the perceptions of others is the 360° or multi-rater feedback questionnaire.[3] These questionnaires are usually based on some form of bespoke or generic competency/ values framework or model of leadership. Raters/respondents include the partici- pant, their line manager(s), direct reports, peers and, in some cases, external contacts e.g. customers, suppliers, etc. (processes involving these wider groups are some- times referred to as 540° feedback). All are asked to complete a questionnaire that rates the participant against the relevant competencies/values or leadership traits. The ratings are usually a mix of quantitative/tick box – on a scale of 1–5 'how frequently' or 'how effectively' does X? – and qualitative/free text – 'what does this person do well?' and/or 'what are this person's areas for development?'

The resultant reports usually group raters/respondents into the categories iden- tified above – participant, line manager(s), direct reports, peers and (where applic- able) external contacts – thus providing anonymity to all bar the participant's line manager, unless the subject happens to have more than one. The usual criticisms of these tools – that (i) 360° feedback that is less than positive has a negative impact on performance (Kluger and De Nisi, 1996); (ii) 'in the wrong hands' they can 'reinforce a climate of mistrust' (Dalton, 2010: 126); and (iii) after nine months managers in one study were only able to 'recall strengths rather than weaknesses' (Gold *et al.*, 2010: 105) – can be found elsewhere. Here, I want to concentrate on four shortcomings of 360° feedback from both a complexity perspective and my personal experience.

First, as Reynolds and Trehan (2003); Brown (1985) and Stacey and Mowles (2016) point out above, 360° feedback questionnaires are based on an understanding of leadership as something that can be reduced to individual behaviours and/or agency. Second, even if leadership was something located in an individual, the qualities and traits identified in 360° feedback surveys are all too often based on the archetype of the tough, white, heterosexual male, leaving little space for anybody who does not fit this picture (Sinclair, 2005). This not only discourages the diversity that most organisations would say they seek, but also potentially feeds the unconscious (and/or conscious) bias of the subject and raters. Third, during the coaching conversations that I have been involved in, as both coach and coachee, the most closely scrutinised element of 360° reports, the element that catalyses most of the discussion, is the free text section in which raters have the opportunity to provide more nuanced, detailed and discursive feedback. And this goes some way to explaining why, fourth, the majority of my development colleagues (even those working from mainstream conceptions of leadership and organisation) view most psychometric tools and 360° feedback instruments as little more than 'dialogue openers'.

I do not deny that many participants on the leadership development programmes that I have been involved in have found the coaching conversations generated by 360° feedback useful, but I contend this has more to do with the opportunity to reflect upon their own thinking/practice, catalysed by the qualitative (rater comments) rather than the quantitative data. This begs the question: is there a more useful way of opening dialogue? As a dialogue opener for this discussion, I want to share a vignette from a colleague who is taking a complexity approach in his practice. Eric Wenzel works as a management consultant, focusing on change management and leadership development, top executive coaching and assessments for senior executives. He heads the Management Diagnostics practice for the German-speaking territories in a global company advising on both people and organisations. The following narrative is taken from Eric's doctoral thesis, which is available online (Wenzel, 2011). At the time of writing, Eric was working for a company that develops and markets 360° profiling tools.

VIGNETTE

While I do not claim that we need to let go of tools altogether, I have begun to resist idealized notions as to what becomes possible through the application of this or that tool in lieu of potentially opening up further conversations.

Let me give an example.

Leadership programs at my current employer are largely based on multi-rater feedback tools, the results of which are explained to larger groups of feedback receivers over the course of two-day seminars. The seminars are followed up by team meetings in which leaders must share their feedback with their team (the feedback givers) and discuss points for improvement of their leadership skills. Usually the discussion around the results is highly constrained by alluding to a specific set of leadership behaviors which are pre-defined and that are said to influence a team's experienced working conditions significantly. Either aspect, the leader's behavioural repertoire and the working conditions are analyzed by the use of various 180° feedback instruments. The experienced working conditions the leader is said to influence to a large degree. It consists of several dimensions which address different areas of people's experience at work such as clarity about the company's vision, standards of excellence or experienced commitment of one's team. The idea is to show very clearly to leaders those conditions in need of improvement and how to bring about the improvement by modifying their leadership and using the 180° graphs as points of reference. I have found myself quickly abandoning the graphs that show a leader's results in team meetings which, however, I am told are supposed to clearly guide those meetings. This is mainly so because I found throughout the first team meetings I facilitated that clinging to these graphs effectively serves to close conversations down.

In participating in the discussions in very different ways from other colleagues, clients and I find ways to address issues such as team identity, issues of power relating or the experiences of mutual (mis)recognition, none of which are captured through our feedback instruments. These aspects of work seem to trouble people quite substantially, however. It is usually believed that mastering the discourse around leadership as it is propagated with these tools takes a while, so it is most surprising for colleagues that literally every manager in the programs I initially participated in has asked me to come back to continue the work with him or her and their teams beyond the assignment I was originally contracted for while none of my colleagues have been asked to do so. While colleagues believe that this is because I have become a master of our tools, the opposite is actually the case. For instance, a recent team meeting I facilitated was quite a shocking experience for the Vice President who is the head of a group of directors. As part of her feedback, she had also received anonymized verbatim comments, one of which was fairly critical of her leadership ability. Quite contrary to her intuition, it turned out in the team meeting that her deputy had made the critical comments, and as she told me later, she had been on the verge of terminating the team meeting when this became clear.

Instead of advising the VP on how to make clear to her deputy that he had failed to live up to her expectations and removing him from his present role as a consequence, I responded to this situation quite differently, and I would consider this to be related to my shifting attitude towards my work. In drawing attention away from the deputy and pointing the VP to her own intense response, our discussion began to gravitate towards her own naiveté and what this meant for the views about other team members she took for granted and about herself. Instead of closing the conversation down by giving clear advice on what to do, I encouraged the VP to explore further her contribution to this situation and to take into account the social complexities this incident revealed. At some point, she even began to recognize the deputy's contribution as a highly courageous act, possibly conveying the most important feedback for her in this whole exercise. I pointed out that in daring to explore the difference he brought to the table, she had become able to tender provisionally her view of her deputy and found a way to complexify her interpretation of the situation, resulting in a more reality-congruent understanding than her initial view might have suggested. She was so surprised by this form of consultancy that she hired me for a team retreat later in the year right away.

[T]he above example seems to be indicative of what this means for my consulting practice. In opening up and exploring further the beliefs we take for granted, the client and I became able to discover a more complex understanding of what had been going on and, importantly, what this meant for the VP's next steps for the future cooperation with her deputy.

Eric's explication of practice is a useful illustration of the difference between a complexity approach to coaching/360°, in which the coach is interested in supporting the coachee to develop an awareness of the social, that is, an awareness of self and others in relation to and with self and others, and the conventional approach, whereby the coach's preoccupation is with developing the coachee's self-awareness, that is, awareness of self and how others might see him or her. For Elias, *self* is the singular and *social* is the plural of *interdependent people* (Stacey in MacIntosh *et al.*, 2006). They cannot be separated. I find 360° feedback tools that look to separate the behaviours of individuals from the social processes in which they emerge unhelpful. This is not to say that we are not responsible for our individual actions and behaviours, rather that they cannot be reduced to individual psychologies. Any explanation of what we find ourselves doing needs to take account of the social interactions in which our actions emerge and the history of social interactions that continue to influence our thinking/practice as we act in the present in anticipation of the future. Coaching is at its most useful when it helps the coach and coachee to develop a more reality congruent understanding of the patterns of power relations they are caught up in.

Power: a detour via detachment

When power is dealt with at all in mainstream literature, it is usually portrayed as something that one person or group of people has and another person or group of people has not. In Gold *et al.*, the discussion of power is reduced to an acknowledgement that in 'formal strategy-making activities, there are always likely to be certain voices that are more privileged and that dominate' (2010: 52). In the paragraph that Carmichael *et al.* invest in its exploration, power is described as a 'position' and as something that leaders can use at their discretion to impose their will and ideas on others or otherwise share (2011: 23). Dalton offers a more nuanced, albeit no less brief, view of power but in relation to organisational development (OD) activities. He cautions OD practitioners to 'recognise the pluralistic power games of organisations and play them skilfully' (2010: 407).

Stuart Lukes' (1974, 2005) understanding of power is representative of explanations found in the mainstream literature. Lukes views power as 'an ability or capacity of an agent or agents, which they may or may not exercise' (2005: 63). That is, power is something that an individual or a group possesses, and then can choose to wield, or not, at will. This understanding of power implies that those with power can simply command those without power to do their bidding. From the perspective of complex responsive processes, drawing on the work of Elias, power is an 'integral element of all human relations', and 'whether power differentials are large or small, balances of power are always present wherever there is a functional interdependence between people' (1978: 74). Elias sees power as a structural process, not a reified 'it':

> We say that a person possesses great power, as if power were a thing he carried about in his pocket. The use of the word is a relic of magico-mythical ideas. Power is not an amulet possessed by one person and not by another, it is a structural characteristic of human relationships – all human relationships.
>
> *(Ibid.)*

Elias uses game models to explore power relations, starting with simple 'two person games' through to more complex 'multi-person games on several levels' (1978.: 76–80). In a two-person, one-to-one relationship, if my perception is that I need you more than you need me (for love, money, status, etc. (ibid.: 88)), then the power differential is in your favour. If you perceive that you need me more than I need you, then the power differential is in my favour. However, although the asymmetry might be great, it will never be 100:0 (even in the relationship between master and slave, the master needs the slave to accept that he or she is a slave even if this can only be achieved through the threat of violence or death), nor will it ever be 50:50. Additionally, relations of power (the differential ratios) are dynamic and the balance of power can shift and switch. Think junior team member being appointed manager, or financially dependent partner winning the lottery. This description of power as a dynamic process of enabling and constraining, of simultaneously co-operating while holding each other to account (Stacey and Mowles, 2016: 402) is a radically different view of power than that found in the mainstream literature. As outlined in Chapter 3, as human beings we are interdependent; we cannot simply do what we want and this is one of the reasons why conceptions of leader-managers as all-powerful individuals are as unhelpful as they are unrealistic.

Elias argues that there are circumstances in which the simple two-person game model might be applied – the 'relationship between a specialist and non-specialist … or a famous painter and patron', for example (1978: 90) – but in reality we are all involved in 'multi-person games on several levels' and this goes some way to explaining why the games that we are caught up in take 'a course *which none of the individual players has planned, determined or anticipated*' and why 'as power differentials lessen between interdependent individuals and groups there is a diminishing possibility that any participants, whether on their own or as groups, will be able to control the overall course of the game' (ibid.: 91; emphasis in the original).

However, it is possible to increase one's influence on the game by becoming more detached in one's involvement and paying attention to the 'dynamics' one is caught up in with a view to anticipating the patterns (next moves) that are emerging in the interplay of everyone's intentions. Becoming more detached in one's involvement and becoming adept at navigating the politics (games) of organisational life is explored more fully in Chapter 6. For the purposes of this chapter, it is worth noting that becoming more detached in one's involvement is not the same as stepping outside of the game. You can never become fully detached; one is influencing while simultaneously being influenced by the game. That is, we are played by the game in the playing of it.

Similarly, to draw attention to the game, particularly those aspects that one might find unjust or absurd, let alone illegal, immoral or likely to injure someone, is to risk exclusion. And this points to another aspect of power that is under-explored in mainstream literature. Stacey and Mowles, after Elias and Scotson (1994), argue that 'power differences establish groupings in which some people are "included" and others are excluded. Power is thus felt as the dynamics of inclusion and exclusion' (Stacey and Mowles, 2016: 406). Inclusion in the grouping called 'managers', for example, automatically leads to one's exclusion from the grouping called 'workers'. I recall a programme participant sharing with the group his very visceral experience of this phenomenon. After successfully applying for an internal promotion, which meant that he would now be managing his former peers, a colleague he had worked alongside for many years took him to one side and said, 'you do realise that this means we can't be friends anymore?' This initial reaction, provoked by the anxiety and uncertainty over what it might mean for their relationship, probably tempered over time, but the point is that the actual/perceived shift in the power differential was something that neither party had intended/anticipated. If one accepts that power is a structural characteristic of all human relationships (Elias, 1978), then one cannot choose to use or not 'wield' power, as Lukes (2005) suggests, the power differential will have an impact on our interactions with others whether we want it to or not, whether we like it or not.

This has important implications for us as leader-managers, particularly in relation to coaching. Authority is usually, but not always, sufficient to tip the power differential in our favour. Wilson et al. argue that from the 'early 1960s onwards, "authority" in its various guises has generally been in decline', while 'elite challenging activities have been rising' (Inglehart, 1977: 3; see also Gitlin, 1993; Wilson et al., 2018: 36). This means that leaders now have to work hard(er) to gain followers' 'compliance and support' (ibid.). However, they also acknowledge that this general trend is 'attenuated in many workplaces' where 'the authority of manager-leaders to hire and fire typically remains intact' and 'highly potent in many cases' (ibid.: 38). This asymmetry in power ratios constrains how open we might be about our 'weaknesses' or 'areas for development' in coaching conversations with line managers who have a material influence on our job opportunities and/or future career aspirations.

The talking up of leadership (Khurana, 2007; Blom and Alvesson, 2015 – see Chapters 1 and 2, respectively) in mainstream and popular management literature has contributed to the illusion/delusion that C/EOs are all-powerful individuals/ groups who control corporate futures. An unthinking acceptance of this can lead to an unhealthy level of deference being expected and/or paid to those in positions of authority/seniority. For Stacey (2012), it is important for leader-managers to dis-avow their colleagues of the dependency that such an idealisation encourages, not least because when 'the idealisation and dependency inevitably fail … denigration and aggression' are sure to follow (2012: 114). Of course, as Stacey and Mowles also point out, acceptance that executive leaders do not control what happens in organisations also calls into the question 'the hugely inflated salaries that many leaders claim' (2016: 515).

As outlined in the Introduction, I do not have the same emancipatory intent as CMS scholars. I do not anticipate a major recalibration of senior management remuneration in the course of my lifetime; there are too many vested interests and current salaries inevitably attract the type of people who would fight to maintain the status quo. No, I am not interested in curbing the excesses of the mega-lomaniacal few (Tourish, 2013), but rather I am looking to prevent the *moderate many* from being seduced by deference into believing that they are, after all, something special and/or should be treated differently than the rest. De Haan and Kasozi observe that 'the risk of overdrive or hubris is particularly great in modern organisations. In these complex, fragmented and global settings, talented individuals may be elevated to leadership positions which nourish, reward and exploit strengths and at the same time fuel particular hubristic processes. Placed in those situations they might conclude, I must be a really exceptional talent because this big, powerful organization is recognizing my contribution and propelling me into ever more senior ranks' (2014: 20).

De Haan and Kasozi define hubris as 'a sense of overbearing pride, defiance or presumption not justified by the circumstances or the perceptions of others' (2014: 20). Aaron James describes those who refuse 'to listen to … legitimate complaints' and challenge the idea 'that we are each to be recognized as moral equals' as ass-holes (James, 2014: 1). In his book *Assholes: A Theory*, James goes on to define an asshole as a person who 'systematically allows himself to enjoy special advantages in interpersonal relations out of an entrenched sense of entitlement that immunises him against the complaints of other people' (ibid.: 4).

I'm not sure what the equivalent term would be in the UK or on the continent, but whatever word one chooses, I think it is important to maintain the profane. This provides the required jolt to catalyse reflexivity. James contends that we all play a part in creating the conditions in which assholes thrive arguing that the 'asshole in power is shaped by his position and its culture as much as shapes it. Much as with our ordinary asshole boss, assholes may wind up in power, not simply because assholes are prone to seek it out but because the position induces a creeping sense of entitlement in those who come to occupy the role' (2014.: 51). James argues that a sense of entitlement deadens 'one's capacities for empathy and understanding' and contends that the corporate asshole's damaging behaviours can outstrip those of the corporate psychopath (ibid.: 53).

Echoing Khurana (2007), James argues that a lack of stewardship demarcates corporate assholes from the rest as they take their responsibility to maximise shareholder value to the extreme. They make it their '*duty* to *minimize* benefits, overall, to consumers and workers' by offering 'the bare minimum incentive to get them to buy a product or show up to work' (2014: 55; emphasis in original). I caution the managers with whom I work to guard against becoming assholes. And I would caution readers to do the same. Furthermore, if you already have the asshole's sense of entitlement, or know that you will effortlessly acquire it should you attain a position of authority, then do everyone a favour, resign and/or stay away from those roles that put you in charge of other people. Should you rise to the dizzy heights of C/EO, or already find yourself there, then enjoy the trappings and the pomp and ceremony that accompany such roles (such traditions have a symbolic significance that it is important to maintain) but always remember:

- You are not Martin Luther King Jr, Nelson Mandela or Mahatma Ghandi. Indeed, were they still living, I contend that they would not recognise the inflated, individualistic and idealistic narratives used to describe their practice/experience.
- You didn't (in most cases) create the organisation that you now find yourself in charge of, it is not your own personal fiefdom to do with what you will. The decisions you make will not only affect the lives of the people you work with but they will also have an influence on the well being of their families and friends and the communities in which you operate.
- The fact that the business you work for makes enormous profits doesn't mean that you are entitled to an inordinately bigger share of the pot than every other employee that has contributed to this success.
- Leave the business in as good (or better) a state than the one in which you found it.
- You are jointly responsible for the triple bottom line – people, planet and profits.
- Don't believe the hype, especially your own (a coach might help with this).

De Haan (2014) argues that coaching might help leaders to avoid the 'shadow side of leadership' which he describes as the negative effects of hubris, derailment, and overdrive. De Haan contends that:

> The best place for a leader to grow compassion and to address the excesses of hubris and relational overdrive is in a tailor-made, confidential and personal relationship, such as can be established in the privacy of executive coaching. By working in such a personal one-to-one helping relationship other

relationships can be brought under scrutiny, and overdrive and derailment patterns can be observed and explored in depth.

(Ibid.: 269)

Orbach argues that 'people at the top are pulling enormous salaries and … if their performance gets overloaded by stress, then it is very expensive to buy them out of their contracts and much cheaper to provide some kind of therapeutic help with the aim to bring them back to peak condition (2008: 17). De Vries *et al.* argue that 'across all industries and at all organizational levels, executives are turning to coaches for support, advice and feedback' (2007: xxiv). Feedback often generated by the qualitative data from 360° feedback processes. As outlined above, from a complexity perspective, 360° feedback processes have four main shortcomings: (i) they reduce discussions of leadership to individual behaviours and/or agency; (ii) the frameworks used are all too often based on the archetype of the tough, white, heterosexual male; (iii) the quantitative data is too abstract to be of use and this means that (iv) the glossy reports produced are often regarded by coaches as little more than 'dialogue openers'. So, how might we have discursive conversations that keep sight of the social and relational (interdependent) nature of leadership without having to navigate our way through abstract frameworks replete with unhelpful archetypes?

Binney *et al.*, have developed a 360° feedback process that does not use any form of quantitative competency-based framework. Instead, they ask just four open questions:

1. What's most important in X's leadership role?
2. What do you value most about X?
3. What would you like him/her to do more of or less of?
4. Looking at the future roles X may have, in what ways do you think he/she needs to develop

(2012: 264)

I suggest that the questions might be even more useful if they did not mention leadership at all. Questions 1 and 4 have the potential to generate answers that simply reflect the habitus, whereby raters will replay mainstream, individualistic and idealistic conceptions of leadership that legitimise and perpetuate archetypes that taking a complexity approach problematises. If one is going to use 360° feedback at all, then a more useful set of questions might be:

1. What does this person do that is most useful to you and the team?
2. What does this person do that is least useful you and the team?
3. What, if anything, would you like this person to do differently?

Taking this a step further, on MSOL and LTC, we support leader-managers to become adept at conversation and relationship with a view to opening up the possibility of superseding the need for anonymous feedback with an open discussion once or twice a year convened by the leader-manager themselves without a facilitator/coach. The questions might then be focused on how the group/team is working and what, if any, contribution the leader-manager is making to this:

1. What works well in this group and what, if anything, does X contribute to this?
2. What doesn't work so well and what, if anything, does X contribute to this?
3. What, if anything, might we do differently?

Working in this way, might reduce the need to employ any form of psychometric/profiling tool as a catalyst for conversation.

Reflections

> Is coaching being used as a tool to sustain an ever problematic and dysfunctional system that requires re-thinking rather than sustaining? Or alternatively is coaching providing a vital reflective space in which individuals can be more humane, thoughtful, creative and strategic at work, a space where critical perspectives are allowed to be aired, where questioning and creativity are encouraged, in order to find innovative ways of moving forward?
>
> *(Western 2012: 26)*

I think it would be fair say that my colleagues and I have been working with coaching as a means of encouraging the latter rather than sustaining the former. Initially, I/we engaged with the discipline/tools and techniques of coaching as a means of enhancing the capacities of the participants on leadership development programmes to engage in conversation and relationships more adeptly while supporting each other in the partnered conversations and whole group community meetings that were at the core of the original RCL programme that preceded LTC (outlined in 'Coaching (and mentoring) at UH: a brief history', above). The conceptualisation of a complexity approach to coaching as a form of 'work therapy' (after Stacey, 2012) emerged in the writing of this book, catalysed by the vivid moment of experience shared in the narrative at the beginning of this chapter and tested since with successive cohorts of participants on LTC. It is a proverbial 'work in progress', but for me it differentiates the complexity approach to coaching from the instrumental and performative approaches that populate mainstream literature. From a complexity perspective, coaching is viewed as a 'vital reflective space' that acknowledges that we are interdependent human beings caught up in patterns of local interaction (games) that we can influence but not control. In the interplay of everyone's intentions, what emerges is paradoxically certain and uncertain, predictable and unpredictable, rational and irrational, conscious and unconscious, co-operative and competitive, creative and destructive all at the same time

However, this is not to idealise conversation and relationship. As Stacey (2012) points out, conversations lead to patterns of interaction that are both ethical and unethical, legal and illegal, good and evil, and there is no way of predicting what will emerge at the outset. I am not claiming that the complexity approach to coaching that I am exploring here is unique (as stated above, the original LTC programme, developed by Sally, drew heavily on relational coaching (de Haan, 2008)), but what I am saying is that taking a complexity approach to coaching problematises perspectives that unthinkingly promote coaching as an unequivocal activity for the good. As shown above, there is a potential for coaching to be experienced and/or employed as a technique of coercive persuasion/disciplinary power, particularly when practised between manager and team member, where the asymmetry in power chances might constrain rather than enable conversation.

In encouraging leader-managers, as participants on leadership development programmes, to engage with coaching, it was neither my intention to develop them as coaches, nor to suggest that they might coach the people who reported to them. My aspirations were much more modest. Bob Garvey argues that at 'the heart of coaching and mentoring activity lie trust, reflection, listening, support and challenge' (2011: 62). In the narrative that opens this chapter, just before the simulation was drawn to a close, one of the options suggested by the speaker/coach to the reluctant coachee was to talk to his or her manager and let their concerns and feelings be known! In taking a complexity approach to coaching, we are looking to increase the chances of this happening without the need for a middleman.

Notes

1   Interestingly, in the UK, at the time of writing, there were calls on the government to commit to promoting equality for mental health in the workplace by considering amending health and safety legislation (first aid at work regulations) so as to require all employers to provide Mental Health First Aid.
2   I am accredited in Belbin Team Roles, Myers Briggs Type Indicator (MBTI), Team Management Systems (TMS), StrengthScope 360, Authentic Leader 360, Thinking Styles and others too numerous to mention.
3   I appreciate there are others, such as Belbin Team Roles, that also offer this, but they also often employ a different set of questions and/or method of assessment than that engaged with by the participant/coachee.

References

Binney, G., Wilke, G. and Williams, C. (2012) *Living Leadership: A Practical Guide for Ordinary Heroes* (3rd edn). Harlow: Pearson Education.

Blom, M. and Alvesson, M. (2015) 'Less followership, less leadership? An inquiry into the basic but seemingly forgotten downsides of leadership'. *M@n@gement*, 18(3): 266–282.

Brinkmann, S. (2017) *Stand Firm: Resisting the Self-Improvement Craze*. Cambridge: Polity Press.

Brown, H. (1985) *People, Groups and Society*. Milton Keynes: Open University Press.

Carmichael, J., Collins, C., Emsell, P. and Haydon, J. (2011) *Leadership and Management Development*. Oxford: Oxford University Press.

Cox, E. (2010) In S. Palmer and A. McDowall, (Eds) *The Coaching Relationship: Putting People First*. Hove: Routledge

Dalton, K. (2010) *Leadership and Management Development: Developing Tomorrow's Managers*. Harlow: Pearson.

de Haan, E. (2008) *Relational Coaching: Journeys Towards Mastering One-To-One Learning*, Chichester: Wiley and Sons.

de Haan, E. and Kasozi, A. (2014) *The Leadership Shadow: How to Recognize and Avoid Derailment, Hubris and Overdrive*. London: Kogan Page.

de Haan, E. and Sills, C. (Eds) (2012) *Coaching Relationships: The Relational Coaching Field Book*. Faringdon: Libri Publishing.

de Vries, M. F. R., Korotov, K. and Florent-Treacy, E. (2007) *Coach and Couch: The psychology of making better leaders*. Basingstoke: Palgrave Macmillan.

Dreyfus, H. and Dreyfus, S. (1986) *Mind Over Machine: The Power of Human Intuition and Expertise in the Era of the Computer*. New York: The Free Press.

Elias, N. (1978) *What Is Sociology?* London: Hutchinson.

Elias, N. and Scotson, J. (1994) *The Established and the Outsiders*. London: Sage.

Flyvbjerg, B. (2012) *Making Social Science Matter: Why Social Inquiry Fails and How It Can Succeed Again*. Cambridge: Cambridge University Press.

Garvey, B. (2011) *A Very Short, Fairly Interesting and Reasonably Cheap Book about Coaching and Mentoring*. London: Sage.

Garvey, B., Stokes, P. and Megginson, D. (2014) *Coaching and Mentoring: Theory and Practice* (2nd edn). London: Sage.

Gitlin, T. (1993) *The Sixties: Years of Hope, Days of Rage*. New York: Bantam.

Gold, J., Thorpe, R. and Mumford, A. (2010) *Leadership and Management Development* (5th edn). London: Chartered Institute of Personnel and Development.

Inglehart, R. (1977) *The Silent Revolution: Changing Values and Political Styles among Western Publics*. Cambridge: Cambridge University Press.

James, A. (2014) *Assholes: A Theory*. London: Nicholas Brearley.

Khurana, R. (2007) *From Higher Aims to Hired Hands*. Oxford: Princeton University Press.

Kluger, A. N. and De Nisi, A. (1996) 'The effects of feedback interventions on performance: A historical review, a meta-analysis, and a preliminary feedback intervention theory'. *Psychological Bulletin*, 119: 254–284.

Lukes, S. (1974) *Power: A Radical View*. New York: Palgrave Macmillan.

Lukes, S. (2005) *Power: A Radical View* (2nd edn). New York: Palgrave Macmillan.

MacIntosh, R., MacLean, D., Stacey, R. and Griffin, D. (Eds) (2006) *Complexity and Organization: Readings and Conversations*. Abingdon: Routledge.

Mead, G. H. (1934) *Mind, Self, and Society*. Chicago, IL: University of Chicago Press.

Mowles, C. (2017) 'Experiencing uncertainty: On the potential of groups and a group analytic approach for making management education more critical'. *Management Learning*: 1–15.

Orbach, S. (2008) 'Work is where we live: Emotional literacy and the psychological dimensions of the various relationships there'. *Emotion, Space and Society*. 1(1): 14–17.

Palmer, S. and McDowall, A. (Eds) (2010) *The Coaching Relationship: Putting People First*. London: Routledge.

Reynolds, M. and Trehan, K. (2003) 'Learning from difference?' *Management Learning*. 34(2): 163–180.

Schein, E. H. (1961) *Coercive Persuasion*. New York: Norton.

Shaw, P. (2010) Be the Change Conference, Copenhagen Business School. Available at https://cast.cbs.dk/media/Udvikling+af+dialog+i+organisationer/1_7190wb9m.

Sinclair, A. (2005) *Doing Leadership Differently: Gender, Power and Sexuality in a Changing Business Culture*. Melbourne: Melbourne University Publishing.

Stacey, R. (2010) *Complexity and Organizational Reality: Uncertainty and the Need to Rethink Management after the Collapse of Investment Capitalism*. London: Routledge.

Stacey, R. D. (2011) '*Leadership as the Agency of Disciplinary Power*'. Unpublished chapter.

Stacey, R. D. (2012) *Tools and Techniques of Leadership and Management: Meeting the Challenge of Complexity*. London: Routledge.

Stacey, R. D. and Mowles, C. (2016) *Strategic Management and Organisational Dynamics: The Challenge of Complexity to Ways of Thinking about Organisations* (7th edn). Harlow: Pearson.

Sveningsson, S. and Alvesson, M. (2016) *Managerial Lives: Leadership and Identity in an Imperfect World*. Cambridge: Cambridge University Press.

Thornton, C. (2016) *Group and Team Coaching: The Essential Guide* (2nd edn). Hove: Routledge.

Tourish, D. (2013) *The Dark Side of Transformational Leadership: A Critical Perspective*. Hove: Routledge.

Wenzel, E. (2011) *An Exploration of Processes of Mutual Recognition in Organization Development Initiatives from the Standpoint of a Practising Consultant*. Unpublished dissertation.

Western, S. (2012) *Coaching and Mentoring: A Critical Text*. London: Sage.

Whitmore, J. (2002) *Coaching for Performance: GROWing People, Performance and Purpose* (3rd edn). London: Nicholas Brearley.

Wilson, S., Cummings, S., Jackson, B. and Proctor-Thomson, S. (2018) *Revitalising Leadership: Putting Theory and Practice into Context*. Abingdon: Routledge.

5

FORUM THEATRE

Introduction

> Well it's just paint in the end, and you push it around until it works – that's all. You get better at it over the years, but you build up your marks and your way of doing things ... You've just got to keep doing it.
>
> *(Prunella Clough, Artist 1919–1999)*

The tools and techniques of theatre have been an integral part of the leadership development programmes that I have been involved in for as long as I can remember, particularly the use of live simulations involving actors. However, working with and from a complexity perspective, the focus of my attention and thus my way of working with these techniques has radically changed. In this chapter, I explore how drama and actors are conventionally used in leadership development, with particular reference to forum theatre (Boal, 1979) techniques, before comparing and contrasting this with the complexity approach that I have been taking in my practice, not only in relation to the use of forum theatre, but also as it relates to understandings of conflict, communication and creativity.

Can I play me?

I am co-leading a workshop for a group of managers. We are four months into MSOL, a year-long, in-house, leadership development programme. The title of this month's workshop is 'Leading the Staff Experience' and we are exploring conversation and relationship with the help of a mediator (Macarena Mata, co-leader for this workshop) and two professional actors (Al and Dawn). The participant asking the question, 'Can I play me?' has just observed a scenario, that she described earlier in the day, being played out by the actors as one of the simulations that they perform during the afternoon session. In the simulation, one of the actors portrays the participant while the other portrays the role of one of the participant's direct reports, someone with whom 'this' conversation regularly recurs.

At the point when the conversation becomes stuck and repetitive, Macarena steps in to pause the action and to prompt the actors to share with the audience how the characters they are portraying are feeling and what sense they are making of what has just transpired. Usually, the next steps are an exploration of (i) what resonates with the participant whose scenario the simulation was based on, and/or the rest of the group; (ii) what is generalisable to the day-to-day conversations that we find ourselves in; and (iii) what changes the group would like to see the actors play out in the next iteration of the simulation. Frequently, in these subsequent iterations, the person whose scenario the simulation is based on steps in to replace the actor portraying him or her. However, in this instance, we are barely through the first of these steps when, rather than making suggestions to the actors, or jumping in to replace the actor playing her, the participant decides to experience what it is like to be the other person in this scenario.

The simulation is iterated for a second time with the participant playing her colleague, one of the actors playing her, and the rest of us forming the audience of what the originator of forum theatre, Augusto Boal, termed 'spect-actors' (1979). Eight or nine minutes into the simulation, Macarena (the facilitator, who in forum theatre terminology is known as the joker) stops the action and asks the participant how she is feeling and what's happening for her. After what seems like a considerable period of silence and stillness the participant replies:

> I know that this isn't the real conversation, and I know that I can only spec-ulate what the person that I am playing actually feels like when we have this conversation … but if she feels a fraction of what I am feeling now, then I need to do something different.

I will leave this narrative hanging for now and return to it later in the chapter when I compare and contrast our (complexity) approach to forum theatre with how it is traditionally taken up in organisational settings. Rae argues that the use of 'theatre and drama as a vehicle for organizational development has become increasingly popular in organizations, whether hiring professional actors to support skills development or, more recently, using drama to address wider organizational issues such as diversity, bullying and harassment or conflict management through the use of a particular form of "organizational theatre", namely forum theatre' (2013: 220). However, in spite of its ubiquity, there is very little to be found in mainstream leadership and management development textbooks about the use of theatre in leadership development. Indeed, as outlined in the Introduction, one of the reasons why I decided to write this book was because mainstream textbooks on leadership and management development inevitably sacrifice depth for breadth. This means that interventions are dealt with superficially, if at all, and are, for the most part, taken at face value with little critique.

Take the textbooks on leadership development that are recommended to UK students, for example. As outlined in the previous chapter, the three leading leadership development textbooks on the reading lists of UK business schools are written by Dalton (2010); Gold *et al.* (2010); and Carmichael *et al.* (2011). Dalton allots two pages to the use of theatre in leadership development, Gold *et al.* allocate just half a page (out of 400) and it is not covered at all by Carmichael *et al.* Furthermore, Gold's half-page is clearly an endorsement of Olivier and Verity's (2008) use of Shakespeare in Executive Development Programmes (Gold *et al.*, 2010: 157), while Dalton uses one of the two pages he allots to this topic to provide a brief overview of dramaturgy and the other to promote an obsolete consultancy service that the Royal Shakespeare Company once offered (2010: 31 and 249, respectively).[1]

Snook *et al.* devote a whole chapter, entitled *Mastering the Art of Leadership: An Experiential Approach from the Performing Arts* by Belle Linda Halpern and Richard Richards, to the use and usefulness of the performing arts in leadership development (2012: 135). And although they do not label what they are doing as forum theatre, I would argue that their rather instrumental use of theatre, drama and actors as a resource for developing in leaders the capacity to influence and to transmit a confident and congruent message/story/vision, is what the majority of conventional leadership development providers currently describe as forum theatre. Halpern and Richards find themselves supporting managers to deliver communications that manipulate the emotions of others, thus capturing 'hearts and minds' (Snook *et al.*, 2012: 148); and I would argue that this more accurately describes what Rae and I have encountered under the guise of forum theatre. Consequently, in this chapter, I will compare and contrast Halpern and Richards' use of drama and actors with the complexity approach that I am taking in my practice.

Halpern and Richards encapsulate the capacities that they are looking to develop in managers as 'presence'. They describe leadership presence as 'the ability to authentically connect with the thoughts and feelings of others in order to motivate and inspire them toward a desired outcome' (Snook *et al.*, 2012: 136). The four-step model of the elements that they feel contribute to presence goes under the mnemonic of 'PRES – Present, Reaching out, Expressiveness, and Self-knowledge' (ibid.). Halpern and Richards contend that the performance arts contribute to the 'content and context' of the leadership development interventions that they are involved in. In terms of content, they argue that 'exercises inspired by acting training can build skill and awareness in the ability to be present, reach out, be expressive and self-knowing – all of which lead to the crucial leadership competency of being able to authentically connect with the hearts and minds of others, in order to inspire them to do great things ... [And] in terms of context, the theatre metaphor is tremendously useful in designing the arc of a complex, multi-modal, and engaging leadership program that offers a robust environment for learning' (ibid.: 148).

To illustrate the type of learning that can occur when working with actors Halpern and Richards share a narrative from their experience in which one of the participants on their programme, Mary Ann, plays out a scenario from her own experience with the help of one of the professional actors. Halpern and Richards report that in the group discussion that follows the simulation, Mary Ann tells the group that the simulation has helped her to realise that 'strategic vulnerability is required in leadership' (Snook *et al.*, 2012: 144). Halpern and Richards summarise this learning with, 'Mary Ann takes away ideas of how she might share herself more with her team, even strategically share that she is not always so sure of herself or share some of her developmental goals' (ibid.).

After rereading the two narratives (the one I share at the top of this chapter, and the one from Halpern and Richards, from which the snippet above is taken), for me the most striking thing is the difference in focus. The respective participants find themselves paying attention to very different things and this shows up in the next steps that each individual identifies. In Halpern and Richards's narrative, Mary Ann's first thoughts are focused on the *self* (in relation to self) and consequently the actions she identifies relate to what she might *do to influence* her team's perceptions of her. Whereas in my narrative, the participant's first thoughts are focused on (self in and with relation to – see Chapter 4) the *other* person and the resultant actions relate to how the participant might need to *be* in order to mitigate the impact she feels that she might be having on her colleague, rather than influencing or manipulating her.

Now, I am fairly certain that Halpern and Richards could provide plenty of narratives in which the participant's focus was reversed, as indeed could I, but it is interesting to note that given a free choice of which narrative to use to illustrate the potential learning from our respective programmes we decided to choose the ones we did. This points to another major difference in the respective pedagogies, a difference that I argue is generalisable to, and representative of, the praxis of many conventional leadership development providers when employing actors/ forum theatre. And that is working with what 'is' rather than working with how one thinks things 'ought' to be and pushing for a premeditated outcome. As established throughout this book, in taking a complexity approach I am encouraging sense-making, reflexivity and practical judgement. In my narrative above, we (the facilitators, actors, and participants) had no preconception of what might arise in the simulated interaction, our sense-making was emergent, and we worked with the uncertainty of not knowing what learning, if any, there might be. In the example from Halpern and Richards, however, the use of forum theatre is much more instrumental; it is the backdrop for a coaching exercise aimed at providing the participant with an abstract paradigm of how things ought to be and an opportunity to practise the steps they need to take in order to achieve the predetermined outcome that they desire.

It takes one to know one

The reason why so much of what Halpern and Richards describe resonates with me is in no small part due to a recognition that the way in which they appear to be utilising the tools and techniques of the acting profession in their programmes is unerringly similar to the way in which I used to employ them in my own practice. When I started out, actors supported the leadership development interventions that I was leading, or participating in as a practising manager, in one of two ways. They either attended 'performance management' workshops to illustrate the dos and don'ts of difficult conversations, thus sparing participants from the anxiety-provoking prospect of the dreaded role play. Or, they were invited to presentation skills workshops to share with participants dramatic techniques to support the development of 'gravitas' when presenting themselves and their ideas to others.

However, over recent years my focus and practice have dramatically changed. This move away from what I am describing as the conventional approach has been greatly influenced by my understanding of organisational life as the patterning of human bodies responding to each other in complex ways, that is, predictable and unpredictable at the same time. However, it would be useful to point out here that the movement in my thinking/practice was, and continues to be, an emergent process. My praxis has changed as a result of taking my everyday experience seriously, working from a more reality-congruent understanding of what is actually going on in the cut and thrust of organisational life and making sense of how I might more usefully play into the interactions that constitute the daily activity that we call work. Hence, in using forum theatre we encourage the actors to simulate what is actually going on for people at work, rather than playing out abstractions of how things ought to be. This means challenging the deceptive certainty of the abstract models and frameworks of leadership and organisation found in the mainstream discourse and engaging with thinkers who are trying to make sense of the ambiguities and paradoxes of leading and organising to provide a more nuanced understanding of work and the human condition. This is an understanding that resonates with my own lived experience, and that of the participants on the programmes that I lead – a perspective that proffers a more complex and practically useful explanation of the everyday politics involved in coming together to get things done.

Prior to this, I spent an inordinate amount of time trying to match my experience of the (messy and ordered, creative and destructive, rational and irrational, exhilarating and frustrating) world of work to the latest management fad that mainstream and popular management literature had to offer and inviting the manager-participants on the leadership development programmes that I was leading at the time to do the same. And, as noted in the Introduction, I would have most probably carried on working in this way, until my growing cynicism and disillusionment proved too much, had I not sat down for a meeting with Professor Ralph Stacey in 2007 to discuss a change management programme that I was involved in. That initial conversation with Ralph encouraged me to re-entertain a liberating, and at the same time, anxiety-provoking thought that I had suppressed many times over the years and that thought was – there are no recipes for this stuff, these models and frameworks of change are nonsense and I don't find them helpful.

Although this conversation was the catalyst that led to my decision to enrol on the DMan programme and engage with Ralph's research more formally, the movement in thought didn't start or end with this discussion. The development of my thinking/practice was, and is, an ongoing, never-ending process. It was not, and is not, like flicking a switch between old thinking and new thinking. Mainstream conceptions of leadership and organisation still dominate the (organisational) habitus and they will always be present in the amalgamation (Flinn, 2011) of thought and experience that informs my praxis. Similarly, my way of working with actors and the techniques of forum theatre described in this chapter is an emergent process started by a chance meeting with (my now good friend and colleague) Macarena Mata, a professional mediator. And at this point, it is important to point out that however 'concrete' our methods and practice appear when written up in print, to echo the Clough quote that opens this chapter, every workshop is a new canvas on which we 'push the paint around until it works'.

A meeting of minds?

I met Macarena, an external consultant, for the first time when she came to the university to work with a group of colleagues and I was called on to help her to set up the audio-visual equipment. As I set up the laptop and launched her slide show I noticed that the title of her presentation, and theme of the workshop, was 'Conflict Resolution'. The half-day workshop was due to start, so I wished her well and left her to it. If there had been more time, I was really interested to ask whether she, as a professional mediator, felt that conflict could be resolved, and if so, whether one could teach people to do this, and in three hours? When it came to the end of the session, I returned to dismantle the audio-visual equipment and took the opportunity to tentatively ask the questions I'd shied away from earlier. I cannot remember exactly what Macarena said at the time, but when I recount this tale to workshop participants I reductively recall her answers as 'Yes and no', 'Yes and no' and 'No and yes'. Whatever her exact answers, the questions provided the catalyst for a discussion that we are still having to this day.

Our main points of agreement in that first conversation were that (i) conflict is not negative: it is an unavoidable part of day-to-day life and has the potential to be constructive as well as destructive; creativity and novelty arise from difference; (ii) some conflicts can be resolved, but more often than not 'resolution' means negotiating a way of going on together in spite of the differences and reaching an accommodation that both parties can live with, or, if this is not possible, feel settled knowing that you've done all you can; (iii) managing conflict is not about getting the other party to see it your way ('winning hearts and minds'), it's about developing the capacity to acknowledge and work with the strong emotions that conflicts stir, keeping oneself safe in the process, seeing each other as human beings, responding rather than reacting, asking oneself 'what else might be going on here?' (see Chapter 7), exploring the interests and needs of both parties with a view to coming to a common understanding and recognising that you have choices; (iv) it is not about manipulating others so that they become subject to your will, rather it is about learning to interact with others in a way that does not denigrate either party's sense of self; and (v) there are no recipes, no easy answers and no guarantees that what you say or do will improve the situation; it may make matters worse and not just worse before they get better.

The understanding that we reached in that initial conversation, which was much more fragmentary than the polished version presented above, was enough for us to agree to work together in order to bring some of these ideas and ways of working to the leadership development programmes I was involved in. That was some eight years ago and we are still working out what it is that we are doing together as our thinking continues to shift and move. The first workshops that we co-facilitated didn't involve actors and we struggled with the challenge of talking about conversation rather than experiencing it. We considered introducing participant role play, but in our experience this is not only anxiety-provoking, for students and facilitators alike, but it is also difficult for participants to remain in character in order to sustain the simulation for any useful length of time. Consequently, our thoughts turned to bringing in actors, but I did not want to work with them as I had in the past. It was around this time that I first encountered forum theatre (Boal, 1979), during an exercise that I participated in, led by Henry Larsen.

Forum theatre

Henry Larsen is Professor of Participatory Innovation at the University of Southern Denmark and before taking up this post he was a member of the Dacapo Theatre Company. Dacapo is a Danish firm of management consultants that has for over twenty-five years been at the forefront of using forum theatre as a means of helping organisations to explore the challenges and opportunities they face. As mentioned above, forum theatre was originally developed by Augusto Boal, a Brazilian theatre director, writer and (latterly) politician. Boal, building on Paulo Freire's ideas in *Pedagogy of the Oppressed* (Freire, 2000) developed his concept of the 'Theatre of the Oppressed'. Boal saw theatre as an opportunity for the audience to get involved with the drama/actors and try out different responses as a means of finding their own agency and in so doing identify spaces for emancipation.

This way of working came to be known as forum theatre in which scenes that are pertinent to the audience are acted out before being stopped by the joker with a view to not only opening up a dialogue and inviting direction from the audience, but also inviting audience members to join the action and interact with the actors as a means of exploring how power is enacted. The main differences between my previous way of working with actors and the way Dacapo worked was that (i) Henry and his colleagues played out scenarios that had been painstakingly developed during several preparatory visits/conversations with the participants involved in the process; and (ii) the resultant scenarios were catalysts for conversation, rather than a means of rehearsing how to 'get it right'.

This resonated with the way in which Macarena and I wanted to position our workshops. Our intention was to explore conversations and relationships in general and those which we found difficult in particular, drawing on Macarena's experience of working with people in conflict. So once we had decided to involve professional actors in our workshops, we spent time working with them as well as a small group of managers preparing and developing a range of generic scenarios that would highlight the kinds of conflict that can arise between managers and their team members, peers and line managers. We could not, nor were we attempting to, do what Dacapo were doing, but we took something from their way of working that we felt was generalisable and worked it into our practice. We set out to do two things. First, we wanted to work with groups of managers in order to explore and make sense of their experience of conversation and relationship. And second, we wanted to help them to become more adept at conversation by developing awareness of self in relation to others and developing the capacities for observing/noticing, listening, questioning, summarising, acknowledging and working with affect.

Rae's research into the use of forum theatre in organisational settings involved not only observation and participation in such events but also extensive interviews with the commissioners, providers, actors and participants involved (Rae, 2013). She found that although the term was freely used by those commissioning such interventions (human resource and development professionals), when probed they were 'unclear about what theatre-based and forum theatre interventions can potentially offer … and were generally less able to articulate how they perceived theatre-based interventions could support organizational learning, and change' (ibid.: 233). One of the espoused aims of forum theatre in organisational settings is 'to provide opportunities for more democratic approaches to learning and development, through offering participants open ended dramatised narratives, usually based on organizational events and allowing participants to take that narrative in a direction which is not necessarily bounded by management intentions' (ibid.: 221). However, Rae found that this was often compromised in practice, more often than not by the jokers whom she argues lacked one or more of three things.

First, Rae found that the jokers in her study often lacked training. One of the actors interviewed by Rae reported, 'We get a day or two days' training maximum as forum, as facilitators. You know, some facilitators, they do exams in it […] you sink or swim' (2013: 227). Second, they lacked, or more accurately were unable to maintain, focus. Rae's jokers more often than not found themselves doubling up as actors due to the budgetary constraints of the commissioning organisation (Boal recommends a minimum of three facilitators – two actors and a joker). And third, and perhaps most importantly, Rae found that the jokers in her study lacked impartiality. In forum theatre, the impartiality of the joker is key. For Boal, the joker must be like the joker in a deck of playing cards. That is, someone who is 'not tied down to a specific suit or value' and has 'no allegiance to performer, spectator, or any one interpretation of events' (ibid.: 222). Rae, however, in her observations and interviews with participants, discovered that the jokers' 'primary focus was on the need to meet the commissioners' expectations', rather than 'responding to the direction of the participants'; instead of opening up learning spaces, the jokers manipulated the simulations in order to ensure that 'events were controlled and managed' (ibid.: 228).

She concludes that 'while employees were engaged in the process and perceived such events as being highly participative, the extent to which the outcomes were emergent rather than pre-determined is open to question' (ibid.: 231). Reflecting on one particular forum theatre event that she observed Rae reports:

> While the dramas brought to life the realities of day-to-day working life – for example, a reluctance to challenge colleagues for fear of making working relationships difficult; the need for a supportive culture in which these issues can be aired – the focus remained on the individual behaviours rather than underlying issues.
>
> *(2011: 11)*

Cohen-Cruz and Schutzman (2006) use the term theatre of the oppressed (TO), rather than forum theatre, to describe Boal's way of working. They argue that there is a tendency to oversimplify and gloss over the complexities and ambiguities that might surface during theatre of the oppressed/forum theatre events where as facilitators/jokers we all too often 'take a how-to approach, forgetting that the "how" needs to be as mutable as the ideas that inform it; we tend to replicate what "worked" in one context into another, forgetting that TO is predicated on a vigilant receptivity to difference across time, circumstance, geography, culture, race, ethnicity, sexual orientation and gender (ibid.: 1). They argue that Boal translated Freire's idea of 'replacing the prevalent banking method of education (filling students' heads with what experts deem important) with a dialogic approach to learning in which students and teachers are interactive partners' developing the concept of the 'spect-actor, who replaces the spectator sitting passively in the dark watching the finished production. As Freire broke the hierarchical divide between teacher and student, Boal did so between performer and audience member' (ibid.: 3).

At this point, it would be relatively easy to use Rae's findings as validation for our way of working. I could claim that we have avoided all of the pitfalls that she identifies by having (i) a 'commissioner' (me) who is fully aware of the potential that forum theatre has to offer to 'support organizational learning, and change' (Rae, 2011: 233); (ii) two professional actors who are able to focus on the job in hand rather than having to double up as facilitators; and (iii) a joker and professional qualified mediator for whom impartiality is paramount. However, such a convenient post-rationalisation would be a misrepresentation of the emergent, messy and fragmentary back-and-forth that has characterised our collaboration over the last eight years. Similarly, I could argue that our way of working does blur the boundaries between teacher/student, performer/audience member, but that we also offer some 'banking' around questioning, listening, summarising and assertive communication.

So how would I describe the difference between the conventional approach to the use of (forum) theatre in leadership development, illustrated by Halpern and Richard's practice, and what I am describing as a complexity approach? First, it's about having a good working knowledge of the philosophy and principles of forum theatre (particularly the roles played by the joker and the actors) and the generative potential of this way of working, as described above. At the same time it's about working from a radically different understanding of conflict, communication and creativity than that found in the dominant discourse, something that I turn my attention to now.

Conflict, communication and creativity

Conflict as the ongoing negotiation of difference

As outlined above, the majority of managers who enrol on the leadership development programmes that I am involved in see conflict as a battle to be won – how do I get the other party or parties to see things my way? This reflects the mainstream characterisation of conflict as 'antagonistic relationships between people' (Grant quoted in Stacey and Griffin, 2008). And the minority of managers who acknowledge the need to listen and put themselves in the other party's shoes, see conflict as an undesirable state that should be replaced by some form of consensus that reconciles difference and brings about harmony. Thus both groups see as something to be overcome, one more thing to get on top of and control, whereas from a complexity perspective, conflict is seen as 'an inevitable aspect of all human relationships' (ibid.: 46). In our ongoing interactions with each other, we compete and we collaborate, but competition and collaboration are not mutually exclusive – they paradoxically co-exist. From this perspective, it is not unreasonable to talk about competitive collaboration, or collaborative competition, as we negotiate a way of going on together that acknowledges but works with the tension. Taking a complexity approach, it is neither possible to eradicate conflict by beating oneself or the other into submission, nor to replace it with some form of utopian consensus or self-suppression. Attempts to eradicate or neutralise conflict (difference), which in organisational settings are present in the many calls for alignment to the strategic plan, shared values, one vision, etc., are not only futile (with totalitarian undertones), but they also discourage the very characteristics that many organisations are looking to foster in their strategic plans, values and visions, namely, novelty, diversity and innovation.

Two colleagues who have taken their experience of conflict seriously are Nol Groot (2005) and Eric Wenzel (2011). [2] Groot, in trying to make sense of his time as managing director of a division of a large services company in the Netherlands, reflects upon his experience of leading organisation-wide contract negotiations with the unions representing workers in the various companies making up the group. During these negotiations Groot attempted to avoid the mistakes of the recent past that were still reverberating around the organisation by 'focusing not on the negotiating position, but on building relationships' (ibid.: 56). To help with the reflexive interrogation of his own thinking about what it means to be in conflict, Groot compares mainstream and complexity conceptions of conflict in the literature and contrasts what he sees as the corresponding approaches 'recommended' by each perspective as a consequence. He uses the term *polarized conflict* to describe mainstream understandings of conflict as 'a social phenomenon involving a struggle aimed at neutralising, injuring or eliminating the values, status, power and resources of opponents' (ibid.: 57). The corresponding recommendation from this mainstream perspective is that conflict should be prevented, repressed or resolved by bringing things out into the open, surfacing the unmet needs of each party and clearing up any misunderstandings (Glasl, 1999). Groot categorises these approaches that ignore, avoid or harmoniously resolve difference(s) as *preventative conflict* (2005: 57).

From the perspective of complex responsive processes, conflict is seen as an ever-present aspect of human relationships. It is the inevitable consequence of people trying to make sense of the world and of themselves as well as competing and co-operating with others where competition and cooperation are two sides of the same coin. Groot uses the term *normative conflict* to describe this view. And if one takes this perspective, then the most useful approach is not to dismiss, run from, or reconcile, but rather to see it as 'an ongoing process of discussing and exploring difference involving both co-operation and competition without necessarily breaking down as hostility of some kind' (2005: 58). Groot describes this approach to the negotiation of difference(s) as *explorative conflict*. He acknowledges that this approach will not necessarily prevent polarised conflict, but in his experience explorative conflict 'can create solutions and prevent people from getting stuck' (ibid.: 60). When it came to leading the negotiations with the unions, Groot's shifting understanding of what it means to be in conflict influenced him to abandon 'standard negotiation procedures' and instead to create 'opportunities for discussion' that avoided the polarised positions of old (ibid.: 78). And for Groot, drawing on Griffin (2002), this involved the recreation and negotiation of identities (ibid.: 158).

This notion of conflict as the negotiation of identity is something that Eric Wenzel (2011) explores in his research. We met Eric in the vignette that accompanies Chapter 4. His doctoral research centred on trying to make sense of what he was being asked to do as a management consultant when invited into organisations. Wenzel often found himself caught in the middle between the senior managers who had commissioned his engagement and the middle managers who would be tasked with implementing his recommendations. Invariably, the mismatch between (senior manager) aspirations and operational realities (facing middle managers) were a constant source of conflict. Building on Groot's work on polarised and explorative conflict, Wenzel explores conflict as simultaneous processes of mutual recognition and mis-recognition, whereby the struggle for recognition involves the negotiation, or re-negotiation, of identity. For Wenzel:

The act of recognition is more than acknowledgement of the other. It is a deep acceptance of the other in his/her right to be different. More importantly, it means accepting ourselves in and through the other. The other is both, different and the same. This may not do away with our anxieties. But it may help us to accept them as a necessary element of the conflictual dimension of human interrelating.

(Ibid.: 65)

Groot's conception of explorative conflict is useful, as I think what Macarena, Al, Dawn and I are doing is exploring conflict, but I find the split between explorative conflict and polarised conflict less so, as the potential for participants to polarise (by repressing, avoiding or seeking an idealistic harmony) even in their exploration is ever-present. It is not either/or, this or that; polarised conflict and explorative conflict simultaneously coexist. Groot's expression of what might be happening in the interaction when one tries to explore conflict is helpful, but the label is not. As soon as one uses a label like explorative conflict to describe an approach to the negotiation of difference, there is a temptation to reify it as a tool or technique that can be used instrumentally, a 'best practice' solution for how to manage conflict. Similarly, it sets up the false dichotomy of polarised conflict as 'bad' and explorative conflict as 'good'; and I know that Groot would be one of the first to acknowledge that in the negotiation of difference there may well be times when positions are or become irreconcilable, or when the most useful next step for one, another or both might be to avoid or repress conflict in order to maintain the relationship, one's job, one's sense of self (identity).

Wenzel's research draws attention to an aspect of conflict that is often glossed over in mainstream literature, something central to Boal's work, and that is power relations. One could argue that the intention of Boal's theatre of the oppressed is to encourage spect-actors to challenge the status quo with a view to shifting the power differentials in favour of the oppressed, thus engendering some degree of emancipation. Here conflict is polarised – them against us. From the perspective of complex responsive processes, the exploration of power relations is not about emancipation but rather sense-making and understanding, which may or may not be emancipatory. For the managers that I work with, the power differential is most often in their favour in relation to the members of their team (their direct reports, subordinates), and most often in favour of the other in relation to their manager (their manager(s), superior(s)).

Thus in our 'theatre of the (what might arguably be more accurately described as) oppressors', rather than seeking emancipation, we are inviting managers to explore difference with a view to reaching an accommodation, a way of going on together, that both parties find acceptable, or if this is not possible, to at least be comfortable that they have done everything they can to allow this to happen. One might ask why this is necessary when the power differential favours the managers? Why not, like Halpern and Richards, teach them how to influence 'hearts and minds'? Well, leaving aside the moral and ethical ramifications of this question, the exploration of difference and/or the encouragement of dissent (Tourish, 2013) are catalysts for reflexivity (Flinn, 2011; Flinn and Mowles, 2014), which in turn might help one to avoid the excesses of hubris (de Haan, 2014) and functional stupidity (Alvesson and Spicer, 2016), outlined in earlier chapters. This requires a very different approach to communication than that found in the mainstream.

Communication as iterative processes of gesture and response

My early understanding of communication was based on the sender-receiver model. Ann Cunliffe argues that the sender-receiver model of communication is based on the premise that:

- there are *independent* and *autonomous* senders and receivers each with a message in mind that they want to convey to the other.
- The sender *first thinks* of what she or he wants to say and the best way of saying it (encodes) *before transmitting* the message.
- The receiver hears/reads the message and *decodes its real meaning*. If the receiver doesn't understand, for whatever reason, he or she will indicate this through feedback, which then enables the sender to rephrase the message or add further information. So communication is a recursive process culminating in an agreement over meaning.*(2009: 54; emphasis in the original)*

Cunliffe argues that in this conception of communication, 'management is about the art of persuasion' (ibid.: 55), about transmitting a message that convinces the hearer to see it your way and do your bidding. This conception of communication is evident in the praxis of Halpern and Richards when they argue that:

> Leaders with presence send a single message. They pay attention to eye contact, body language, voice variability, pacing, silence, the use of space to express a uniform message. Concerned? They pause. Excited? They speak faster. Eager? They lean forward. They use language and story to reach the hearts and minds of their audiences – to make sure their message lands. You know good acting when you see it because you believe what you see and that transports you into the story. You know good leadership for the same reasons.
>
> *(Halpern and Richards in Snook et al., 2012: 138)*

Cunliffe accepts that there are times when we might prepare what we have to say in advance, occasions where we might learn a speech by rote, or write something down and read it word for word. However, she argues that once we enter into a conversation, what we say will be a 'mix of previously thought words and sentences, along with improvisations as [we] respond to the other person' (2009: 55). Cunliffe draws on the work of Bakhtin and his conception of dialogism where meaning emerges in the 'interaction and struggle' (Bakhtin, 1986: 92). This is markedly different from the sender-receiver model and similar to the understanding that informs the complexity approach to communication.

Informed by the work of the American pragmatist philosopher, George Herbert Mead, I see communications/conversations as iterative processes of gesture and response. Mead (1934) argues that consciousness and self-consciousness emerge in the conversation of gestures between engaged human beings, where a gesture calls out a response in the gesturer that is similar to the response that same gesture calls out in the other. This means that a gesturer can, to some extent, anticipate the response that they are likely to call out in the other; modifying what they are saying as they are saying it. Thus the gesturer is gesturing to themselves and the other, at the same time. Both are responding to each other according to their life histories. So rather than understanding communication as a message being repeatedly trans-mitted by an autonomous sender to an equally autonomous receiver, until the receiver understands the sender's original meaning, Mead posits that meaning emerges in the iterative social process of gesture and response since the gesture can never be separated from the response:

> The response of one organism to the gesture of another in any given social act is the meaning of that gesture, and also is in a sense responsible for the appearance or coming into being of the new object – or new content of an old object – to which that gesture refers through the outcome of the given social act in which it is an early phase.
>
> *(1934: 78)*

If you recall an occasion when you caught yourself adjusting mid-sentence how and/or what you were saying because the verbal or non-verbal reaction of the person you were speaking to did not appear to be eliciting the response you had hoped for, then you will not only begin to appreciate Mead's insight, but you will also see how inadequate the sender-receiver model is for explaining what is actually happening when we communicate with each other. Understanding the various responses we are having to the gestures we are in the process of making to another allows us to anticipate, and to some extent predict, the response we might be about to call forth in the other. Mead described gestures that are to a degree shared as being significant symbols, that is. acts of communication (a frown, for example) that are generally understood by the people with whom we interact. Significant sym-bols make it possible for us, as human beings, to make sense of each other. Mead considered the vocal gesture as the most useful significant symbol, and the develop-ment of sophisticated vocal gestures, that is, language, as central to the development of consciousness.

This ability to take the attitude of the other allows us to play out the possible outcomes of our actions as private role plays. Indeed, Mead described humans as role-playing animals. He further argued that as we engage in more and more interactions the mind 'evolves in increasingly complex ways' (Stacey and Mowles, 2016: 345), to the point where we are able to take in the attitude of many others, which Mead (1934) describes as the 'attitude of the generalised other'. That is, we are able to take in the attitude of the whole group/society in generalised form, thus enabling us to predict the reception (response) our words and deeds (gestures) are likely to provoke. This acts as a 'powerful form of social control through self-control' (Stacey and Mowles, 2016: 345). However, Mead was also at pains to point out that his theory is not a form of social determinism. That is, there is no guarantee that the responses my gestures call forth in me will call forth the same responses in you. This is because the response that my gesture calls forth in me is partly the result of my experience of the thousands of interactions that I have had during my lifetime, and the response it might call forth in you is partly the result of your corresponding life experience. My gestures are themselves responses to the millions of gestures that have been made to me in the hundreds of thousands of conversations I have already had, in addition to the silent conversations (role plays) I have with myself. And this takes no account of the potential for you to have a spontaneous response to my gesture: something evoked in you for the first time. Indeed, I cannot even guarantee my responses to my own gestures. A good example of this is when we might find ourselves inadvertently blushing when we disclose something.

This is a radically different view of communication from the sender-receiver models contained in mainstream and popular management literature. Communication is not seen as an event, as a parcel of data conveyed from one person to another, rather as an iterative process of sense-making and negotiation whereby meaning is not merely contained in words, policy documents or directives, but also in how such things are being taken up by people in local interaction. So, for example, as outlined in Chapter 3, the meaning of an address by a CEO is not in his or her gift as it will be interpreted differently in the many and varied local interactions that take place as individuals and groups try to make sense of what they've heard. So, one can see that using actors to rehearse one's part in a future conversation makes sense from the sender-receiver perspective, but none whatsoever from the perspective of complex responsive processes. For me and Macarena, the use of actors/forum theatre is not a dress rehearsal but rather an opportunity to develop self-awareness and explore what it means to improvise and become adept at conversation. Organisational consultant Michael Shiel contends that in these situations, the role of the leader is to stay in the conversation with a view to drawing attention to 'surprises, irregularities and misunderstandings' and 'encourag[ing] new patterns of thinking and knowing to emerge in joint exploratory learning'. This involves developing the ability to pay attention to the processes of communication, 'as well as being fully present to the changing patterning of the silent conversation with oneself' (2005: 183).

If we compare and contrast mainstream and complexity understandings of communication using the Martin Luther King Jr narrative from Chapter 2, then the sender-receiver model of communication might explain King's 'I have a dream' detour as a message that King sends to an expectant crowd who are passively waiting to receive it. From the perspective of complex responsive processes, it is a response to the gesture from Mahalia Jackson, where the response cannot be separated from the gesture. The meaning of Mahalia Jackson's ('Tell 'em about the 'Dream', Martin') gesture only becomes apparent in King's response. Jackson's gesture is itself a response to the *present* (her own gestures and responses and those of King and the crowd), drawing on the *past* (her own previous gestures and responses and those of King and different crowds when he has shared previous versions of the 'I have a dream' speech), in anticipation of the *future* (her desire to influence King). From the perspective of complex responsive processes this is described as the living present. That is, temporal processes of interaction where our experiences and actions in the present are influenced by and influence our accounts of past experience at the same time as influencing our (anticipated) future actions (Flinn and Mowles, 2014: 2) and those of others. This understanding of communication and the living present has radical implications for thinking about creativity and the creation of (new) knowledge.

Creativity as social processes of knowledge creation

Rae experienced and explored two uses of forum theatre in her research, one that looked to encourage individual change and the other that was more concerned with bringing about change at organisational level (2011: 16). Leaving aside the split of individual and organisational (which I hope by now you have realised is problematic if you take anything but a functionalist approach), one might characterise the use that I have been exploring above as being focused on the development of individuals. The use of forum theatre in organisational change, be that a change of culture, values, strategy, purpose, or supporting transitions to new structures or ways of working, is usually referred to as organisation(al) development (something I plan to explore in my next book).

I have experienced the use of forum theatre in this way as a participant several times, but I have much less experience of facilitating such events. However, somebody who has a great deal of experience, as outlined above, is Henry Larsen. The following vignette provides an insight into how Henry and his former colleagues work with forum theatre techniques to encourage reflexivity (see Chapter 3), that is, to help participants to think about how they are thinking with a view to exploring what might be useful for future interactions.

VIGNETTE

'So let us introduce ourselves to each other at the tables', I said to the audience. A man who was sitting with his wife at my table started to talk about their two children. Although all was well now, a few years ago the social workers had wanted to remove their children. He and his wife had sought help from the social workers to deal with their very difficult children but they and the social workers had formed a very bad relationship. As a result, after three years, the social workers decided to take the kids into care. The man had gone to the press and finally they were allowed to change to another institution and new social workers. Within a year, they were helped so much that they were able to deal with their children without any help from 'the system'. He also mentioned that he himself had been in a children's home for 17 years. He felt that this had been used against him in the situation.

The conversations took place as a meeting in the initial phase of a research project about user involvement in the social services and the legal rights of the citizen. This particular day was about the contact of parents with 'the system'. The participants at this meeting were social workers, foster parents and assessors, and also parents who had either lost, or come close to losing, their children. We were supposed to work with the participants as an alternative to the widely used 'focus group' interviews. The idea that was by dramatising some aspects of people's stories we could uncover issues that would not come out in interviews. No one in the room had ever tried this before, and I felt anxious and tense but at the same time an intense desire to find some way to explore the theme: How do we understand client involvement and legal rights?

We had split into three groups. While the man was talking I could see that other groups were finishing their round. My colleagues and I had a plan but I felt drawn to the man's story. So I called the actors, who were sitting at the other tables. I expressed that I would like to see performed on stage the story of what the 'good' social workers had been doing and I asked the man to say something about it. He hesitated. 'We were just sitting there, and they appreciated us and helped us be parents'. 'What did they do?' I asked. He could not explain. 'What were you doing?' I asked. 'Well, we played some games with the children', was his reply. Obviously the man could not explain his relationship with the social worker, but we set up a situation with three actors, one playing the nine-year old child who was very noisy and challenging, one playing the father and one playing the social worker.

Usually the man would direct the actors, but obviously he was not able to do that. The actors had not heard his story from the beginning and they were confused. I sensed that we all felt that this was risky. The actors started playing cards and after a while I stopped them: the actor playing the kid had been really challenging in his role. 'What was different', I asked the man. 'The kid is OK', he said, 'and the father is OK too, sitting not knowing what to say to the child. But the social worker is wrong. She just observed and did not take part in the play. It was taken on video, and afterwards we watched it together and talked about what I could do.' The man's speech was nearly fluent now.

The actors played again now with the 'social worker' watching. At a moment when the child was behaving badly the 'father' took a glance at the 'social worker', she smiled and kept quiet. 'Yes, this is good', the man said, 'it is just the way it was when he ('the father') looks at her ('the social worker'), and she sits there and just smiles. I really remember it and it gave me the confidence to calm down and not be angry about the child's restlessness. We worked with this and gradually I learned how to relate to the boy'. He spoke more and more, talking fluently in a much richer language.

'Didn't she take notes?' asked a member of the audience. 'No', he said. 'There was a large board and she could write on that. In the beginning it distracted me but after a few sessions it did not disturb me. We could talk about it afterwards, and because what she wrote was visible on the board, I never felt that she had a hidden agenda'. Another member of the audience commented that what she had seen on the stage was not a good situation because no limits were set for the boy and that should not be allowed. The man replied that basically she was right, but first of all he, as a father, had to find a way to be there and cope with the situation and that was just what came out of the relation to the social worker. He explained that just by having her there and being inspired by her reactions, he found his own way of reacting in the situation with his children. 'After some months the situation changed and within a year we did not need help any more', he said.

Reflecting on this narrative six months later, Larsen added:

Everyone in the room was engaging animatedly in what was going on, we were moving into a conversation that was at the very heart of the theme we were working with, and we were processing it together, in iterations of talking and playing. The actors contributed with experiences that in the fullest sense were embodied and emotional. They reiterated these situations by playing them again, taking the momentary conversation into consideration. So through iterating and reiterating in different ways we were all working with the theme of the day. In this way, the man was drawn into a new conversation that gave him an insight that was novel, just as the situation was novel. What happened affected the situation about the theme we were working with and its progress towards a way of understanding that which had not been understood – or understood in a different way – previously.

(Ibid.: 31–35)

This way of working with forum theatre is starkly different to my experience of how other organisational and leadership development specialists work with it. The difference is that Dacapo use forum theatre as a catalyst for exploration, a space where knowledge (understanding, sense-making, way of thinking) is co-created in the workshop. That is not to say that everybody walks away with the same knowledge (understanding, sense-making, way of thinking), but they do not leave with the same point of view that they entered with. Change doesn't happen as a result of the intervention, but in the midst of it. Rae argues that 'forum theatre, given its antecedents, is likely to be at its most effective if it can be used as method of providing a stimulus for participants to access and view their own experiences and form emotional connections to those experiences' (2011: 231). This goes beyond the transmission or acquisition of pre-determined knowledge that informs conventional approaches towards an emergent approach to knowledge creation. Rae found that for all the talk of a dialogical approach to learning and development, the language of the practitioners and commissioners was much more didactic (ibid.: 232).

Reflections

The practices that Macarena, the actors and I have developed, and the choices that we have made since starting to work together, have generated intended and unintended consequences. The unintended but most welcome consequence of having Macarena (a vastly experienced mediator) as joker, is impartiality. In mediation it is not about one party agreeing to do the other party's bidding. It is not about manipulation or coercion. Mediation is about supporting both parties to come to a mutual understanding that enables them to arrive at an accommodation that both can live with. It's about negotiating a way of continuing to work/live together, or not as the case may be, in spite of differences. The mediation process encourages both parties to see each other as human beings, rather than enemies, to acknowledge each other's interests and needs, find some common ground and come to an accommodation that views difference and conflict as a fact of life, not something to eradicate. This also means that the actors, Dawn and Al, both experienced forum theatre facilitators themselves, can concentrate on embodying the characters that they have been asked to play rather than being distracted by the duties of facilitation.

The actors bring their ability to respond to each other, the participants and the joker in character, both during and after the simulations. They are not guided by me, as the 'commissioner', to manipulate conversations in order to achieve given outcomes or learning objectives. This means that scenarios that we have been playing with for years are different every time. How the characters respond on the day is influenced by the group we are working with, by how Al and Dawn are feeling on that day, and by how Macarena and I are interacting with everyone. The actors respond as the character they have created on the day would respond, not as this character responded last time they played this scene. Also, they are adept at speculating what their characters might do following the interactions. This means that what they agree to in the simulation, and what they speculate will happen next when prompted by the joker, are often two separate things. Similarly, they might appear unmoved in the conversation, but subsequently inform the joker, and the rest of the audience, that something has shifted for their character, but they didn't want to admit or signal that to the other party involved in the simulation.

Again, I am not holding up this way of working as a potential exemplar, or suggesting that our practice mitigates all of the tensions that Rae found in her research. We quite often have our impartiality tested as we find ourselves rooting for one or other of the characters in the simulation, or pushing for a particular technique to be employed, and as a senior manager in the institution where the workshops take place, I might find myself intervening on a matter of policy or procedure. And I am not saying that some of the managers who we work with don't leave disappointed that we have not furnished them with a recipe or *n*-step plan for how to have difficult conversations. Nevertheless, the majority of participants find this to be one of the most useful sessions of the programme. I hope that the above narrative has illustrated the emergent and emerging nature of our current way of working. What works for us won't necessarily work for you. So, I am not suggesting that you go and employ the services of a mediator as joker, for example. What I am encouraging you to do is reflect on your own practice, and see what, if anything, is generalisable from our experience. I would also encourage you to compare mainstream conceptions of conflict, communication and creativity with a complexity approach and consider which you find to be more congruent with your own day-to-day experience.

Notes

1 It was not my intention to record this level of detail for each of the interventions under review in this book until it became apparent that this is (i) a useful illustration of the superficiality with which all of the interventions under review are covered (bar coaching, to which Gold *et al.* dedicate some fifteen pages); and (ii) indicative of how such perspectives, tools and techniques are more often than not accepted at face value and seldom critiqued.
2 I am introducing these authors because they are practitioners who take a complexity approach in their practice, work outside of the UK (in different cultures), and explore themes that have helped me to make sense of conflict as it arises in organisational settings. An added bonus is that their unpublished doctoral theses, and the doctoral theses of most of the authors who have given me permission to use narratives from their experience as vignettes in this book, are also available for free via the internet.

References

Alvesson, M. and Spicer, A. (2016) *The Stupidity Paradox: The Power and Pitfalls of Functional Stupidity at Work.* London: Profile Books.
Bakhtin, M. (1986) *Speech Genres and Other Late Essays.* Trans. V. W. McGee. Austin, TX: University of Texas Press.
Boal, A. (1979) *Theatre of the Oppressed.* London: Pluto Press.
Carmichael, J., Collins, C., Emsell, P. and Haydon, J. (2011) *Leadship and Management Development.* Oxford: Oxford University Press.
Clough, P. (2016) Quotation from *Prunella Clough, Unknown Countries*, an exhibition at the Jerwood Gallery, Hastings.
Cohen-Cruz, J. and Schutzman, M. (Eds) (2006) *A Boal Companion: Dialogues on Theatre and Cultural Politics.* Abingdon: Routledge.
Dalton, K. (2010) *Leadership and Management Development: Developing Tomorrow's Managers.* Harlow: Pearson.
de Haan, E. and Kasozi, A. (2014) *The Leadership Shadow: How to Recognize and Avoid Derailment, Hubris and Overdrive.* London: Kogan Page.

Flinn, K. (2011) *Making Sense of Leadership Development: Reflections on my Role as a Leader of Leadership Development Interventions.* University of Hertfordshire, unpublished thesis.

Flinn, K. and Mowles, C. (2014) *A Complexity Approach to Leadership Development: Developing Practical Judgement.* Leadership Foundation for Higher Education stimulus paper.

Freire, P. (2000) *Pedagogy of the Oppressed.* London: Bloomsbury Publishing.

Glasl, F. (1999) *Confronting Conflict: A First Aid Kit for Handling Conflict.* Stroud: Hawthorn Press.

Gold, J., Thorpe, R. and Mumford, A. (2010) *Leadership and Management Development* (5th edn). London: Chartered Institute of Personnel and Development.

Grant, A. (2008) In R. Stacey and D. Griffin (Eds) *Complexity and the Experience of Values, Conflict and Compromise in Organisation.* Abingdon: Routledge.

Griffin, D. (2002) *The Emergence of Leadership: Linking Self-Organisation and Ethics.* London: Routledge.

Groot, N. (2005) *Senior Executives and the Emergence of Local Responsibilities in Large Organisations: A Complexity Approach to Potentially Better Results.* University of Hertfordshire, unpublished thesis.

Halpern, B. L. and Richards, R. (2012) 'Mastering the Art of Leadership: An Experiential Approach from the Performing Arts'. In S. Snook, N. Nohria and R. Khurana (Eds) *The Handbook of Teaching Leadership: Knowing, Doing and Being.* London: Sage.

Larsen, H. (2008) *Spontaneity and Power.* Saarbruken: VDM Verlag Dr. Muller.

Mead, G. H. (1934) *Mind, Self, and Society.* Chicago, IL: University of Chicago Press.

Rae, J. (2011) *A Study of the Use of Organisational Theatre: The Case of Forum Theatre.* Durham University, unpublished doctoral dissertation.

Rae, J. (2013) 'Facilitating learning spaces in forum theatre'. *European Journal of Training and Development,* 37(2): 220–236. Shaw, P. (2002) *Changing Conversations in Organizations: A Complexity Approach to Change.* London: Routledge.

Shiel, M. (2005) In D. Griffin and R. D. Stacey (Eds) *Complexity and the Experience of Leading Organizations.* London: Routledge.

Snook, S., Nohria, N. andKhurana, R. (Eds) (2012) *The Handbook of Teaching Leadership: Knowing, Doing and Being.* London: Sage.

Stacey, R. and Griffin, D. (Eds) (2008) *Complexity and the Experience of Values, Conflict and Compromise in Organisation.* Abingdon: Routledge.

Stacey, R. D. and Mowles, C. (2016) *Strategic Management and Organisational Dynamics: The Challenge of Complexity to Ways of Thinking about Organisations* (7th edn). Harlow: Pearson.

Tourish, D. (2013) *The Dark Side of Transformational Leadership: A Critical Perspective.* Hove: Routledge.

Wenzel, E. (2011) *An Exploration of Mutual Processes of Recognition in Organization Development Initiatives from the Standpoint of a Practising Consultant.* University of Hertfordshire, unpublished thesis.

6

EXPERIENTIAL EXERCISES

Introduction

In this chapter, I turn my attention to the type of on-programme leadership development activities designed to encourage experiential learning, that is, exercises, simulations and (live) case studies. I contend that these activities do hold the potential to generate some salient lessons; however, they are often not the ones that are promised in advance by the consultants/cies that specialise in the design and delivery of such interventions. The same can be said for large-scale interventions, ranging from ropes courses and orienteering through to full-blown expeditions in the great outdoors, where the lessons that are often overlooked are the opportunities to hone the capacities for sense-making, reflexivity and practical judgement. I also showcase reflective narrative writing as a valuable means of intensifying and deepening one's thinking and exploring the parallels between one's experience on leadership development programmes and one's day-to-day practice.

That's edutainment!

It's Thursday morning. I have just sat down to have breakfast in the hotel restaurant. I am looking out for my two colleagues. We arranged to meet up early, as usual, to reflect upon yesterday's session and prepare for today's before events and the restaurant are swamped by the arrival of the partners and the twenty-four programme participants. It is day four of the five-day leadership development programme that we run for a global management consultancy. 'We' are a leadership development consultancy specialising in experiential learning. As client director and programme manager, it is my responsibility to ensure that things run smoothly and that participants have an 'awesome' learning experience. The five-day (four whole and one half-day) programme is topped and tailed with one-to-one coaching sessions informed by a competency-based 360° feedback questionnaire/ report. As usual, my colleagues and I have been working with three partners from the client company to co-facilitate the programme. Each one of us is paired with one of the partners and each pairing has been working with the group of eight participants we were allocated before the start of the programme to work with throughout. This is something like programme sixteen of the twenty that we run each year.

Lewis arrives first, closely followed by Clive. If previous mornings are anything to go by, we have about twenty minutes before others arrive. Lewis kicks off our conversation:

'Did you get the call last night?'
'Yes, I did', I respond. 'And I let them know in no uncertain terms that I wasn't impressed'.

Wednesdays are half-day sessions, an opportunity for some rest and/or recreation during what can be an intense and full-on week. There is usually some form of activity organised for the participants – skiing (in ski resorts), water sports (if we happen to be at a beach location), hiking (if the hotel is situated in a forest in the middle of nowhere). As faculty we are always invited to join in the recreational activities but we are not expected to attend. Arrangements for dinner also differ on Wednesday evenings, with participants and faculty being left to their own devices rather than being scheduled to dine together at the hotel and engage in the post-dinner ritual known as 'Points' (more of which later). Last night we decided to leave the participants to do their own thing and we dined at a local restaurant with the partners before retiring to bed at a reasonable hour. During the night I was woken by the telephone ringing. I picked up the receiver and glanced at the bedside clock – 2.34 am. At the other end of the line was one of the programme participants who greeted me with:

'Kevin, we're all down by the pool, partying, come and join us'.

With as much composure as I could muster, I said that I would not be joining the 'pool party' and reminded him that we had a 9.00 am start and that I expected everyone to be there, on time, 'bright-eyed and bushy-tailed'. I then went back to sleep.

'I told them where to get off, too', said Lewis.
'Oh – I joined them for an hour', said Clive, sheepishly. 'Well, they'd already woken me up, so I thought I might as well'.

This incident occurred over a decade ago. The company I worked for at the time specialises in experiential learning and the activities used during leadership development events range from discrete twenty-minute mental and/or physical

games, through climbing, sailing and orienteering challenges, to full-blown expeditions in the great outdoors. As the programme referred to in the narrative above
was run off-site at various hotel locations around the globe (that is, without access
to ropes courses, boats or the great outdoors), we used short, discrete experiential
exercises to explore aspects of leading and leadership during the programme. The
vivid moment above played no small part in intensifying the doubt and disillusionment I was already experiencing in relation to mainstream conceptions of
management and leadership and leadership development, and not long after this
episode I left the company to join UH.

What I came to realise, and subsequently to explore in my doctoral research
(Flinn, 2011), was the fact that for the first eight years of my career as a leader of
leadership development (1998–2006), I had been unthinkingly 'spoon-feeding'
(Raelin, 2009) participants the same mainstream conceptions of management, leadership and organisation that I had been spoon-fed as a manager and student of
management. In other words, I had been fronting programmes that had been
designed by third parties (usually highly paid consultants and/or consultancies)
which contained a great many of these abstract frameworks, models and theories of
leadership and organisation. Raelin argues that this 'spoon-feeding' approach,
which views knowledge as something 'tangible and permanent, requires it to be
transferred from the mind of the knower into the mind of the current or future
user' (ibid.: 402). Raelin, a lecturer in management education, contends that this
practice 'is reinforced by the longstanding assumption that the role of the teacher is
to rescue learners from their state of "not knowing"' (ibid.: 408).

Raelin contends that this 'empty vessel' approach to teaching persists because
learning has become a commodity, and thus students and/or their parents expect
teachers to pass on the knowledge that they possess and for which they are 'paying
good money to procure' (2009: 408). He argues that this way of thinking/working, is
based on a 'representational model that parses management practice into a set of
detached, predictable, and teachable categories that can capture and explain management in spite of its inherently messy, fluctuating, and accidental nature' (ibid.:
403). On the programmes that I was involved in during the early part of my career,
the disparities between mainstream conceptions of how things *ought to be* (see
Rodgers' Act 4 in Figure 3.1) and the day-to-day reality of *how things are* (Rodgers'
Act 1) were more often than not rationalised as something lacking in the participants, the 'system', or both. What was actually lacking was any form of critique. In
my doctoral research (Flinn, 2011), I was interested to explore why this approach
to corporate training persisted, and why employers, once they had procured my
services, did not seem to be interested in the content, just so long as the ratings on
the 'happy sheets' were good (happy sheets being the evaluation questionnaires
completed by participants at the end of a workshop/event/programme). Seemingly, happiness/satisfaction was their primary concern, and if learning happened
along the way, then that was a bonus to be welcomed.

Returning to the narrative above, Clive's 'sheepishness' was influenced by his
anticipation of the response that his '*Oh – I joined them for an hour*' gesture would

provoke. He knew that Lewis and I, influenced by the preceding history of gesture and response in previous iterations of this ongoing conversation, would know that the main reason that Clive attended the pool party was to ensure that he did nothing to jeopardise his happy sheet scores at the end of the week. The client organisation we ran the programme for/with set very high expectations for this 'flagship' programme. Faculty had to achieve an individual score of at least 4.6 out of 5 on the evaluation sheet completed by all participants at the end of the programme. Those faculty members (partners from the client company included) who achieved scores above 4 but less than 4.6 would be 'talked to', and those receiving less than 4 would be invited to 'take a rest' from the programme. For Lewis and me, as permanent employees, being asked to 'take a rest' would not be pleasant, but it would not mean unemployment, whereas for associates such as Clive, who were only contracted for each programme, it would mean loss of job/livelihood. Consequently, this was not the first time that Clive had engaged in unscheduled activities in order to ingratiate himself with participants. On this occasion, Lewis and I said nothing further. There was nothing more to say.

Many of the themes that I have been exploring in the preceding chapters are present in this narrative – gesture/response, emergence, interdependence, power, inclusion/exclusion – but for me the most interesting theme was the effect (unintended consequence) that measurement, in the form of happy sheet scores (participant happiness), had on all involved. First, participant enjoyment (entertainment) had become more of a focus than participant learning (education), hence the use of the term 'edutainment' in the title.[1] And second, and more importantly, the pressure to maintain 'the numbers' had led to a level of standardisation in the programme content that I found problematic. As part of my induction to the programme manager role, I was 'apprenticed' to the previous incumbent. This programme manager's 'numbers' (happy sheet scores) were 'legendary'. He routinely achieved personal scores of 5 out of 5. He was adept at playing the game. He was meticulous in his preparation/facilitation and he was an outstanding host of 'Points'.

'Points' was part of the programme before my mentor became programme manager, but it is fair to say that he quickly made it his own. At the start of the programme, the twenty-four participants were split into six teams of four (two fours making up the eight that a pair of faculty worked with as a group during the week), with the six teams competing for points which were awarded by faculty. The points scored each day were announced to teams after dinner each evening and, under the direction of my mentor, this had burgeoned from a quick five-minute update to a thirty-minute performance. At the end of the week, the team with the most points was awarded a prize. However, events were always engineered to ensure a two- or three-way tie between the teams, so that on the final evening the tied teams had to perform 'skits' (sketches), with the winning team being the one whose skit produced the most applause from the rest of the group. Invariably, we (the three faculty from my organisation) were invited to perform our own skit, and in this respect my mentor was in his element (a missed vocation, no doubt).

Performance carried over into his facilitation of the experiential exercises we used throughout the week-long programme, as a means of exploring leading and leadership. The exercises were a mix of physical, cerebral and construction-type activities, or some combination thereof, lasting anywhere between twenty and ninety minutes. As part of my induction, my mentor provided me with a list of the lessons that 'had to be' generated from each exercise and a script for the debrief that followed each activity. As mentioned above, my introduction and experience of development up to this point was to spoon-feed materials created by third parties, so I did not see anything unusual in what I was being presented with here. However, when I took over the management of the programme, I found this approach to be quite bizarre. For me, it was not so much the futility of determining the indeterminate, it was, moreover, the missed opportunities for learning if one stuck to the script.[2] I saw the year out, but I had already decided to leave. I was a 'successful' programme manager, my 'numbers' averaged 4.7 and I was a big hit during 'Points', but there was little, if any, opportunity for personal/professional growth and the experience left me questioning the value of experiential exercises for which learning outcomes are chosen in advance.

Post-script

My mentor's praxis in relation to experiential exercises/learning, outlined in the narrative above, was not representative of the thinking/practice exhibited across the organisation. The way of working that emerged on that particular programme was influenced by many factors, not least the unintended consequences of focusing on the 'numbers'. Thankfully, I got to work on other programmes and my overall experience of my time there contributed greatly to my thinking practice and the company continues to do fantastic work. If I were to retrospectively take a complexity approach to this incident, I would share the above narrative with all involved before sitting down as a collective to make sense of what we were doing together. I contend that the potential learning would be greater than that from routinised activity.

Before looking at how taking a complexity approach to experiential activities had led to their repatriation in my thinking/practice, I want to explore some conventional (Gold *et al.*, 2010: Carmichael *et al.*, 2011; and Dalton, 2010) and critical (Raelin, 2009, 2016) perspectives on the potential learning from small- and large-scale experiential activities.

Learning from experience(s)

Gold *et al.* argue that 'the value of experiential learning is the emergent sense-making that depends on the response and interpretation of managers to whatever is selected as experience. However, such interpretations are never neutral and are subject to the cultural, social and political factors that provide part of the context for activity' (2010: 153). They further argue that if done well, 'exposure to challenging activities allows emotions to be revealed and new possibilities for action to be considered as critique of previous ways of working' (ibid.). Carmichael *et al.* focus on the subjective nature of experiential learning drawing on the thought of John Dewey (1925) to argue that 'we all experience objects and events differently, since our previous experience and consequent interpretations of past events lead us to construct differing understandings of current or recent events – so learning is subjective or unique to the individual' (Carmichael *et al.*, 2011: 157).

Dalton argues that games and simulations 'with proper facilitation and discussion … are valuable for giving people an appreciation of the strengths and weaknesses of the team process' (2010: 246). However, he also explores the disadvantages of such activities arguing that they 'can foster a misleading sense that ambiguous business conditions can be structured so that the right answer emerges' (ibid.). He concludes that 'to work, the games have to be related to clear learning objectives and participants need to be good at abstracting from reality, accepting the artificiality of the situation and imagining its relationship to real life (ibid.).

Raelin echoes Dalton's criticism about the artificiality of games, arguing that simulated experience, 'be it from cases or from actual simulations such as in-box exercises, is just that – simulated, not real' (2009: 403). He acknowledges that such activities allow 'students to observe and discuss how others act in real situations, or to have them observe and discuss how they have acted under simulated conditions' but they falter as a 'holistic form of learning' as they do not 'take account of such real-time and relational contingencies such as unplanned disturbances, non-deliberate coping strategies, defensive routines, or just plain failures and surprises' (ibid.).

Outdoor management development/Outward Bound

> Outward Bound has found that using a proven methodology of experiential and theory-based learning, combined with the conscious use of metaphor, can build high-performing teams and leaders faster and more effectively than any other approach. Outward Bound's team-building programs strengthen organizational culture, accelerate organizational performance and improve results – results that may include profitability, market share and increased efficiency … or simply a more cheerful mood around the water cooler.
>
> *(Raynolds et al. 2007: 225)*

Gold *et al.* (2010) touch on outdoor management development (OMD) describing it as a 'well-known form of experiential activity' that owes a great deal to 'military approaches' to development. They argue that although many organisations use OMD, there are doubts about the 'transfer of learning … back to work' (ibid.: 153). Again, they purport that this can be mitigated by the quality of facilitation arguing that if 'completed successfully' OMD can 'boost self-confidence' and instil 'a willingness to undertake even greater challenges' (ibid.). Dalton also explores

OMD drawing similar conclusions to Gold *et al.* (2010) and arguing that the 'quality of the learning experience is likely to be proportionate to the quality of facilitation', signified for Dalton by staff who are 'experienced in outdoor activities' and sufficiently 'psychologically skilled' to support participants through 'stressful experiences' in which they 'may feel vulnerable' (2010: 254). Dalton also argues that, done well, OMD can 'encourage entrepreneurial values of robustness, self-reliance, risk-taking and self-confident leadership' (ibid.: 253). He also questions whether the learning from OMD is 'transferable': 'The big problem with OMD is demonstrating that the emotionally stimulating learning derived from climbing rock faces really translates into improved working in the office on Monday morning' (ibid.: 254).

I agree with Dalton, Gold et al. and Raelin up to a point. The experiential games, simulations and (live) case studies that one encounters on leadership development programmes are not the same as the actual experience of interacting with the people with whom one works in the context one works in, but for me that does not make the simulated experiences artificial or unreal. This would only be the case if one was claiming that simulated experiences are the same as one's work experience and in my lived experience, both as a facilitator and as a manager-participant on leadership development programmes, experiential games/activities are deliberately designed to discourage this type of direct comparison. As I argued in the Introduction, there is nothing intrinsically wrong with games, simulations and (live) case studies; their utility depends on the approach, focus of attention and quality of the attendant and ongoing sense-making. However, I do agree that opportunities for useful learning are often missed when learning communities avoid the exploration of what is actually going on between them and/or post rationalise their experience with reference to idealistic mainstream models, as Paul finds himself doing in the narrative that opens Chapter 3.

The anxiety-relieving effects of fun and false certainty

In my doctoral thesis (Flinn, 2011) I draw on the work of Gibson Burrell and Larry Hirschhorn, respectively, to argue that 'fun and the false certainty provided by idealised models and theories helps to relieve the anxieties of leaders who are struggling to cope with the complexities and uncertainties of their everyday life in organisations, this, in turn, helps to maintain stability and ensure that there is no challenge to the status quo' (Flinn, 2011: 46). At the time, I categorised this as coercive persuasion with a kindlier face.

Hirschhorn (1995) argues that it does not really matter which theories and models are shared. He argues that almost anything will act as a 'transitional object' (after Winnicot, 1965) that has the potential of helping learners to make the transition from dependency to independence (Hirschhorn, 1995). He contends that the exploration of the relationship between the facilitator and participants on a leadership development programme offers a greater potential for learning than any of the models or theories that might be discussed, but that this is avoided due to the anxieties it might provoke. He argues that:

> [L]earning about management can itself promote significant anxiety … as managers find it hard to evaluate employees, confront peers, or correct superiors. Paradoxically management training frequently conceals and disguises this interpersonal dimension by offering managers a set of techniques and methods with which they can in fact bypass the interpersonal domain … Thus management training functions as a social defense [against anxiety] at two distinct levels. It offers defensive techniques, and it functions itself as a mechanism for containing anxiety by in fact denying it.
>
> *(Ibid.: 106)*

This argument is echoed by Raelin who contends that teachers/facilitators 'collude in allaying learner anxiety by structuring the curriculum to minimize unexpected or anxiety-provoking occurrences and by controlling the class to prevent destabilizing dynamics' which might take the form of emotional outbursts or even silences (2009: 408). He argues that the 'last thing expected from teachers is to confront students with their own state of not knowing and to help them face the fears that such not knowing can produce', as to do so would be an 'abdication of one's responsibility as a teacher to meet students' dependency needs' (ibid.). Taking a complexity approach to leadership development means problematising idealised models and theories of leadership and rather than covering over the complexities and uncertainties of everyday life in organisations, and shielding participants from anxiety-provoking affect, a complexity approach looks to support leader-managers to acknowledge and work with emotion (their own and that of others – see Chapters 4 and 5). Indeed, some of the most useful learning opportunities come from the exploration of what goes on within the group, among group members and between group members and the programme leader(s). The way in which I approach this in my practice, with the groups of leader-managers with whom I work, is discussed in more detail below.

Gibson Burrell, Professor in Organisational Theory at the University of Leicester, believes that the 1990s saw a return to the post-war search for the 'contented workforce' with organisational development attempting to use team-building days and Outward Bound-type activities to reintroduce pleasure into the organisation (Burrell in Alvesson and Willmott, 1992: 86). In the string of measures that it is claimed will be enhanced should you engage in an Outward Bound activity (see the quotation above), it is interesting to note that the final potential benefit mentioned is a 'more cheerful mood around the water cooler' (Raynolds *et al.*, 2007: 225). When I first started out in management development, in 1998, 'fun' was nearly always identified as a learning objective by participants and procurers alike. Twenty years on, not much has changed. 'Fun' is still one of the first objectives cited by procurers of development programmes when planning a workshop or away-day. Indeed, only recently, 'fun' was one of the first objectives identified by a participant when asked what he or she wanted from the away-day event that I was facilitating.

Since joining UH and taking a complexity approach to my work, the leadership development activities that I am responsible for are no longer 'off the shelf' programmes designed by third party consultants, where the learning objectives/ outcomes and content have been pre-empted and scripted in advance, rather they are emergent learning opportunities shaped by me (sometimes with the help of colleagues) in collaboration with delegates as participatory members of the learning communities that we create together. What happens between us as a group is, by agreement, regarded as legitimate experience to explore and reflect upon (see Ava's narrative below). On the face of it, the structure and content are indistinguishable from conventional leadership development programmes, including engagement with the type of experiential exercise under discussion in this chapter. The differ- ence lies in what we pay attention to and how this relates to our day-to-day experience. As a precursor to exploring the lessons that are often overlooked in conventional leadership development programmes, particularly in relation to the use of experiential exercises, I want to share with you a vignette from a colleague who has been taking a complexity approach in his practice. Sam Talucci is Pre- sident of Talucci Consulting Group and Senior Faculty at the National Outdoor Leadership School. Sam leads experiential activities that are at the extreme end of the spectrum, i.e. they are full-blown expeditions in the great outdoors.

VIGNETTE: TRAVELING FROM LITTLE PINES COL TO PINE VALLEY

The day starts at 06:00. It is that moment of penumbra right before the sun makes its appearance. As light illuminates the valley, Pacific coast fog banks and low clouds roll inland – up and over the ridgelines in a symphony of move- ment. The morning activities involve preparing and eating breakfast, breaking camp, pack packing and, once we are all ready, a briefing by the two leaders of the day. Today it is Andres and Shane. These two leaders could not be more different. Andres is of Hispanic heritage. He grew up in South Central Los Angeles, survived the madness by being a gang member and was able through the fire service apprentice program to change the trajectory of his life. Shane grew up in the American Midwest, graduated from university and is looking for the opportunity to lead his own team this summer. Andres and Shane deliver the briefing for the day finishing with the assessment that it all looks fairly straightforward. The straightforward part catches my attention because every time I hear that word the day turns from clear-cut to a complicated epic. Chris and Leonard are traveling with Andres' group and I am traveling with Shane's group.

The first part of the day plays out as planned. And then the bad weather from the Pacific rolls in. A constant drizzle turns into rain and the temperature drops – ideal conditions for hypothermia. Shane's group reaches the saddle above Pine Valley at 13:30. As per the briefing early that morning, this is where the two groups are supposed to rendezvous and make the decision about descending into the valley or continuing up over the ridge that rises from the saddle another 2000 ft. We look around the saddle and the other group is not to be found. Our group members call out. No response. We break up into scouting groups, one heading up the ridge one heading down into the valley. By this time, the drizzle has turned to a steady rain and the temperature is in the low 40s. We have left 'straightforward' behind.

Eventually we establish that Andres' group is about 900 ft above us on the ridge. Shane brings our group together. We get our packs and move up the ridge to rendezvous with Andres' group. As they wait for our arrival, they set up a tarp in an attempt to stay dry. My colleague Chris stands under his open golf umbrella. I check in with Chris and he explains how Andres' group was not paying attention to the maps and they missed the saddle. How did that happen? The saddle is a major and very obvious physical feature. From a terrain standpoint, you have to descend down into the saddle and then ascend up and out of it. This particular group ascended out and up 900 ft.

The two groups come together. Andres and Shane speak. And then they spend the next 40 minutes in a discussion with the whole group as to what they should do now. Chris and I stand there and observe getting more humid and cooler as we watch the students become wetter and colder. It appears, as we listen to the process, that Andres and Shane are attempting to create a consensus decision and it is not working. Chris and I check in and decide we needed something to happen soon as the temperature was continuing to drop. I step in and ask, "So how is this working for all of you?" With intermittent groans, I heard a probing reply, "This is not working." It was followed by the inevitable inquiry, "What would you do?" I said, "Well, if I were on a personal trip in this weather I would be back at the road-head sitting in my car with the heat on." We all had a light laugh. I ask them to think about what is going on with the group, the deteriorating weather conditions, where they can set up shelter and so on. Then I step back out of the conversation. A number of strong voices state objections to camping in the saddle because of the presence of snags [dead trees]. However, with the eventual consent of the objectors, the decision was finally made to return to the saddle and camp.

When we arrive at the saddle, Andres and Shane are looking a little weary from the process and there are many very wet and cold people. Then, just as everybody is taking their packs off, Robert, Jeremy and Dan declare that they are not going to camp on the saddle because of the snags. They announce that they are going to scout out to the west, along the slope of the ridge. The group is immobilized again – not knowing if they are going to move again or set up camp. It takes about 25 minutes for them to come to the conclusion that camping on the western slope of the ridge is a really bad idea. We set up camp: prepare hot drinks, cook some food and get people to change into warm, dry clothes. The rain abates for a while. It is dark by the time everybody is fed. Chris and I decide that we need to do two individual group debriefings and then we will bring the two groups together to debrief the larger, unified group. An aspect of the learning is to examine how we are functioning and making sense as the environmental conditions deteriorate, as our physical capacity is being challenged by low energy and as our patience wanes. The AARs (debriefings) are not as fruitful as we would have liked and we use this factor to illustrate how this is actually the most critical time to be engaged in our best practice. Chris and I finish with the large group and plan a meeting in the morning to revisit the AARs.

The night is punctuated by heavy rains and wind. We wake to a steady drizzle. We meet the next morning and check in as a group. Andres and Shane want to revisit what happened the day before; they are perplexed. They followed what they had learned about decision making and yet some members of the group chose to do something different once we got to the col. A lively discussion ensues and the participants struggle to connect what they had been taught with what actually happened ... what started to emerge for them was that decision making and communication are not linear ... what we have taught is in keeping with the mainstream understanding of communication and decision making as a component of a leadership-training program. Based on this type of content, the participants come away thinking that they have done something wrong or have not used the models correctly.

[...]

What emerged in this narrative is the ongoing struggle and difficulty groups are involved in when making sense of and reflecting on what is happening, how it is happening and why it is happening. The reason this difficulty is present, I would argue, is due to the underpinning rationalist causality of certainty, our linear concept of time and that we take these ideas for granted and do not chose to examine or think about the implications that are embedded in this way of making sense of our interactions. The premise is that the leader and group will develop rational decisions that will lead the group (including the leader) to get it right at this very moment in time. It can lead to outcomes that are confusing for the leader and the group because their focus is on the idea that there must be a right answer as opposed to the possibility that there might be multiple answers. Some answers are more satisfying than others; for example, the third-day-in-the-rain decision to first camp in the saddle after which some group members decided to start scouting for a different place to camp. The leader and some group members in the debrief wondered how they got it wrong.

Another way of making sense of this is to take up transformative causality of uncertainty ... In approaching leading, decision making and communication in this manner, participants are allowed the opportunity for a novel way of starting to make sense of their interactions ... In the end, what ties this all together for me is paying attention to practice (the day-to-day interactions I am involved in) and method (how I think and make sense of the practice I am involved in).

(Sam Talucci 2012)

Sam and his colleagues do not claim that the experiential exercises that they engage in on expeditions are in any way replications of the interactions that participants find themselves involved in back at work, even though they lead groups of leaders (including Navy SEALs and (forest) firefighters) that do actually find themselves in territories and situations similar to those found on the expeditions run by the National Outdoor Leadership School. No, they look to see what, if anything, is generalisable from the expedition experience to what participants find themselves doing in organisational settings, particularly in relation to their roles as leader-managers.

What strikes me about Sam's narrative is the focus and timing of the reflections/ debriefs. The debriefs do not focus on whether the decisions taken were appropriate and/or in line with the rules/steps contained in the models and frameworks for decision making that they had studied in the classroom, rather they concentrated on what was happening between group members and the programme leaders. And the debriefs not only take place after the event, but also in the midst of the activity. This echoes the conceptions of 'reflection-on-action' and 'reflec-tion-in-action' developed by Donald A. Schon in his seminal 1983 work, *The Reflective Practitioner: How Professionals Think in Action*. In his thesis, Sam draws on Schon and explores what for him are the similarities and differences between reflection 'in' and 'on' action and reflexivity and phronesis (Talucci, 2012).

Reflection is a major element of what is probably the most popular framework of experiential learning, Kolb's learning cycle (2015) comprising concrete experi-ence, reflection/observation, abstract conceptualisation and active experimentation. For Schon, 'reflection-on-action' is reflection after the event and 'reflection-in-action' is reflection during the event (1983). He describes reflection-in-action as a four-step process: routinized action, encounter of surprise, reflection and new action (ibid.: 49–69). During the leadership development programmes that I lead, and particularly when we are engaging in experiential exercises, simulations and (live) case studies, we do reflect both during and after a given activity; however, there are three significant differences between these conventional perspectives on experiential learning and reflection and a complexity approach.

First, on conventional programmes, reflection is taken to mean introspection and Stacey describes this as 'reflecting on one's own thoughts and feelings and forming beliefs about one's own mental states' (2012: 111). This is often described as a form of stepping back and taking an objective view of one's experience. From the per-spective of complex responsive processes, one cannot step outside of one's experi-ences to view them objectively nor understand one's actions in isolation from the social processes in which they emerge. Taking a complexity approach means accepting that the most we can do is become 'more detached in our involvement' (Elias, 1956) and pay attention to the interdependent patterns of interaction that we find ourselves caught up in. From the perspective of complex responsive pro-cesses of relating, this type of reflection, as a form of sense-making, is a social phenomenon.

Second, in taking a complexity approach to leadership development I am look-ing to encourage reflexivity, that is, thinking about our thinking. For Stacey, reflexivity 'is the activity of noticing and thinking about our participation toge-ther … how we have come to think as we do … the history of our traditions of thought (2012: 111). This means moving from being a reflective practitioner to becoming a 'reflexive practitioner' (ibid.: 112). Stacey argues that reflexive practice goes beyond reflective practice because:

> It involves people in more than reflection together on what they are doing, and that more is inquiring into how they are thinking about what they are doing. It involves asking ourselves who we are, what are we doing together, why are we doing it and how are we thinking about all of these questions.
>
> *(Ibid.)*

And third, taking a complexity approach to experience and reflection means rather than waiting for a surprise or for something out of the ordinary to occur, we take time out to reflect and be reflexive as a matter of routine. As outlined in Chapter 3, reflection/reflexivity is not something that should only happen as a result of difference and/or disruption; what I am calling reflective curiosity (the amalgama-tion of sense-making, reflexivity and practical judgement) is something we should initiate even when things seem to be going swimmingly.

Raelin argues that management educators have done little to embrace 'practice-based and critical approaches' preferring instead to stick with the 'promotion of reductionist and mythological active learning strategies which, though useful, are unlikely to lead to the acquisition of prudential wisdom' (2009: 401). In a recent article he argues that class-room learning is not 'apt preparation for the practice of management' (ibid., 2016) and calls for more work-based learning:

> Compared to traditional classroom learning often delivered in off-site settings, work-based learning summons participants to live engagements during which they can reflect on their experience so as to expand and create knowledge while at the same time improve their practice. Accordingly, they develop particular habits and attitudes that give rise to an adoption and appreciation of leadership as a collective practice.
>
> *(Ibid.: 43)*

In his description of work-based learning, Raelin includes things like action learn-ing (see Chapter 7) and coaching (see Chapter 4). He does not dismiss classroom learning or experiential exercises out of hand:

> This is not to suggest that being exposed to simulated experiential activities solving problems in a classroom setting is inopportune. Classroom learning of this experiential nature can be preparatory for the ultimate application of the desired metacognitive critical skills in naturalistic settings. However,

work-based learning sees the location of learning as shifting from a single place to the sites of collective practice.

(2016: 46)

If I understand Raelin correctly, his argument goes something like this: didactic classroom experiences are not the most effective way of preparing participants for the messy, politically charged and contingent, social/collective and relational practice of leading/leadership, so instead of engaging in abstract activities such as experiential exercises and simulations, management educators would be better served by employing activities such as action learning and coaching. And my response, which by now you might be able to anticipate, is that it depends on the approach, focus of attention and quality of the attendant and ongoing sense-making. Coaching and action learning, centred on heroic, individualistic and idealistic conceptions of leadership, can also be experienced as abstract and instrumental (see Chapters 4 and 7) and simulations (see Chapter 5) and experiential exercises can be experienced as powerful opportunities for the development of awareness of self in and with relation to others and the enhancement of the capacities for sense-making, reflexivity and practical judgement.

If I had been writing this chapter immediately after my experience of experiential exercises on the programme described in the narrative that opens this chapter, and previously, then I would have found it difficult to disagree with Raelin's challenge to their efficacy. However, since taking a complexity approach to leadership development these activities have witnessed a reprieve, partly due to the change in approach/focus outlined above, but also because of the quality of reflection and reflexivity that participants on MSOL have exhibited both during the programme as a group and after in the reflective narrative accounts of experience they have written as part of the assessment for accreditation.

Experiential exercises reprieved

The magic of stories is that the more specific you are, the more universal they seem to get.

(Frank Cottrell Boyce, screenwriter and novelist 2008)

As previously stated, I am not trying to convince you that experiential exercises should be part of the development programmes that you might be(come) involved in. I am simply exploring what taking a complexity approach looks like for me and the participants with whom I work. However, before doing so, I feel it is important to point out three things. First, experiential exercises only take up a fraction of the twelve days that comprise MSOL. Second, the longitudinal nature of the programme means that participants have time to build relationships which increases the potential for the interactions following these exercises to be supportive and challenging, reflective and reflexive, honest and insightful. And third, MSOL also involves variations of the work-based learning technologies that Raelin calls for – coaching, action learning, project work – and, for those participants completing the assessment element of the programme required for accreditation, reflective writing.

I want to open up the exploration of a complexity approach to experiential exercises (simulations and (live) case studies) by sharing two of the reflections written by MSOL participants following their separate engagement with one such activity on MSOL. A third narrative will be shared later in the chapter to illustrate how our interactions as a group figure in the learning. After each workshop, participants are invited to write up to 500 words reflecting on something that struck them during the session. These are first-person narrative accounts of experience. Participants are expected to explore why this theme/incident/vivid moment of experience seems important, any parallels with their day-to-day practice, and what influence, if any, this is having or might have on their thinking/practice. All three of the narratives below have been submitted in partial fulfilment of the assessment required for accreditation. Successful students are awarded a Postgraduate certificate in Business and Management from the Business School at UH. I have chosen narratives written by participants on MSOL during 2016/17, all of whom are line managers at the University. One is a recent graduate, another has just completed the programme and is in the process of pulling together a portfolio of work for accreditation, and the third had just started out on the programme. They have each given me their permission to share their reflections verbatim, with some of the names being changed to protect anonymity.

Intensifying learning through reflective narrative writing: Chris, Tori and Ava

Chris and Tori's reflections were sparked by their separate experiences of leading an activity called Shoestring Theatre, an exercise that we engage with early in the programme. I have also included Chris's rejoinder, following his involvement in an exercise exploring creativity and collaboration a few months later, as an excellent example of reflexivity.

Chris's narrative

> In nominating myself for the third leadership task that day, I was allocated directing the Shoestring Theatre Company's production of 3 short scenes from a play/show with a preparation/rehearsal time of 30 minutes. I was out of my comfort zone but was helped somewhat by the fact that everyone in my team was also out of their comfort zone. What I noticed about myself from the experience of going through those 30 minutes was that I ended up being very directive and feeling comfortable inhabiting this place. I told myself that I was doing this to avoid chaos when delivering the 3 short scenes to the rest of [the] group.

Another (more critical) voice inside me was providing a different narrative – i.e. that I was only 'paying lip service' to the idea of leadership and that really I felt most at ease telling others what to do, and that I was then 'massaging' this stance by subsequently asking individuals 'how does that sound to you?'

With some additional time to reflect on the experience, I can allow some compassion for myself and see a bigger picture (although my critical voice can still be heard, murmuring that this is 'letting myself off the hook'). I came up with good ideas – to use humour to reduce anxiety among the cast and to engage the audience / to use a narrator for each of the scenes to guide the process / to give people choice around which plays/shows to present / to give people choice around roles and to equally participate myself / to manage time and to provide momentum and containment. The experience also reconfirmed to me that leadership is not the exclusive preserve of 'heroic' figures and that I can carry out leadership tasks.

Excerpt from Chris's reflection following a later session on creativity:

A final point ... the module on creativity 'worked' for me because on the day it enabled me to come up with a new insight about myself that startled me: I went beyond where my thinking has often taken me before ('the quality I need to develop is courage') to a different place internally ... 'what if I didn't minimise other people's points of view that I don't agree with?'

Thinking this thought represents a place of creativity – a departure point to doing things differently. I am asking myself to be more expansive, to not reduce issues so readily to the black and white but to tolerate the shades of grey that represent not knowing and compromise.

Tori's narrative

For this week's learning log, I would like to reflect on a particular challenge of leadership: leading a team when you as the leader are hesitant about, or perhaps even strongly opposed to, the task at hand. I have chosen this subject because during our leadership exercises in Module 2, I had to lead the Shoestring Theatre exercise. This was a task which was not at all comfortable for me, but perhaps even worse my whole team felt the same.

After the exercise, we as a group reflected on what would be the best approach as a leader in these situations. Do you pretend to be fully engaged and enthusiastic about the project, in the hope that enthusiasm is infectious? Or do you admit freely that you are as troubled with the task as they are, in the hope that honesty breeds trust? During the Shoestring Theatre exercise I took the latter approach. I admitted freely that I was uncomfortable with the task, but it had to be done and we were all in it together. Fortunately, in this situation, the approach worked and we all engaged fully in the task (and if we're honest actually enjoyed it a little!). The end result may not have been a work of art, but the process of teamwork, commitment and collaboration was in itself a triumph.

This situation was a bit of fun and my approach fortunately paid off. But the task did get me thinking, what happens when the task at hand isn't a bit of fun? When the task is highly arduous, or the implications distressing? What happens if your chosen approach as a leader backfires?

In my day-to-day work, my team is required to act in accordance with government funding regulations, and this means that we regularly have to make difficult decisions about a student's funding entitlement. The decisions that we make can have major implications for a student's financial situation, their ability to stay at university, and consequently their whole future. When I introduce this responsibility to a new starter in the team, the response is always one of extreme unease. How can we, in just doing our job, be responsible for making such decisive decisions, with such potentially distressing implications? As a team leader, I struggle with the responsibility myself, and therefore struggle to ratify the responsibility to my team. However, the responsibility is one that I cannot shirk, and essentially this is what I say to my team. I have always taken the approach of being honest about my misgivings. Taking any other approach in this situation would make me seem unfeeling and callous, and I don't believe that this is the way to earn the respect of your team (which I'm not suggesting is imperative for every leader, but it certainly is for me). So I suppose my reflection this week is about the importance for me of taking an honest approach to leadership – of being honest with my team and honest with myself. If I lead with honesty, the end result may not be one that I am entirely content with, but I will always be content with myself.

On MSOL, I look to build in opportunities for the group to reflect during (reflection-in-action) and after (reflection-on-action) the exercises we engage in. This can take the form of stopping in the midst of the activity and inviting the participants to reflect and explore what is going on for them in relation to and with others and/or looking for the parallels between what is happening and participant experiences in other settings. From a complexity perspective I am looking to encourage leader-managers to become more 'detached in their involvement in the game' (Elias, 1956), literally in this case, with a view to exhibiting how they might more consciously do this during the games that they find themselves caught up in on a day-to-day basis.

Eric Dunning, a colleague of Norbert Elias when they worked together in the sociology department at the University of Leicester, and Jason Hughes (2013) argue that a 'detour via detachment' (Elias, 1956) 'can lay the foundations for a process of "secondary involvement", for returning to a more "involved" position in which – if the detour has been successful – armed with potentially *more* reliable, *more* reality congruent or *more* "object-adequate" knowledge ...[one] will have the potential to intervene in the social world in a manner that has more intended relative to unintended consequences than would be possible hitherto' (Dunning and Hughes, 2013: 13; emphasis in the original). Dunning and Hughes argue that Elias's 'central thesis in this respect is that the more fantasy-laden the basis for such interventions, the more likely such interventions are to have a higher degree of unintended relative to intended consequences' (ibid.: 47).

What I take from this is how important it is for leader-managers to do all they can to maintain awareness of how things are (the operational realities), recognising that this becomes more and more difficult the bigger and more complex an organisation becomes and the higher one rises in the corporate hierarchy. However, it is also important to remember from a complexity perspective that (i) one might reduce the unintended consequences, but not eradicate them; (ii) some unintended consequences might turn out to be welcome; and (iii) 'small differences can escalate into major, completely unpredictable changes, so creating new forms and destroying others at the same time' (Stacey and Mowles, 2016: 297). Becoming more detached in our involvement via these timeouts also allows us to be reflexive about the ideologies that are influencing our interactions. That is, we can ask questions about how we have come to think that a leader should not tell others what to do/be strong, etc. And we can explore whether these ways of thinking are serving us well or not.

I contend that some of the claims that Raelin makes for practice-based learning are accessible in classroom simulations in which 'planned engagement and collective reflection on that experience can expand and even create knowledge while at the same time serving to improve practice' (Raelin, 2009: 402). The above narratives illustrate the potential for experiential exercises to provide vivid moments of experience (Shaw, 2010) that can act as catalysts for collective sense-making, reflexivity and practical judgement. In these instances, learning/knowledge cannot be predetermined in advance, rather it is co-created (see Chapter 5) in iterative processes of reflection and sense-making. Additionally, reflective narrative writing encourages the type of reflexive curiosity that is exhibited by both Chris and Tori in the narratives above, during their experience of leading this experiential exercise 'in the classroom' they are each confronted by their own thinking (ideology) in relation to what it means to lead. 'Through the interplay between action and feedback, learners acquire more valid social knowledge, more effective social action, and greater alignment among self-knowledge, knowledge-of-other, and action' (Raelin, 2009: 46).

On MSOL, in addition to the short discrete exercises, like the one that Chris and Tori reflect on in their narratives, the simulated conversations explored in Chapter 5 and 'change exercise' in Chapter 3, we also explore collaboration and improvisation with the help of poetry and engage in a significant post-programme community project as a programme finale (mentioned in Ava's narrative below). On LTC we have worked with dance, music and t'ai chi. I do not want to overplay the usefulness of experiential exercises, simulations and (live) case studies (see 'Reflections' below), but in taking a complexity approach I find them to be useful triggers for the reflexivity that participants exhibit both on the programme and in their reflective narrative accounts following the workshops. As briefly mentioned above, in addition to these structured and planned activities, we also take seriously what transpires between us as a group – not only what happens between the participants themselves but also between the participants and myself as programme leader (see also Chapter 7). As participants get used to exploring what is happening between us during experiential exercises and realise how valuable this can be in making sense of leading, they become more comfortable reflecting on our interactions more generally, and vice versa. The one feeds the other enabling the exploration of our similarities and differences in thinking and approach.

In their article entitled 'Learning from Difference', Reynolds and Trehan argue that 'learning from difference is to be encouraged because the experiences of difference in the classroom will probably have their counterpart in working and managing within organizations' (2003: 177). However, they caution against not trying to overtly or covertly resolve differences as they arise, but rather to learn from them (ibid.: 177). Taking a complexity approach means drawing attention to the relations of power and the patterns that are emerging in the game. It also means accepting the asymmetry in power relations between me as programme leader and the leader-managers on the programme. This is not always comfortable for me or the participants, as illustrated by Ava's narrative.

Ava's narrative

I am not good with endings and so I was apprehensive about the last session. Beforehand, I had been thinking about the individuals I have been studying with on this course, over the past ten months, and how I could thank them for helping me to develop my own leadership, from working with and among them, as well as through their shared experiences during our 'community meetings'.

On entry to the room, I was disappointed by a series of little changes to the session which included: some group members were not able to attend the session (change of people); our community meeting would be at the end of the day (change of time) and the session would be led by Helen not Kevin (change of teacher). Normally, these three changes would not have affected me but at this last session, they seemed to have an impact. Why?

As the session on planning our community project advanced, I realised that I was upset about the imminent loss of community – the group community, the learning community and most importantly the 'community meetings'.

On reflection, I understand that the 'community' on this course represented much more than sitting with other people and having a chat for me. It came to represent an important space where I, or others in the group, could have meaningful conversations, listen without judgement and offer support without the usual barriers of job role, position at UH and wage bracket. In this arena, I was able to talk freely and share feelings about frustrations or celebrations in my day-to-day management.

I am reminded of an early session on the course where we had to draw our leadership style. I found myself drawing a CND sign, with wings and in the centre of the piece was a safety net. The piece was my attempt at creating of a safe place for my team to try out new ideas and not be afraid to fail. Interestingly, I think the place I have been trying to create for my team has been slowly developing around me through this leadership journey, in the emerging community spirit of the group. From the early stages where we agreed the boundaries of the group, I feel that we developed our own safe environment to express ourselves, develop, grow, share ideas, emotions and most importantly, work together.

So as it turns out, I do not need to thank my colleagues just yet, as we will be working together on our community project for the next six months. Instead, I can continue to contemplate how best to describe the sense of belonging and empowerment I have been left with, from the community spirit we created.

The community project referred to is the (live) case study that participants complete at the end of the programme. The term 'live' is used to differentiate experiential, real time activities from the typical, type-written case studies employed on conventional leadership development programmes. In the Introduction I noted that what I find myself doing in my own practice with those I work with, in the contexts in which I operate, is not something that you can take and apply to the contexts in which you work with the people with whom you find yourself interacting. The same argument applies to the abstract, impression managed, 'best practice' case studies beloved of traditional business schools.

Pierre Bourdieu refers to the contexts that we find ourselves in – the 'series of institutions, rules, conventions, categories, appointments and titles which constitute an objective hierarchy and which produce and authorise certain discoveries and activities' – as 'cultural fields' (Webb et al., 2002, 21–22) and 'cultural capital' as 'a form of value associated with culturally authorised tastes, consumption patterns, attributes, skills and awards. Within the field of education, for example, an academic degree constitutes cultural capital' (ibid.: x). And finally, habitus is understood as 'the values and dispositions gained from our cultural history that generally stay with us across contexts [fields] … These values and dispositions allow us to respond to cultural rules and contexts in a variety of ways (because they allow for improvisations), but the responses are always largely determined – regulated – by where (and who) we have been in a culture' (ibid.: 36). Bourdieu identifies three forms of social capital: (i) economic (material wealth in the form of money, stocks and shares, property, etc.); (ii) cultural (knowledge, skills, education, qualifications, etc.); and (iii) symbolic (status, prestige, etc.) (1982: 14). Thus in order to gain and maintain a position of influence within a given field, one must accumulate the relevant (recognised) economic, cultural, and symbolic capital (Flinn, 2011).

Bourdieu's conceptions of capital and field are useful in making sense of the contexts and communities in which we find ourselves, that is, the interdependent mix of values, norms, beliefs, power relations, and ways of thinking that constitute local communicative interaction. In the narrative above, Ava points to the sense of safety she feels 'without the usual barriers of job role, position at UH and wage bracket'. This gives her the confidence to 'talk freely and share feelings about frustrations or celebrations in my day-to-day management'. Reflecting on our interactions as a learning community, the 'game that is MSOL', throws into relief the other games that we are caught up in at the university and which forms of social capital might give players an advantage in the game. Who gets to speak first and/or the most? Who doesn't? Who gets listened to, and who gets ignored? Who do I, as programme leader, seem to favour? As shown above, becoming more detached in our involvement, noticing the patterns that are just emerging and being able to anticipate the next couple of steps, might give you some advantage in the game. Similarly, awareness of what and how social capital confers advantage in the game might give one enough information to plan one's next moves or to challenge the game in the knowledge that challenging the game might lead to one's exclusion.

Michel de Certeau (1984) carried out an analysis of Bourdieu's own political adroitness, which de Certeau describes as Bourdieu's 'strategic moves' in the 'scholarly game' of academia. From this he generalised 'three aspects of strategic thinking' that contribute to a player's 'cultural literacy':

1. a self-reflexive understanding of the person's own position and resources within the field(s) or institution(s) in which they are operating;
2. an awareness of the rules, regulations, values and cultural capital (both official and unofficial) which characterise the field of activity;
3. an ability to manoeuvre as best as possible, given the handicaps associated with, for instance, a lack of … capital.

(Ibid.: 57)

Crozier and Friedberg (1980) also adduce game models to make sense of organisations. They argue that power relations are 'inevitable' and this means that we must continue to live in a world of conflict, manipulation and ambiguity because '*no society can rely on its supposed virtuousness to insure harmony*' (1980: 248; emphasis in the original). They argue that individual agency is not sufficient to cause a significant shift in the power differential. They contend that the only way to bring about equity is to develop more leaders:

A greater number of persons must be allowed to join in the game. They must be granted a greater autonomy, freedom, and range of options. Only power can fight power. The greater threat of abuse comes not from allowing an actor to take initiatives, but rather from suppressing the freedom to do so in order to restrict all initiative to a monopoly of certain actors or higher authorities.

(Ibid.: 248)

Echoing Crozier and Friedberg, De Haan and Kasozi argue that it is 'where many can be involved in leadership that better decisions are made, where the positive impact of decisions is greater, and the excesses and extravagance of leadership are avoided' (2014: 3). A more modest way to cause a shift in power relations, then, is to invite as many people as is usefully possible to join the decision-making process.

Reflections

Exploration of the events that happen in the classroom, whether or not they are simulated, can enhance the development of reflexive curiosity and the capacities of, sense-making, reflexivity and practical judgement. This can help to develop the cultural literacy/feel for the game required to play and/or challenge it more skilfully. Of course, useful lessons do not always materialise and some exercises fall flat, irrespective of the quality of the reflection. At UH, we still ask participants to complete programme evaluations (happy sheets), and for the experiential exercises we use on MSOL we ask participants to rate learning and enjoyment separately. As one would anticipate, opinions vary with responses against each activity ranging from high enjoyment/low learning, through low enjoyment/high learning, to high enjoyment/high learning. As noted above, the longitudinal nature of the programme and the development of what Ava refers to above as a 'safe space' contributes to the engagement in and subsequent usefulness of experiential exercises, yet not everyone is able or inclined to commit to programmes comprising twelve days (as both MSOL and LTC currently do). In the next chapter, I explore what I have been doing to accommodate colleagues who fall into this category and take a reflexively curious look at action learning (Revans, 1980).

Notes

1 There are obvious parallels here with the commodification of higher education that Raelin (2009) describes above, but that will have to wait for another time.
2 To this day, when asked what the learning objectives and/or outcomes will be for the programmes I am involved in (which happens often in higher education institutions), I usually respond that I have absolutely no idea what people will learn, but I can tell you about the themes we might explore.

References

Alvesson, M. and Willmott, H. (1992) *Critical Management Studies*. London: Sage.
Bourdieu, P. (1982) *Language and Symbolic Power*. Cambridge: Polity Press.
Carmichael, J., Collins, C., Emsell, P. and Haydon, J. (2011) *Leadership and Management Development*. Oxford: Oxford University Press.
Cottrell-Boyce, F. (2008) 'Losing My Religion'. *The Guardian* (Aug.). Available at: www.theguardian.com/film/2008/aug/19/drama.religion
Crozier, M. and Friedberg, E. (1980) *Actors and Systems: The Politics of Collective Action*. Chicago, IL: University of Chicago Press.

Dalton, K. (2010) *Leadership and Management Development: Developing Tomorrow's Managers*. Harlow: Pearson.

de Certeau, M. (1984) *The Practice of Everyday Life*. Trans. S. Rendall. Berkeley, CA: University of California Press.

de Haan, E. and Kasozi, A. (2014) *The Leadership Shadow: How to Recognize and Avoid Derailment, Hubris and Overdrive*. London: Kogan Page.

Dewey, J. (1925) 'Experience and Nature', The Paul Carus Foundation Lectures 1. Chicago, IL: Open Court Publishing Company.

Dunning, E. and Hughes, J. (2013) *Norbert Elias and Modern Sociology: Knowledge, Interdependence, Power, Process*. London: Bloomsbury Academic.

Elias, N. (1956) 'Problems of involvement and detachment'. *British Journal of Sociology*, 7(3): 226–252.

Flinn, K. (2011) *Making Sense of Leadership Development: Reflections on My role as a Leader of Leadership Development Interventions*. Unpublished thesis.

Gold, J., Thorpe, R. and Mumford, A. (2010) *Leadership and Management Development* (5th edn). London: Chartered Institute of Personnel and Development.

Hirschhorn, L. (1995) *The Workplace Within: The Psychodynamics of Organizational Life*. Cambridge, MA: MIT Press.

Kolb, D. A. (2015) *Experiential Learning: Experience as the Source of Learning and Development* (2nd edn). Upper Saddle River, NJ: Pearson.

Raynolds, J., Lodato, A., Gordon, R., Blair-Smith, C., Welsh, J. and Gerzon, M. (2007) *Leadership the Outward Bound Way*. Seattle, WA: The Mountaineers Books.

Raelin, J. A. (2009) 'The practice turn-away: Forty years of spoon-feeding in management education'. *Management Learning*, 40(4): 401–410.

Raelin, J. A. (2016) 'Work-based (not classroom) learning as the apt preparation for the practice of management'. *Management Teaching Review*, 1(1): 43–51.

Reynolds, M. and Trehan, K. (2003) 'Learning from difference?' *Management Learning*, 34(2): 163–180.

Revans, R. (1980) *Action Learning: New Techniques for Managers*. London: Blond and Briggs.

Schon, D. A. (1983) *The Reflective Practitioner*. New York: Basic Books.

Shaw, P. (2010) Be the Change Conference, Copenhagen Business School. Available at: https://cast.cbs.dk/media/Udvikling+af+dialog+i+organisationer/1_7190wb9m

Stacey, R. D. (2012) *Tools and Techniques of Leadership and Management: Meeting the Challenge of Complexity*. London: Routledge.

Stacey, R. D. and Mowles, C. (2016) *Strategic Management and Organisational Dynamics: The Challenge of Complexity to Ways of Thinking about Organisations* (7th edn). Harlow: Pearson.

Talucci, S. (2012) *Leadership Development as Reflexive Practice*. Unpublished thesis.

Webb, J., Schirato, T. and Danaher, G. (2000) *Understanding Bourdieu*. London: Sage.

Winnicot, D. W. (1965) *The Maturational Processes and the Facilitating Environment*. London: Hogarth Press.

7

ACTION LEARNING SETS

Introduction

> The need to develop skilful group discussion has rarely been more pressing.
>
> *(Christine Thornton 2016)*

I have been creating spaces for 'skilful group discussion' (Thornton, 2016: 6), where groups and teams come together to make sense of what they find themselves doing in organisational settings, for almost two decades now. And as I reflect upon what I have found myself doing, as a facilitator of these spaces/sessions during the course of my career, it is tempting to split the development of my thinking/ practice into three very distinct phases – before, during and after the DMan. However, this would merely be a convenient post-rationalisation of what has been a much more fragmented and fragmentary development process. A more accurate description is that for many years I have been endeavouring to help individuals, groups and teams to think together, and over the last decade I have found myself exploring and experimenting with group analytic thinking/practice with a view to doing this in a more 'skilful' way.

In this chapter, I explore my current thinking/practice in relation to working with groups and teams, comparing and contrasting this complexity approach with my former praxis, centred as it was around action learning (Revans, 1980). However, rather than arguing that taking a complexity approach problematises the use of action learning as a leadership development activity, I contend that there are more similarities than differences between the complexity approach that I am taking and Revans' (ibid.) philosophy, and that action learning has its place. In contrast to previous chapters, the reflective narrative from my experience appears toward the end of the chapter as a series of short reflections, following on from a vignette from a colleague who is also taking a complexity approach to working with groups of managers. The discussion of the emerging themes is weaved between the narratives as they arise.

From Learning Reviews to Community Meetings

During the first year of my doctoral studies, which I commenced in 2008, I was introduced to a research method and way of working that is greatly influenced by group analytic thinking and practice. Indeed, the DMan was originally developed as an informal collaboration between UH and the IGA in the UK. At the DMan quarterly 'retreats' that were integral to our studies we worked in small and large groups, called learning sets and Community Meetings, respectively. My learning set (and doctoral research) was supported by two supervisors (one of whom is a trained group analyst) and the whole group Community Meeting was supported by all five members of faculty (which included another qualified group analyst).

The tangible differences between the group work that I had been exposed to on previous leadership development programmes and the DMan – starting and ending *exactly* on time, exploring the emotions that were manifest (as well as some that were not), and routinely exploring our answers to the question 'What else might be going on here?' – left me both confused and intrigued. In 2009, in an attempt to gain a better understanding of this psychodynamic approach to working with groups, I joined an experiential group at the IGA. This experience did not provide all of the answers that I sought, but it did give me the confidence to start to work differently with the groups of managers who I was working with on one of the leadership development programmes that I lead at UH, MSOL, and to develop a new programme for senior managers at UH, LEGs, in collaboration with two of the professors from the DMan programme, Ralph Stacey (a qualified group analyst) and Chris Mowles.

MSOL workshops are held monthly[1] and each of the ten workshops explores a particular theme. Themes include Making Sense of Leading … Yourself, Teams, the Staff Experience, the Student Experience, Creativity and Change. As my thinking/practice shifted, influenced by experience on the DMan and in the experiential group, I changed the title of the session that opened up each workshop from Learning Review to the Community Meeting. Learning Reviews had become little more than a ritual opportunity for participants to shame each other for not having 'found the time to apply any of the learning from the previous workshop'. I wanted the Community Meeting to be a space where participants could share their experiences and experience of leading at UH. Thus, this mirrored the process that I encountered on the DMan, where the structure of the Community Meeting would emerge during the ebb and flow of conversation, in the absence of any agenda.

From Community Meetings to LEGs

In 2009 I was tasked with putting together a development programme for the senior management team at UH. The senior team at the time was a mix of academic (Vice Chancellor, Pro Vice Chancellors, Deans of Faculty, Heads of School) and professional managers (Directors of professional service departments, for example, Human Resources and Finance). My experiences on the DMan, the IGA experiential group and MSOL gave me sufficient confidence to suggest to the Vice-Chancellor that Professors Ralph Stacey and Chris Mowles should to be involved in the development of the programme. The Vice-Chancellor agreed and Ralph and Chris were intrigued enough to accept the opportunity of working with colleagues in their own institution in a somewhat unconventional way. We developed something we called LEGs. Each group was made up of six managers and a convenor. The convenors were Ralph, Chris, two other colleagues from the business school, who were not involved in the DMan but who were advocates of the way of working, and me.

The purpose of the groups was to provide an opportunity for methodically exploring what it means to lead, by engaging in ongoing, reflective conversations about their experience and experiences of leading at UH. Each group met once a quarter for a period of eighteen months. Prior to the first meeting, participants were sent a document explaining what an LEG is not, along with a description of the role of the convenor.

The following excerpt from the introductory email sent to participants ahead of their upcoming conference gives a flavour of my/our intent:

What an LEG is not:

- It is not a 'talking shop', although conversation will be at its core.
- It is not an Action Learning Set, although each member will have the opportunity to discuss what is currently important to them in their role.
- It is not intended to produce action plans, although actions will inevitably follow.

The role of the convenor:

- The convenor is a participant in the discussion. His/her role is not to guide, or input. It is for this reason that we have avoided calling them facilitators. What the convenor will bring will be difference, an outside view, and some structure to the sessions. There will be one convenor per group, and each group will have a different convenor.[2]

In light of the focus of this chapter, it is interesting to note (and to be reacquainted with) my unequivocal insistence that an LEG is *not* an Action Learning Set.

These early forays into working with groups in a different way left me simultaneously disappointed and hopeful. Disappointed by my failure to encourage some group members to explore anything other than simplistic, cause and effect fixes and solutions to what were, on the whole, intractable problems, and hopeful because I glimpsed the transformative potential that groups have for helping individuals to become more aware of (a) themselves in relation to others; (b) the interdependent nature of their involvement in the activities they undertake in work settings; and (c) the need for more nuanced thinking about how to navigate the paradoxical situations and highly charged political landscapes they find themselves caught up in.[3]

LEGs ran for eighteen months before winding down when two of the five convenors retired (or more accurately in Ralph's case, semi-retired). It would be fair to say that some participants really valued the space and still talk about LEGs to this day, others thought they were useful for engaging with colleagues in a different way/context and we never found out what the remainder thought of them, but as they had already voted with their feet and stopped attending some months before the programme ended, one can guess. Community Meetings on MSOL continue apace, and it was the overwhelming appreciation for this space, expressed by current and past MSOL participants, that led me to further explore group analytic ways of working. I completed the IGA's National Foundation Course in Group Analysis in 2014, and in 2015 I enrolled on its inaugural Diploma in Reflective Organisational Practice programme and following graduation this year I joined its inaugural Creating Large Group Dialogue in Organisations and Society programme.

As explained in the Introduction, by cataloguing the various development programmes that I have and will be involved in, I hope to illustrate that I have engaged with and taken seriously the perspectives and disciplines that I explore in these pages. In this chapter, I examine action learning and group analytic thinking as it relates to working with groups and teams in organisational settings. For Stacey (2012), one of the many shortcomings of conventional approaches to leadership development is that they do not pay enough attention to the exploration of group dynamics. This resonates with my experience as both participant and leader of leadership development programmes. The only reference to group process that I encountered as a participant on leadership development programmes, and previously shared as a facilitator, was Tuckman's four stages of team/group development – forming, storming, norming and performing (Tuckman, 1965).[4] And as far as I can tell this still appears to be the 'go to' framework for understanding group process on traditional development programmes.

Stacey (2012) argues that expert leaders do not close down conversations too quickly, rather they seek to widen and deepen communication and orchestrate opportunities for exploration and sense-making (see Chapter 3). He contends that a sensitivity to group dynamics can help managers to develop the practical judgement required to know when to 'open up and when to close down' conversation (ibid.: 114). Mowles argues that group analysis 'aims to make group members more aware, better at noticing and more skilful in their interactions with others' (2017b: 6); capacities that are integral to sense-making, reflexivity and practical judgement. Disillusionment with mainstream understandings of leadership and organisation and the dominant discourse in relation to leadership and organisation development, discussed at length in Chapters 2 and 3, had been the catalyst for exploring alternative perspectives and sustained my perseverance with group analysis.

The Reflective Practice in Organisations (RPO) programme explored many of the same themes that were covered in the National Foundation Course in Group Analysis, but it was during this programme that this way of thinking/working made sense to me and started to show up in my thinking/practice in a noticeable and meaningful way. I still have a long way to go. I know enough to know that I do not know enough, but in my experience this does not mean that those who have had little if any exposure to group analytic thinking should shy away from trying to help the groups they work with to make sense of the context in which they find themselves. Mowles argues that group analytic thinking is useful in helping to 'better frame [the] enduring problems in organizational life' and this can help managers to 'work against the tendency to rush to action without reflection' and 'address the profound feelings which are often provoked by being in relation with others, often in conditions of uncertainty' (2017a.: 221). Later on in this chapter, I will explore those aspects of group analytic thinking that I am currently finding useful, but before this, I want to take a fresh look at the Action Learning Set process as pioneered by Reg Revans.

Action Learning Sets

> The central idea of this approach to human development, at all levels, in all cultures and for all purposes, is today that of the set, or small group of comrades in adversity, striving to learn with and from each other as they confess their failures and expand upon their victories.
>
> *(Reg Revans 1980: 16)*

Following modest beginnings as a development intervention for managers at the British Coal Board in the 1940s, action learning and action learning sets (Revans, 1980), and/or some variation thereof, have become a ubiquitous element on leadership development programmes around the world. I was first introduced to action learning as young manager and then again as a less young facilitator. The quality and usefulness of the conversations, as a participant and a facilitator, varied wildly. Action learning was most useful when participants and facilitators kept to the principle of asking the presenter questions to open up their thinking in order to help them to consider different perspectives and alternative understandings of their day-to-day experience. It was less useful when participants and facilitators offered instrumental solutions to the intractable problems shared by the presenters.

Gold *et al.* (2010), Carmichael *et al.* (2011) and Dalton (2010) all provide fairly standard descriptions of action learning as 'one of the most powerful methods of development to emerge from the 1970s and 1980s' (ibid.: 212). All three offer case studies and describe action learning as a process through which groups of managers agree to 'meet over a period of time … to help each other by asking questions, discussion, exposure to critical comment … reflection and action planning' (Gold et al., 2010: 194). All three caution against the variability of practice and process as well as the 'tendency for it to be seen as a panacea for all manner of development problems' (Dalton, 2010: 216). Carmichael et al. (2011) reflect that it has gone in and out of fashion over the years putting its lack of consistent sticking power down to it not being seen as a good fit in 'command and control' cultures where 'it may be seen as too soft for the rigours of macho-oriented business managers' (ibid.: 227). Both Dalton (2010) and Gold et al. (2010) draw attention to the recent interest in more critical approaches to action learning 'which makes more explicit the tensions, power dynamics, emotions and dominance factors' in the set and the wider organisation (ibid.: 196).

When it came to revisiting action learning, following the process that I have sought to model in previous chapters, that is, going back to the source of the ideology, perspective, tool or technique under review with a view to comparing and contrasting conventional approaches with my way of working, I was quite taken aback. Revans' original hypothesis, that if 'one learns best from whatever it is that one may be trying to do [then one] can learn to do it better by the very act of thinking how they do it' (1980: 7), took me by surprise. For Revans, action learning works on the principal that the most effective thing a manager can do, is to reflect on his/her day-to-day experience:

> Action learning suggests that, since he has to do this in any case, he might just as well find out how he is doing it at that moment and, with what he discovers, try to do it a little better the next day, or next week, or even next year.
>
> *(Ibid.: 251–252)*

I am pushing it a little, but I do not think that I am overplaying it when I say that Revans' approach, in talking about taking experience seriously and sharing narratives of practice in a learning community with a view to making sense of what might be going on and deciding on a next step, is not a million miles away from what I found myself doing on the DMan and it is very similar to what I find myself doing on a daily basis when working with groups of managers as a leader of leadership development programmes. Indeed, I'd be comfortable with either of the above quotations as descriptors for what we find ourselves doing during the Community Meeting element of MSOL.

If we count taking experience seriously as similarity one, then for me, there are three more major similarities and one glaring difference between Revans' (original) philosophy and a complexity approach to working with groups. The second similarity is that Revans is evangelical in his conviction that management is not a science. He quotes extensively from an article by Badawy, who argues that:

> The accumulated evidence suggests that management education is in trouble … Management education is largely based on theoretical, neat and

unrealistic models of administrative behaviour. It does not deal with the realities of organisational life. Management graduates, as a result, are mired in the
code of rationality.

(1978: 75)[5]

The third similarity is that Revans believes that many of the problems that we
encounter as managers are not technical but rather relational and reflect the power
relations in play:

[T]he problems central to the pits ... were not those of mining technology but
of the relations of management and worker. My own belief ... is that these
relations will be improved by action learning in which all in the pit work
together on the identification, analysis and treatment of their common
problems.

(1980: 17–18)

The fourth and final major similarity between Revans' perspective and a complexity approach is that he contends that it is impossible to influence much beyond
the local patterns of interaction that constitute our working relationships. His
experience of working within the coal industry convinced him that 'beyond such-
and-such a size, pits become unmanageable. Little that we understand very clearly
can be done to make an efficient or happy unit out of one that is already too large'
(ibid.: 20–21).

And the one major point of departure? Interestingly, Revans is quite dismissive
of groups expending time and energy reflecting on group dynamics, which is one
of the things that I am arguing is of fundamental importance. Under the heading
'Group Dynamics and Other Task-Free Exercises', Revans expresses his concern
that explorations of group dynamics might divert attention away from the primary
task of action learning, that is, identifying and taking the actions back in the
workplace:

Indeed, in very recent years, there is now the chance that what had been
developed as action learning, a consortium of top managers regularly meeting
to discuss among themselves the effect of trying out their interpretations of
reality back upon the reality itself, may now revert to mere group discussion
unverified by subsequent real world comparison.

(2011: 82)

He acknowledges that group dynamics 'aimed at trying to demonstrate to others
who they imagine themselves to be, why they say the things they say and act the
things they act' can be helpful to managers, but also argues that 'it is quite fanciful
to imagine that this new understanding also equips them to master the imperious
demands of external and objective responsibility' (ibid.: 83). He further cautions that:

We must be wary, now that action learning seems to gain acceptance, that the set is not cut off from reality, sold as a part-time discussion group of four or five top managers meeting to exchange their unverified misconceptions as to what may be going on under their command.

(Ibid.: 69)

If you have got here having read the preceding chapters of this book, it should come as no surprise that a complexity approach to leadership and leadership development involves taking group dynamics seriously. In other words, if one accepts that organisations are not systems, but patterns of human interaction, whereby global patterns emerge (are formed while simultaneously forming) in the many local interactions in which phenomena such as leadership are co-created, then an understanding of 'what else might be going on here?' could prove to be very useful. I see Revans' ambivalence as a defence against the anxiety provoked by what he perceives as a threat to the integrity of the action learning process. However, his concern that interventions like this might lead to sets becoming little more than 'part-time discussion group[s]' does strike a chord with me. The LEG that I convened back in 2009/10 did veer towards discussion group, at times, and came dangerously close to becoming the type of 'talking shop' that I had insisted LEGs should not be. So are Revans' fears well founded, and do reflective spaces like the LEGs and the Community Meeting run the risk of becoming all talk and no action? To open up this debate, I want to share a vignette from a colleague who has been working with groups in a more discursive way.[6]

All talk and no action?

Chris Mowles is Professor of Complexity and Management, and Director of the Doctor of Management Programme, University of Hertfordshire. He also works as a consultant with senior management teams, supporting them in particularly difficult situations. Clients include the NHS, the Department for International Development, the United Nations, the International Fund for Agricultural Development and many large international non-governmental organisations (Oxfam, Save the Children, WaterAid, etc.). Chris has Group Work Practitioner status with the IGA and continues his training there.

VIGNETTE: LEARNING SETS

Over a two-year period [I] took part in a complex organisational intervention designed both to evaluate and develop a therapy service in a Scottish NHS region, part of which was aimed at developing the department's leaders. The therapy service comprised 150 full-time equivalent employees covering a dispersed rural area. Like many public sector organisations, this department had been affected by a series of reorganisations, alongside which it had experienced problems of staff retention, a higher than average number of complaints about poor service, and attention from local politicians as a consequence. Routine difficulties of management and leadership were compounded by a new matrix organisational structure, which was organised through five local hubs and at the same time required regional service coherence. Eight service leaders were answerable to their local managers but were also instructed to lead and develop the service regionally.

Ours was not the first organisational intervention to have tried to improve service performance. Previously, a team of consultants had produced a report comparing and contrasting what they found in this particular department against what they considered to be 'best practice' in similar therapy departments. They produced a list of recommendations setting out what the department and its leaders should be doing – a list which was accepted by the leadership team but which they had struggled to implement. By contrast, in our consultancy intervention we were concerned to start with what managers and leaders were actually doing now, rather than what they ought to be doing. We considered that the development of leadership and management practice would be central to supporting this particular department to develop. Although the benchmarking process which resulted from the previous report was undoubtedly helpful, it gave little assistance to the leadership team in knowing how to develop what they were already doing in their particular context and how to address the department's principal concerns. It was this latter perspective that we were keen to work with.

Alongside a review of waiting lists, service delivery and other service-specific matters, we also set up four learning sets of eight people, one comprising the leadership team, which met every three months for half a day to discuss the way in which team members were working in their local environments and how they were working together. Participants in the groups were encouraged to keep journals about what was going on for them at work if this helped, but there was no obligation to do so. The only requirement was to come prepared to talk about what was going on for them at work; what preoccupied them, and to describe what their role in the process was. It was a method designed to attend to the constantly emerging patterns of power and interdependence that arise in any organisation and to make the everyday practice of leadership the heart of the enquiry. Participants in the process were required to reflect upon aspects of their work which they found problematic, perplexing or damaging to their sense of professionalism, and the way that they were co-creating these patterns of interaction with others. So, one focus for the leadership team became the extent to which the team itself was functioning, which we returned to again and again.

Not only were participants in the learning sets invited to pay attention to their relationships with others, they were also encouraged to consider themselves more widely as researchers of the working practices in the organisation they had been appointed to lead. In encounters with their colleagues, and where differences emerged, they sometimes came up hard against their own assumptions about what they were doing and why they were doing it. There was no intention that staff involved in the learning sets should necessarily produce solutions to those problems which in many organisations can bring intractable and repeated difficulties, such as those caused by constant reorganisation. Instead they were encouraged to deliberate together without the pressure of an immediate requirement for action and to engage more intensively in conversations about the way they were working. The intention was for leaders and managers to gain new insights into their practice in order to create the possibility of their working differently.

[...]

Insights from the complexity sciences problematise the idea of linear cause and effect. It would be a claim too far, then, that this particular intervention with the leadership team, and managers in the other learning sets, directly led to improvements in service and in leadership practice over the two years. However, what we did notice was an enhanced ability of the leadership team to engage confidently with each other, despite differences and antagonisms, and to tackle some of the enduring difficulties in the wider organisation less defensively. They became more fluent in describing what they were doing and why, and began to notice more coherently how they were interacting with others.

(Mowles in Flinn and Mowles 2014)

To explore the importance of reflecting on group dynamics in the action learning set process, and pick up on the themes arising in Chris's narrative, I want to share something of my experience of studying for the IGA's inaugural Diploma in Reflective Practice in Organisations (RPO). More specifically, I want to examine four of the many aspects of group analytic thinking/practice that I have found useful in my practice. As part of the accreditation students are obliged to complete thirty hours of practice as a convenor of reflective practice group (RPG) sessions. The RPG sessions that I reflected on during my involvement were the Community Meetings held with the three groups of managers that attended MSOL during the duration of the RPO programme. In my narratives of some of these sessions that appear below, names have been changed in order to protect colleagues' anonymity. The elements of group analytic thinking/practice that I think are useful to leader-managerss and leadership-management developers are:

- dynamic administration (Behr *et al.*, 2005);
- journalling and creating spaces for reflection;
- letting go and adapting to the context and/or type of group you are working with (Thornton, 2016);
- endings.

Let's give it another five minutes

Prior to commencing the RPO programme, my time-keeping during Community Meetings was inconsistent. When I arrived at UH in 2007, I was advised that colleagues 'hardly ever show up on time'. Explanations for this involved the twin rationalisations of (i) academic lectures starting at five minutes past the hour and (ii) colleagues working to 'university time'. Thus, I would often find myself at the beginning of each workshop/Community Meeting uttering the phrase that opens this section. Subsequently, I would start the Community Meeting when I deemed that anticipated latecomers had been given sufficient time to accommodate potential traffic problems, personal crises, etc., and finish the session when I felt that the conversation had 'run out of steam'. Consequently, Community Meetings might start anywhere between 9.00 and 9.15 a.m., and finish somewhere between 9.25 and 9.45 a.m..

Dynamic administration

Behr *et al.* define dynamic administration as 'the various activities which the conductor performs in order to create and maintain' the group analytic setting (2005: 42). They go on to add that this 'includes such apparently mundane tasks as arranging the furniture in the room and drafting letters to group members' and this is important because they 'have dynamic significance and have to be woven into the material which forms the analytic process' (ibid.: 42). Schlapobersky argues that in relation to dynamic administration the group conductor's responsibilities fall into two categories: (i) 'the construction of the group, including "composition and selection"'; and (ii) 'managing the group's settings and boundaries' (2016: 237).

However, he also acknowledges that construction, composition and selection are less manageable for experiential/process groups, particularly those that are 'composed from the membership attending what might be a course or a conference'. Although he doesn't refer specifically to leadership development groups, I would argue that the same constraints in relation to construction, composition and selection apply. Drawing on the work of Behr *et al.* (2005), [7] Schlapobersky identifies the following twelve principles of dynamic administration:

1. Dynamic administration is the means by which the conductor creates and maintains the setting of the group
2. The conductor:
3. Provides structures for the group in time and place
4. Mediates communication between the group and the outside world
5. Guards the group's boundaries and manages its times
6. Gives definition to boundary events like late arrivals or premature departures so they can be explored therapeutically
7. Helps ensure all actions are woven into the texture of the group's dynamics
8. Takes responsibility for furniture and furbishment of the room including its circle of chairs

9. Handles notices about absences and provides messages to the group from absentees
10. Provides out-group contact with relatives on the one hand and with fellow professionals on the other
11. Maintains correspondence with other clinicians concerned with the well-being of group members
12. Maintains a memory for the group in terms of its dynamic history and the dynamic history of its members
13. Fee-payment issues for groups in private practice are an integral part of dynamic administration.

Stripping out those principles that I would think are more relevant to group analytic/therapeutic settings, that is, principles 9, 10, 11 and 12, I argue that taking a complexity approach to group work involves paying attention to most aspects of the remaining seven responsibilities of the group conductor. The consistent and conducive room/environment and circle of chairs have been part of my way of working since MSOL commenced back in 2008. However, I now ensure that Community Meetings start and end on time. At the start of each session I update the group on any known absentees or prearranged latecomers. And following the session, I check in with any 'unauthorised' absentees. I have come to understand the importance of dynamic administration in helping to create a 'safe' space for both the group and myself.

As noted above, I had participated in several groups that had been run along group analytic lines (DMan, Experiential Group, Foundation Course) and I had never really understood the convenor's compulsion for starting and ending on time. Even though I had engaged with the theory on a number of occasions, I had not grasped the importance of dynamic administration to the smooth running of the group. In holding and containing anxiety, dynamic administration promotes the conditions required for exchange (learning) (Thornton, 2016: 32). My initial motivation for sticking to the allotted time was compliance with the 'rules' of working in a group engaged in analytic/reflective practice. This resonates with the argument that one might initially find oneself 'sticking to the letter of the law' as a means of moving from 'novice to competent beginner' (Dreyfus and Dreyfus, 1986. See Chapter 3).

My compliance soon turned to advocacy as I witnessed the positive effects that adhering to the principles of dynamic administration seemed to be having on both me and the groups I was working with. Starting and ending on time, informing the group of any known absentees or prearranged latecomers, following up with 'unauthorised' absentees made a huge difference. Over the months I noticed fewer latecomers, fewer long silences and greater contribution from individual group members. This enabled me to relax and focus on what might not be being said, identifying the parallels between group needs and what might be needed in the wider organisation, etc. As you will by now no doubt be aware, I am not suggesting cause and effect, or indeed, linearity. Group member participation inevitably fluctuated and some of the patterns of interaction that I am describing as 'positive effects' would most likely have occurred over time as the group got to know me and each other better. However, if I compare my experiences with earlier MSOL groups, my acting into the space differently did have some influence.

My engagement with the theory of dynamic administration not only helped me to make sense of what I am being asked to do as a convenor of RPGs, but also to explore the parallels that convening has with leading-managing. As facilitators/ convenors and leader-managers, we are in charge but not in control (Streatfield, 2001). This is a paradox that we find ourselves navigating daily. In his book, *The Paradox of Control in Organisations* (2001), Philip Streatfield recounts his experience as a supply chain director at SmithKline Beecham. On taking up the role, Streatfield was charged with improving the yield on the production line for a capsule tablet, a cold remedy known as Contac 400. He explains:

> The process involved spraying sugar solution onto sugar crystals and building up a pellet with coating powders including the drug substance. I was told that knowing when the pellets were wet enough to apply the powder, and yet not too wet, was the key to meeting the specification. How did the operators know this? They watched and felt the beds of pellets and just knew when a batch was going to turn clumpy (too wet) or when powder would fly off up the extracts (too dry).
>
> *(Ibid.: 14)*

Streatfield goes on to describe multitudinous attempts to identify the optimum time for the operators to spray, based on scientific investigation under the tenets of Total Quality Management (TQM), only to discover that yields based on these principles were never as good as the yields produced by the operators continuing to spray at the time that they 'just knew' it to be right. Drawing on the complexity sciences and the perspective of complex responsive processes of relating, Streatfield identifies what he terms the paradox of control. That is, as the manager he is in charge but not in control of the production process. Behr et al. argue that in the early stages of group formation the conductor is often 'on the receiving end of omniscient and omnipotent projections' (2005: 91). They contend that in these situations the conductor has 'to disabuse the group gradually of these fantasies, and at the same time introduce them to the analytic culture' (ibid.). Streatfield, in acknowledging that to achieve optimal results he has to share the responsibility for production with the production team, not only came to disabuse the group of these fantasies but also *himself.*

This is a good illustration of the sense-making, reflexivity and practical judgment (see Chapter 3) that I have been pointing at throughout this book. In the midst of being caught up in repetitive (stuck) cycles of activity based on the deceptive certainty of rational control (in this case, TQM) Streatfield is able to become more detached in his involvement to make sense of the situation in which he finds himself, reflexively challenge his own thinking and exhibit the kind of practical judgment required to articulate a next step that resonates with others. He recognises the operators and they simultaneously recognise him. And it is in this mutual process of recognition that he emerges as a leader. However, this is also a good illustration of the futility of trying to separate leadership and management. As argued in Chapter 2, if one thinks of leadership as making sense of the context in which one finds oneself (and articulating a next step that others recognise and support), and of managing as coping with that context and the intended and unintended consequences of the next step, then as illustrated in this example it is in the midst of coping with each new next step that Streatfield makes sense of the context. Thus management and leadership, and leading and managing are two sides of the same coin – they occur simultaneously and cannot be split.

And this paradox can be seen in the role of the group analytic conductor. Behr *et al.* describe the situation in which the conductor has sole 'responsibility for creating and maintaining the setting' but in which 'the analytic task is shared with the rest of the group [allowing] for a creative interplay between the conductor as the guardian of the group's stability and the group as the agent of therapeutic change' (2005: 43). This resonates with Streatfield's description of his role as 'guardian of the line':

> This did not mean abdicating my authority as a manager. There were unofficial rules that kept everyone in line. Those who did not pull their weight, or who abused the rules expected to be pulled back in line. I learned that it was part of my role to be guardian of the line that we were together constructing, articulating that line and disciplining those who crossed it.
>
> *(2001: 21)*

For my practice, this means that there are opportunities to explore the parallels between what happens between me and the group, and what happens between them and the groups that they manage. The effective exercise of dynamic administration does not lead to control, but in containing some of the anxiety of not knowing, it allows conductors and managers, participants and teams, to more readily engage with the primary task, and not get caught up in potentially destructive unconscious processes. As illustrated by Ava's narrative, in Chapter 6, small changes/not adhering to what has been agreed in terms of dynamic administration can impact on participant experience, particularly when anxiety is already heightened by the thought of endings (see 'Endings' below), as it was in Ava's case.

Note taking and creating spaces for reflection

As part of the RPO programme, we were assigned a supervisor with whom we worked in small groups (a supervisor plus three students) to make sense of what we were experiencing in our (reflective group) practice. This involved keeping a journal of our experience(s). Not wanting to be distracted and distracting by taking notes during the Community Meetings, I began to offer a comfort break at the end of each session, during which I would note themes and my initial reflections on Post-it notes. I would then sit down in the evening after the workshop and expand on these first thoughts. For example:

Journalling

We started at 9.00 a.m.. Most of us were there on time, with Margaret and Linda arriving late. I updated the group about two members who had been in touch to say they were ill (Alan and Julie), and initiated a quick round of introductions to welcome and integrate those members that were new to the group. I (re)introduced the session (Community Meeting) as 'a space for us to think about and share our thoughts and experiences of managing and leading at UH'.

Libby, who often speaks first, opened with a question: 'Do senior managers come on this programme?' I asked, 'What's the question behind the question?' and this opened up the discussion into her and other participants' experience that the collaborative approaches to leadership that we have been exploring on the programme seemed to be in short supply the further up the hierarchy you looked. This led to a rich conversation about hubris, and the potential for shame if senior managers shared their uncertainties with colleagues on a programme like this (some of the group said they would welcome this while others felt that this would be too anxiety-provoking for all parties).

The conversation moved on to the difficulty of challenging authority, and Mary shared an experience of being challenged by the Vice-Chancellor in a senior executive meeting and not being backed up by her line manager (a member of the senior executive team). I introduced the themes of power, collusion and co-creation. That is, how we are all influencing while simultaneously being influenced, thus co-creating patterns of interaction (Stacey) that might not be useful to anyone involved (the Abilene paradox[8]). We then discussed the challenges of bureaucracy and standardisation and the potential for this to constrain innovation. I suggested that this is another paradox whereby boundaries and structures enable and constrain at the same time.

The conversation moved on to what senior managers might do to reduce their administrative burden, and I brought the group back with the comment that 'it is interesting that we have spent a lot of time during this session talking about what senior managers should or could be doing. What do you make of this?' We then began to talk about our own agency in the situations we find ourselves in, problematised 'quick' or 'easy fixes', and wondered what this meant for our own practice.

We finished at 10.00 a.m. (the comfort break allowed me to scribble some notes about the session)

Although I had become accustomed to the value of writing reflective narratives as part of the DMan process and had subsequently been inviting managers on leadership development programmes to do the same (see Chapter 3), I had stopped doing this myself, and yet the reflections I wrote during the RPO programme were invaluable in identifying themes, patterns, parallel processes and instances of potential projection and transference. Additionally, the support of the supervision group set me wondering why we, in most cases now, routinely think of providing supervision for coaches, but we don't necessarily do the same for those colleagues involved in other forms of leadership development.

Letting go and adapting to the type of group you are working with

One of the attractions of the RPO programme was the emphasis on organisations. The IGA programmes on which I had participated previously (the experiential group and the National Foundation Course) had understandably been dominated by people who worked in clinical settings, and the convenors of the groups I worked in had kept to strict group analytic (Foulkes, 1975) ways of working, that is, only appearing in the room at the very moment the session was due to start, calling time at the end of the session and leaving immediately, and in the middle maintaining their role as the blank screen on which group members' projections and instances of transference might be more easily identified. Similarly, the interpretations offered by the convenors entered territory that would not be welcomed by the participants with whom I was working on leadership development programmes.

This previous experience led to me offering minimal contributions to the early MSOL Community Meetings that I had started to run along RPG lines. This enforced minimalism was partly the result of my wanting to ensure that the groups did the work, and partly the result of my anxiety about wanting to offer the 'perfect' interpretation of what might be going on in the group. In comparing and contrasting the complexity approach taken on the DMan programme with the group analytic method, Mowles argues that one of the key differences is that 'faculty members are just as likely to make personal disclosures as are research students. This is partly to acknowledge that this is a group committed to doctoral research rather than therapy' (2017a: 225). One of the lessons that I have had to relearn is that managers in work settings might need some help in finding their voice in groups. Consequently, I reintroduced a number of strategies to relieve their anxiety and open up the conversation. The following narative is a good example of what I am pointing to here.

How are you arriving?

Following on from a previous workshop on creativity, I began the session by inviting the group to choose an object from the table (that I had set up at the back of the room) that signified something for them about how they were arriving. I did this partly as a reminder of the types of tools and techniques that we had explored in the previous session, and partly as a means of ensuring that everyone was encouraged to take the opportunity to speak during the Community Meeting, something that some participants were still finding it difficult to do.

9.00 a.m.–10.00 a.m.

The objects, about twenty in number, were random items that I had accumulated over the years and brought together as a resource for use in this type of exercise – a model New York taxi, a broken key, a battery, a writing slate, a tea bag, etc. As a further prompt, I added that this was not an invitation for all the participants to tell us which mode of transport they had used that morning – car, bike, etc. – but rather what was on their minds at the start of the workshop.

Margaret chose as her object a set of Post-it notes and introduced the item with 'I feel that I have stickies on the brain'. I asked what that felt like. Margaret explained that it felt terrible. A peer was in the habit of micro-managing Margaret on joint projects and left little room for Margaret to challenge her because she always preceded her 'interference' by stating 'I know that I am a terrible micro-manager, but …' This opened up a rich vein of conversation about the multiple pressures that we find ourselves buffeted by, and the difficulty of challenging someone when they are apologising for the very behaviour that you would like them to address, before launching into that very behaviour.

3.45 p.m.–4.30 p.m.

Towards the end of the day, I decided to forego the usual coaching sessions in favour of a second RPG session at which I invited the group to return to the table at the back of the room and pick an object that said something about how they were leaving. They did this and joined me in the circle.

Everyone picked a different object than the one they had chosen in the morning.

Margaret ('stickies on the brain') chose the blank slate. For her, it signified ideas, and she said that she was 'going away with some ideas for next steps'.

For me, the blank slate was a powerful metaphor for getting rid of the stickies on brain.

Letting go of my (now conscious) need to act like a 'group analyst' and replacing it with the freedom to act like a convenor of reflexive practice groups, proved beneficial both for me and the group. My anxieties, arising from attempts to do what I felt that I ought to be doing, rather than what I felt that I needed to be doing for the group, reduced significantly. This allowed me to concentrate on holding and containing the group's anxieties, which in turn provided the space that the group might need to get on with the primary task. Thornton argues that the variety of contexts one finds oneself in a convenor 'requires you to think vigorously about the purpose, context and membership of each group with whom you work; doing so enables you to craft, with each group, appropriate methodologies, depth, and frankness of engagement' (2016: xix).

I had to accept that I was not working with open-ended analytic groups, but with time-limited stranger groups that might need encouragement, such as the catalyst of the random objects, to reach a level of safety that allowed for disclosure and exchange. Thornton's reminder that 'all teams are groups, but not all groups are teams' (2016: 11) was timely and useful. The groups that I was working with could be described, in Thornton's terms, as 'learning groups', i.e. groups that have 'come together as relative strangers for the purpose of individual learning' (ibid.). For Thornton:

> [The] richness of learning arises from the fact that learners set and work actively on *different* learning goals. In such a group, members can share profound insights and significantly refine their interpersonal and collaborative skills; in fact, in a successful learning group, these outcomes are inevitable.
>
> *(Ibid.; emphasis in the original)*

One size does not fit all, and one has to adapt one's approach to fit the context, the group, and the individuals therein. I have recently started to work with a number of senior management teams at the university, several women-only groups (as part of an initiative to encourage more female colleagues into senior management roles), the entire management team (thirty plus) of one of the professional departments at the university, a supervision group for university coaches, and an external RPG comprising of an eclectic mix of people from the local community. Each one of these groups has required me to negotiate a way of working/convening that is tailored to their needs and one that is constantly reviewed and recalibrated as the process emerges.

Endings

The fourth element from group analytic thinking that has found its way into my practice is the importance of endings. The end was signalled early during the RPO programme – 'we are half-way through the programme' or 'we have three more sessions in which to explore these themes', etc. – and the importance of leaving the group with some positive memories of their experience was also highlighted.

Saying goodbye

> Given that this was the last workshop, I decided to hold the Community Meeting at the end of the day. So rather than having the usual 9.00 a.m. start for our Community Meeting, we held it from 3.00 p.m.–4.00 p.m. I negotiated this change with the group at the start of the session and as I shared my rationale for this, namely my dissatisfaction with the nature of endings that had occurred (or more accurately hadn't occurred), it catalysed a short discussion about parallel processes across the organisation. Nancy and Sue shared their disappointment about the regularity with which they learned of departures long after colleagues had gone, and usually as a result of emailing them and receiving an automatic reply detailing their retirement, new job, etc. Sue had

to leave before 3.00 p.m. so she said her goodbyes during the course of the day.

3.00 p.m.–4.00 p.m.

I provided cakes and fruit to celebrate the end of the programme and as people settled into their seats in the circle, I introduced the session as an opportunity to look in the 'rear view mirror' and notice 'how far we had come'; as well as an opportunity to look to the future. The session was quite humbling with colleagues taking turns to share what their involvement in the programme had meant to them and how my facilitation/leadership of the programme had made a major contribution to this. I batted the first couple of compliments away, but was then able to accept them with a little more grace.

Pleasingly, and without any prompting from me, colleagues then went on to share their appreciation of each other's contribution to the programme/learning community. Mary singled out the change that she had seen in Alex during the course of the programme, apologising for the maternal nature of her comments (Alex is in his mid-twenties and Mary is in her mid-forties). Alex took these comments in the way that they were intended and went on to acknowledge the changes that he had identified in himself, as well as those that had been commented on·by those around him. This led to a further round of sharing those elements of the programme that had been challenging but useful, as well as the fun and laughter that we had had along the way. The end of the hour came quickly with colleagues sharing how much they would miss this space, as well as how better prepared they felt to go on without it.

Thornton argues that the effective coach, working with individual clients, should have 'knowledge in at least three fields: psychological literacy to understand the client, good interpersonal skills to facilitate the learning process, and a grasp of business/organizational life that enables a joint understanding of the work context to develop, with the client ... plus knowledge of a fourth field, group dynamics' (2016: 11). To coach/convene groups, she further argues that 'an understanding of applied systems and complexity thinking is also indispensable, or s/he will have little understanding of the reach of her/his interventions with teams' (ibid.: 13).

Engaging with group analysis and group analytic ways of working has helped me to enhance all four of the attributes that Thornton deems necessary to work with individuals, and my studies for the DMan, drawing on the perspective of complex responsive processes of relating (Stacey, 2012; Griffin, 2002, Shaw, 2002; Stacey and Mowles, 2015), have given me an excellent grounding in the fifth. This has given me confidence to create and act into the RPG spaces that I find myself in, not with any illusions that I have the answers, but rather with the more helpful knowledge that I don't, and that is OK. This also means that I can spend my energies creating a safe space that contains and holds the group anxieties enabling them to do the work in which exchange and learning is possible, but not guaranteed. This last point is ably illustrated by Ava's experience (see Chapter 6).

In addition, participation in the programme has helped me to be (i) more nuanced and adaptive in my approach and aspirations for the various types of group that I find myself working with – be they learning groups or work teams; (ii) more aware of the importance of note taking and reflection for thinking, linking, processing and understanding; (iii) an advocate for dynamic administration and alert to the parallels this has for management/leadership; and (iv) much more deliberate in my approach to contracting, and beginnings and endings.

From LEGs to RPGs and back again

In relation to the activity under review in this chapter, i.e. group work, it is difficult to say where a complexity approach starts and group analytic ways of working end. The DMan was developed in collaboration with members of the IGA and Ralph Stacey is a trained group analyst himself. Chris Mowles describes the DMan group at UH as:

> [A] type of therapeutic community where the therapeutic aspect of what we are doing together is de-emphasized in favour of research, making links with organizational life, and completing a doctorate … Nonetheless experiential groups, reflection, reflexivity and communicative interaction are at the heart of what the programme offers as a way of coming to terms with the hurly burly of organizational life.
>
> *(2017a: 222–223)*

Exploring reflection, reflexivity and communicative interaction and the hurly burly of organisational life are at the heart of what I find myself doing in the leadership development spaces that I am responsible for. The title of this section – 'From LEGs to RPGs and back again' – reflects the sense that I am making of my engagement with group analytic ways of thinking/working, particularly over the last three years. On reflection, my immersion in the discipline meant that for a while I tried to work in a group analytic way or more accurately in a way that I understood to be group analytic, hence I dropped the use of the term LEG in favour of RPG for the groups that I started to work with during my RPO studies.

However, recently my position has shifted. I am back to asking the question that I struggled with so much in the early days on the DMan: what else might be going on here? And what, if anything, does group analytic thinking/practice offer? But not only group analytic thinking but also 'insights from the complexity sciences, the process sociology of Elias (1939, 2001), Elias and Scotson (1994), pragmatic theories of communication (Mead, 1934), experience and values (Dewey, 1934, 1958), a complex understanding of time and action (Joas, 1996; Mead, 1932, 1934) and paradox' (Mowles, 2015, 2017a: 223). Consequently, for the two new groups that I have started to work with recently, I have reinstated LEGs as a more accurate title/descriptor for what we might find ourselves doing together.

As noted above, Stacey (2012) argues that a sensitivity to group dynamics is a critical component in the development and exercise of one's capacity for practical judgement. He explains this sensitivity as 'an ability to interpret what is going on in a group' (ibid.: 114). Stacey argues that the 'inevitable ambiguities and uncertainties of organizational life are bound to make people feel anxious' and this anxiety can lead to 'high degrees of dependency on their leaders and managers, waiting for instruction on what to do, thereby slowing down the responses to ambiguity and uncertainty' (ibid.). Thus in contrast to Revans, who views the exploration of group dynamics as a diversion that might prevent action being taken, Stacey sees the processing of what might be going on in the group as a prerequisite for action, particularly if the anxiety levels are such that they are preventing the group from thinking. This sentiment is shared by advocates of critical action learning whereby the exploration of affect and the acknowledgement of unconscious processes, power relations, tensions and contradictions are important in order to offset the potential for group dynamics to lead to 'inaction' (Vince, 2008).

Reflections: talk is action

> Relationships and the mental state of groups are not a luxury to be invested in when it can no longer be avoided, but a pre-condition for anything being done or delivered in every organisation, be it of large, small, or medium size.
>
> *Gerhard Wilke, 2014: xvi*

It seems trite to say that talk, or conversation, is action, but whatever we get done in organisations, we get done in iterative patterns of communicative interaction, that is, conversations, ongoing processes of gesture and response (see Chapter 5). In the organisational settings in which you work, how many times have you heard the following phrases?

- This hasn't been thought through.
- That meeting was a complete waste of time.
- A bad decision is better than no decision.
- There's an elephant in the room.
- Let's not open up that can of worms.

A reading of Revans' early publications suggests that the whole point of action learning is to be critical (in particular, challenging the (academic) notion of management/administration as science), social (focusing more on developing the relationships between set members and their colleagues rather than the capabilities of the individual) and to generate new learning (which involves letting go of current thinking or unlearning). His equation for learning is $L = P + Q$, where L stands for learning, P for programmed knowledge and Q for questioning insight. For me, Revans was encouraging reflexivity, that is, thinking about one's thinking in the company of others with a view to letting go of ways of thinking/doing that might no longer be serving us well. However, I contend that the reason this often does not happen in conventional action learning set spaces is due the fact that the insights offered by participants are steeped in the type of mainstream, instrumental, linear cause and effect type of thinking that taking a complexity approach to leadership development problematises. Rather than acknowledging and working with paradoxes, conventional approaches look to collapse them with a form of 'this and then that' logic. Bolden *et al.* think that this way of thinking is more prevalent in the West, where:

> For many people their first impulse upon being confronted with a paradox is to try to 'resolve it', to render down the conflicting statements so that they agree and the apparent contradiction can be made to go away. We are hardwired to regard anything difficult as a problem needing to be fixed.
>
> *(2016: 3)*

I can understand Revans' anxiety that conversations can end up being abstract and divorced from the operational realities of organisational life. Indeed, this is a good description of the shortcomings of the dominant discourse that I have been pointing to throughout this book and the main reason for the complexity approach to leadership and organisation resonating with me in the first place. Conventional approaches to action learning have lost sight of the fact that Revans refutes mainstream thought and academic conceptions of management as science. I contend that this is what Brook *et al.* (2016) are pointing to in their calls for a 'new', critical form of action learning. Thornton argues that properly led groups 'can help people face hard realities together, fostering resolve and generating creative, realistic solutions to business challenges. Groups can help individuals overcome stress and other 'knee-jerk' responses to threat or change, and so work productively once again' (Thornton, 2016: 5).

I am also alert to the potential for RPG spaces and talking to become idealised, thus ignoring or covering over the destructive forces that group processes can surface (Nitsun, 2015). Working in this way is not for everybody – participants and programme leaders alike. However, I have witnessed how useful this way of working can be in helping managers to enhance their capacities for sense-making, reflexivity and practical judgement, knowing when to poke the elephant and open up the can of worms, as well as when not to (Wilke, 2014), in the knowledge that the meaning of such a gesture will only ever emerge in the responses it provokes. Mowles argues that:

> [M]ethods derived from the group analytic tradition ... have the potential for creating more skilful managers who may be more insightful in groups and about groups, and who may have more resources for working against more general individualising tendencies which can produce feelings of atomisation and helplessness.
>
> *(2017b: 12)*

As I have stated on numerous occasions throughout this book, there is nothing intrinsically wrong with the tools, techniques and methods employed on traditional leadership development programmes, including action learning, but how useful they are in helping managers to go about their day-to-day activities depends on the approach, the focus of attention and the quality of the attendant and ongoing sense-making, reflexivity and practical judgement.

Notes

1 Workshops are scheduled around my availability and that of the training room. This means that workshops are hardly ever scheduled to take place on the same day each month, and the gap between sessions can be anything from three to five weeks.
2 This excerpt is taken from the communication sent to the Senior Management Team prior to their Conference in March 2009. The document was sent as background information for a planned conference session to discuss Senior Management Team development in general and the proposed LEGs in particular.
3 For a more comprehensive exploration of MSOL, see Flinn and Mowles (2014). And for a more expansive exploration of LEGs, see Flinn (2011).
4 I do not have the space to provide a thorough critique of Tuckman (1965), but this is one of those concepts where it pays to go back to the original source material. Tuckman's original research was a meta-analysis of all of the journal articles he could find relating to group process. The majority of studies related to therapy groups , T-groups and groups that had been set up and observed under laboratory conditions. There were very few papers in his analysis that related to group process in work settings. Indeed, in the original article, Tuckman provides the caveat that his theory might not be generalisable to group process in organisational settings. And in an update of this research some years later (Tuckman and Jensen, 1977) he casts some doubt on whether the 'storming' phase is generalisable outside of therapeutic settings.
5 Echoes of Collins and Hansen, Kellerman and Pfeffer (Chapter 1) are not lost on me, nor I suspect on you.
6 This narrative is taken from a Leadership Foundation for Higher Education Stimulus Paper that we wrote together (Flinn and Mowles, 2014), and it is interesting to note that Chris called the groups he was working with at that time learning sets, hence my use of the term from the end of the previous paragraph as the title.
7 This appears as *Table 9.2* in Schlapobersky (2016) and is adapted from Behr and Hearst (2005: 42–54).
8 The Abilene paradox is a term coined by Jerry Harvey (1988) to describe what can happen among a group of people when each member mistakenly believes that their own preferences are counter to the group's and, therefore, does not raise objections resulting in an outcome that is counter to the wishes of many (or all) members of the group.

References

Badawy, M. K. (1978) Design and content of management education: American style. *Management International Review*, 3: 75–81.
Behr, H. and Hearst, L. (2005) *Group-Analytic Psychotherapy: A Meeting of Minds*. London: Whurr.
Binney, G., Wilke, G. andWilliams, C. (2012) *Living Leadership: A Practical Guide for Ordinary Heroes* (3rd edn). Harlow: Pearson Education.
Bolden, R., Witzel, M. and Linacre, N. (Eds) (2016) *Leadership Paradoxes: Rethinking Leadership for an Uncertain World*. Abingdon: Routledge.

Brook, C., Pedler, M., Abbott, C. and Burgoyne, J. (2016) On stopping doing those things that are not getting us to where we want to be: Unlearning, wicked problems and critical action learning. *Human Relations*, 69(2): 369–389.

Carmichael, J., Collins, C., Emsell, P. and Haydon, J. (2011) *Leadership and Management Development*. Oxford: Oxford University Press.

Dalton, K. (2010) *Leadership and Management Development: Developing Tomorrow's Managers*. Harlow: Pearson.

Dewey, J. (1934) *A Common Faith*. New Haven, CT: Yale University Press.

Dewey, J. (1958) *Experience and Nature*. New York: Dover Publications.

Dreyfus, H. D. and Dreyfus, S. D. (1986) *Mind over Machine*. New York: Free.

Elias, N. (1939) *The Civilizing Process*. Blackwell: Oxfordrepr. (2000).

Elias, N. (2001) In M. Schröter, E. Jephcott and M. Schroter (eds) *The Society of Individuals*. New York: Continuum International Publishing Group.

Elias, N. and Scotson, J. (1994) *The Established and the Outsiders*. London: Sage.

Flinn, K. (2011) *Making Sense of Leadership Development: Reflections on My role as a Leader of Leadership Development Interventions*. Unpublished thesis.

Flinn, K. and Mowles, C. (2014) *A Complexity Approach to Leadership Development: Developing Practical Judgement*. Leadership Foundation for Higher Education stimulus paper.

Foulkes, S. H. (1975). *Group Analytic Psychotherapy: Method and Principles*. London: Karnac (reissued 1986).

Gold, J., Thorpe, R. and Mumford, A. (2010) *Leadership and Management Development* (5th edn). London: Chartered Institute of Personnel and Development.

Griffin, D. (2002) *The Emergence of Leadership: Linking Self-Organisation and Ethics*. London: Routledge.

Harvey, J. (1988) 'The Abilene paradox: The management of agreement'. *Organizational Management*. American Management Association, 17(1): 19–20.

Joas, H. (1996) *The Creativity of Action*. Cambridge: Polity Press.

Mead, G. H. (1932) *The Philosophy of the Present*. New York: Prometheus Books.

Mead, G. H. (1934) *Mind, Self and Society from the Standpoint of a Social Behaviourist*. Chicago, IL: University of Chicago Press.

Mowles, C. (2015) *Managing in Uncertainty: Paradox and the Complexity of Every Day Organizational Life*. London: Routledge.

Mowles, C. (2017a) 'Group analytic methods beyond the clinical setting: Working with researcher-managers'. *Group Analysis*, 50(2): 217–236.

Mowles, C. (2017b) 'Experiencing uncertainty: On the potential of groups and a group analytic approach for making management education more critical'. *Management Learning*: 1–15.

Nitsun, M. (2015) *The Anti-group: Destructive Forces in the Group and Their Creative Potential*. Hove: Routledge.

Revans, R. (1980) *Action Learning: New Techniques for Managers*. London: Blond and Briggs.

Revans, R. (2011) *ABC of Action Learning*. London: Gower.

Shaw, P. (2002) *Changing Conversations in Organizations: A Complexity Approach to Change*. London: Routledge.

Schermet, M. A. and Klein, R. H. (1996) 'Termination in Group Psychotherapy from the perspectives of Contemporary Object Relations Theory and Self Psychology'. *International Journal of Group Psychotherapy*, 46(1): 99–115.

Schlapobersky, J. R. (2016) *From the Couch to the Circle: Group-Analytic Psychotherapy in Practice*. Abingdon: Routledge.

Stacey, R. D. (2012). *Tools and Techniques of Leadership and Management: Meeting the Challenge of Complexity*. London: Routledge.

Stacey, R. D. and Mowles, C. (2015) *Strategic Management and Organisational Dynamics: The Challenge of Complexity to Ways of Thinking about Organisations* (7th edn). Harlow: Pearson.

Streatfield, P. J. (2001) *The Paradox of Control in Organisations*. Abingdon: Routledge.

Thornton, C. (2016) *Group and Team Coaching: The Essential Guide* (2nd edn). Hove: Routledge.

Tuckman, B. W. (1965) 'Developmental sequence in small groups'. *Psychological Bulletin*, 63 (6): 384.

Tuckman, B. W. and Jensen, M. A. C. (1977) 'Stages of small-group development revisited'. *Group & Organization Studies*, 2(4): 419–427.

Vince, R. (2008) 'Learning-in-action' and 'learning inaction': Advancing the theory and practice of critical action learning. *Action Learning: Research and Practice*, 5(2): 93–104.

Wilke, G. (2014) *The Art of Group Analysis in Organisations: The Use of Intuitive Experiential Knowledge*. London: Karnac.

Zinkin, L. (1994) 'All's well that ends well. Or is it?'*Group Analysis*, 27: 15–34.

8

NO RECIPES, JUST RULES OF THUMB

Introduction

> A work is never completed except by some accident such as weariness, satisfaction, the need to deliver, or death: for, in relation to who or what is making it, it can only be one stage in a series of inner transformations.
>
> *(Paul Valery 2015)*

I am neither 'weary' nor 'satisfied'. I have thoroughly enjoyed the process of writing and there are enough loose ends to keep me busy for some time yet. However, there is a 'need to deliver' and I am happy to leave the loose ends hanging as something for you to get hold of – a way into the complexity approach to leadership development that I set out here. W. H. Auden's paraphrase of the Valery quotation comes closer to how I am thinking/feeling as I sit down to write the concluding chapter of this book:

> A poem is never finished; it is only abandoned
>
> *(W. H. Auden 1994)*

And in this case, the definition of 'abandon' that I have in mind is to give up control and/or to pass on.

As this is the final chapter, it is tempting to provide some form of synopsis of the preceding pages. This is probably the unconscious (now conscious) influence of expectation generated by the social object, that is, the game of (academic) writing. To be included in the game, one might be expected to provide a precis of what has gone before. However, this might discourage the type of engagement I am looking to provoke, so I am going to resist. So, if you have arrived here before reading the rest of the book, read it. It is not overly long, it is accessible and (I hope) interesting enough to reward you for the investment of your time and energy. And if you have read what has gone before, I hope that it has been a catalyst for your own reflexive curiosity and that you *have* found it accessible and interesting.

No recipes, just rules of thumb

> All anyone can ever do, no matter how powerful, is engage intentionally and as skilfully as possible, in local interaction, dealing with the consequences in an ongoing manner as they emerge. Many practical activities such as organisational change programmes, strategic planning, the nature of leadership, the meaning of control, and so on, need to be re-thought if one takes this perspective.
>
> *Stacey and Mowles (2016: 300)*

If one accepts that organisations are not systems but complex responsive processes of relating, that is, emergent patterns of interaction between interdependent human beings simultaneously co-operating and competing to get things done together, then you will understand that there are no prescriptions for how leader-managers might go about engaging in this. However, that is not to say that there is nothing generalisable. Consequently, to conclude, I will share some of rules of thumb that I think are useful to leader-managers, students/participants and leaders of leadership development, respectively, in the knowledge that many of you will fall into more than one category and some of you into all three.

Leader-managers

1. If you must differentiate between management and leadership, think of leadership as making sense of the context in which you find yourself (and articulating a next step that others recognise and support), and of managing as coping with that context (and the intended and unintended consequences of the next step). However, it is in the process of coping that one makes sense of the context, so management and leadership, leading and managing, are two sides of the same coin, they occur simultaneously and cannot be split. This is one of the many paradoxes of organisational life.
2. Leadership is a social and relational phenomenon. It is through our recognition of others that we come to be recognised as leaders. You will not always be able to recognise, or be recognised by, everybody (articulate a next step that all agree with) but this does not mean that we should exclude those who do not recognise us (disagree with the next step). However, this is sometimes unavoidable and/or necessary.
3. Do all that you can to maintain an awareness of how things actually are (the day-to-day operational realities), recognising that this becomes more and more difficult the bigger and more complex an organisation becomes and the

higher one rises in the corporate hierarchy. To help with this, De Haan and Kasozi (2014) recommend inviting as many people as is usefully possible into the decision-making process, while Dunning and Hughes (2013) contend that greater reality congruence means fewer unintended consequences. However, taking a complexity approach means keeping in mind that (i) you might reduce the number of unintended consequences, but never to zero; (ii) some unintended consequences turn out to be welcome; and (iii) it only takes one. In other words, 'small differences can escalate into major, completely unpredictable changes, so creating new forms and destroying others at the same time' (Stacey and Mowles, 2016: 297).

4. Organisations are not systems (complex adaptive, biological or any other), they are patterns (complex responsive processes) of interaction (of relating) between people, and as such they cannot be controlled, stepped outside of, or steered in a given direction.

5. There is instrumentality in some technical aspects of the leader-manager role, but when it comes to people, there is no recipe. The capability that one might usefully develop is reflexive curiosity and this involves the capacities for sense-making, reflexivity, and practical judgement.

6. Don't be an asshole (James, 2014). And if you already have the asshole's sense of entitlement, or know that you will effortlessly acquire it should you attain a position of authority; then do everyone a favour and stay away from roles that put you in charge of other people. And if you do get to be a C/EO, enjoy the trappings and any accompanying pomp and ceremony, but remember, just because the business that you work for makes vast profits doesn't mean that you are entitled to an inordinately bigger share of the pot than every other employee who has contributed to this success.

Students/participants

1. Take your experience seriously. Compare and contrast the theories, models and frameworks you encounter on leadership development programmes with your lived experience. If there is a mismatch, rather than simply thinking that you have it wrong, challenge what you hear and read and look to/for perspectives that resonate with your reality – see 2, below.

2. If you are asked to complete a piece of (academic) writing, by all means read mainstream and popular management literature, but also engage with critical, complexity and alternative perspectives – see 1, above. And remember, all the glistens is not to be found in Gold et al. (2010), nor in Carmichael et al. (2011) or Dalton (2010). Textbooks often have to sacrifice depth for breadth and can be short on critique and alternative points of view.

3. Do not rely on third party interpretations of the thought of others, including those interpretations of the work of others that I have made in this book; always go back to the original source and make up your own mind – see 1 and 2, above.

Leaders of leadership development

1. Be conscious of the potential for the programmes that you lead to be experienced by participants as a form of coercive persuasion (Schein, 1961), whether this is your intention or not – see Chapter 3. Stacey argues that the 'aim of coercive persuasion is to break down the personalities of people and reconstruct them in ways that are chosen by the most powerful' (2012: 7). He maintains that this 'can never be ethical' and that he 'cannot see how it can have any legitimate place in organizational life' (ibid.: 7).

2. Whether we take a conventional, critical or complexity stance in our thinking/practice, as leaders of leadership development we have a responsibility to share a plurality of perspectives with programme participants (Flinn, 2011), not only to ensure that they develop sufficient cultural literacy to navigate the day-to-day politics (games) of organisational life, but also to avoid the risk that in pushing our own perspective we are not simply replacing 'one hegemony with another' (Ford and Harding, 2007) – see 1, above.

3. Taking a complexity approach to leadership development involves practising reflexive curiosity, as well as encouraging it in others (see 1 and 2, above). This means regularly asking ourselves the questions 'who are we and what are we doing together', 'who are we becoming and is this useful to us and those around us?' This involves more than simply adding the current buzzwords to the titles of our programmes and/or articles and books.

4. As leaders of leadership development we are also, in effect, leader-managers and students/participants on the programmes that we run, consequently, it might be useful to take account of the rules of thumb for manager-leaders and students/participants, above.

Reflections

> Never before has leadership come under more criticism and distrust than in this second decade of the 21st century. After ... leadership debacles in practically every walk of public and private corporate life, there has been an ever-growing consensus that it is time to reassess leadership ... for industry, organizations and for both individuals and society at large.
>
> *(de Haan and Kasozi 2014)*

The opportunity to spend some time engaging in reflexive curiosity regarding my thinking/practice has been a really valuable experience and a fantastic opportunity to take a close look at some current conventional, critical and (not so current) alternative thinking in relation to leadership and leadership development. Surprises? The first surprise is that there is no mention of Henry Mintzberg, an author whose thinking I really rate.[1] The second surprise is that there are so many mentions of Mat Alvesson, most noticeably in Chapter 2. Alvesson is currently one of the most prolific and interesting writers on leadership, both in his own right and in the many collaborative projects that he has engaged in.[2] The third surprise is how the process of 'from novice to expert' outlined by Dreyfus and Dreyfus (1986) resonates with my lived experience. In trying to integrate group analytic thinking/ways of working into my practice (see Chapter 7) I realised, and not for the first time, that rather than trying to do things 'by the book' I might more usefully exercise practical judgement. The fourth and final surprise is the how much leadership writing has a 'back to the future' feel about it. Many authors, both conventional (Kellerman, 2012) and critical (Kempster and Carroll, 2016), in calling for leader-managers to take account of people and planet as well as profit, echo the principle of stewardship that was integral to the management education offered by the first business schools in the 1880s (Khurana, 2007).

The search continues

In taking a complexity approach to leadership development, I am not arguing that improvising our way through the politics of day-to-day life in organisational settings is something new, but rather that this is what we are all already doing irrespective of the illusory stories of instrumental rationality and deceptive certainty we might otherwise tell ourselves and others. I am suggesting that if we take a moment to reflect upon our lived experience of life in organisations, then we might realise this. How we then play into the situations and contexts in which we find ourselves might change slightly but not necessarily for the better. Whatever we do and however great our power chances might be in the doing of it, we cannot control and/or predict the future because we cannot control or predict the interdependent moves of everybody else in the local and global games that we are caught up in, let alone the multitudinous local and global games that we are not directly involved in. However, it might mean that we have a more reality congruent expectation of ourselves and others – whether this contributes to 'collective well being' (Wilson *et al.*, 2018) or more equitable salary differentials is anyone's guess.

My main reason for writing this book was to offer managers, students and leadership development practitioners an insight into the perspective of complex responsive processes of relating (Stacey, 2001; Griffin, 2002; Shaw, 2002; Mowles, 2011; Stacey and Mowles, 2016) – in other words the complexity approach of this book's title. Seeing authors, like Collins and Hansen (2011), suggesting that they are taking complexity seriously and highly influential mainstream authors like Kellerman (2012) and Pfeffer (2015) flirting with criticality but not committing, provokes me to make the plea 'accept no substitutes'. For me, taking a complexity approach is not a fad, it is an approach that I have been taking for the last decade, working with the perspective that Stacey, Griffin and Shaw started to articulate more than a quarter of a century ago. Taking a complexity approach (to leadership development) does not mean providing answers, but it does mean offering an understanding of human interaction that, if taken seriously, will allow us to 'engage intentionally and as skilfully as possible, in local interaction, dealing with the consequences in an ongoing manner as they emerge' (Stacey and Mowles, 2016: 300).

For my own part, I remain in 'search mode' (Smith, 2001). I plan to take a closer look at some of the practice based theories of leadership (Tengblad, 2012; Raelin, 2016) explored in Chapter 2, I am keen to do more with reflective narrative writing in LEG spaces, I am eager to make more of the approach to 360° feedback that I outlined in Chapter 4 and I want to think about how to incorporate more diverse archetypes of leadership into the programmes that I lead.

Notes

1 His thought-provoking TWOG (Tweet2Blog) is available at www.mintzberg.org/blog.
2 Indeed, you will have noticed that the leadership research coming out of Scandinavia in the last decade or so has significantly influenced my own research/sense-making.

References

Auden, W. H. (1994) *Collected Poems*. Ed. E. Mendelson. New York: Faber and Faber.

Carmichael, J., Collins, C., Emsell, P. and Haydon, J. (2011) *Leadership and Management Development*. Oxford: Oxford University Press.

Collins, J. and Hansen, M. T. (2011) *Great by Choice: Uncertainty, Chaos and Luck – Why Some Thrive despite Them All*. London: Random House.

Dalton, K. (2010) *Leadership and Management Development: Developing Tomorrow's Managers*. Harlow: Pearson.

de Haan, E. and Kasozi, A. (2014) *The Leadership Shadow: How to Recognize and Avoid Derailment, Hubris and Overdrive*. London: Kogan Page.

Dreyfus, H. and Dreyfus, S. (1986) *Mind over Machine: The Power of Human Intuition and Expertise in the Era of the Computer*. New York: The Free Press.

Dunning, E. and Hughes, J. (2013) *Norbert Elias and Modern Sociology: Knowledge, Interdependence, Power, Process*. London: Bloomsbury Academic.

Flinn, K. P. (2011) *Making Sense of Leadership Development: Reflections on My Role as a Leader of Leadership Development Interventions*. Unpublished thesis.

Ford, F. and Harding, N. (2007) 'Move over management: We are all leaders now'. *Management Learning*, 38(5): 475–493.

Gold, J., Thorpe, R. and Mumford, A. (2010) *Leadership and Management Development* (5th edn). London: Chartered Institute of Personnel and Development.

Griffin, D. (2002) *The Emergence of Leadership: Linking Self-Organisation and Ethics*. London: Routledge.

James, A. (2014) *Assholes: A Theory*. London: Nicholas Brearley.

Kellerman, B. (2012) *The End of Leadership*. New York: HarperCollins.

Kempster, S. and Carroll, B. (Eds) (2016) *Responsible Leadership: Realism and Romanticism*. Abingdon: Routledge.

Khurana, R. (2007) *From Higher Aims to Hired Hands*. Oxford: Princeton University Press.

Mowles, C. (2011) *Rethinking Management: Radical Insights from the Complexity Sciences*. London: Gower.

Pfeffer, J. (2015) *Leadership BS: Fixing Workplaces and Careers One Truth at a Time*. New York: HarperCollins.

Raelin, J. A. (Ed.) (2016) *Leadership-as-Practice: Theory and Application*. London: Routledge.

Schein, E. H. (1961) *Coercive Persuasion*. New York: Norton.

Shaw, P. (2002) *Changing Conversations in Organizations: A Complexity Approach to Change*. London: Routledge.

Smith, D. (2001) *Norbert Elias and Modern Social Theory*. London: Sage.

Stacey, R. D. (2001) *Complex Responsive Processes in Organizations: Learning and Knowledge Creation*. Abingdon: Routledge.

Stacey, R. D. (2012) *Tools and Techniques of Leadership and Management: Meeting the Challenge of Complexity*. London: Routledge.

Stacey, R. D. and Mowles, C. (2016) *Strategic Management and Organisational Dynamics: The Challenge of Complexity to Ways of Thinking about Organisations* (7th edn). Harlow: Pearson.

Tengblad, S. (Ed.) (2012) *The Work of Managers: Towards a Practice Theory of Management*. Oxford: Oxford University Press.

Valery, P. (2015) *The Collected Works of Paul Valery*. Vol. 1: *Poems*. Princeton, NJ: Princeton University Press.

Wilson, S., Jackson, B. and Proctor-Thomson, S. (2018) *Revitalising Leadership: Putting Theory and Practice into Context*. Abingdon: Routledge.

INDEX

Abilene paradox 162, 170n8

Action Learning 12, 148–70; action learning as leadership development activity 148–9; Action Learning Sets 152–5; adapting to type of group 163; administrative burdens, reduction of 162; appreciation of working together, sharing of 166; authority, difficulty in challenging 162; beginnings 165–7; coaching effectiveness, Thornton's knowledge fields for 166; community meetings, emergence of structure of 149; Community Meetings, from learning reviews to 149; complexity approach. action learning and 148–9; complexity approach, group dynamics and 155; complexity approach, similarities and difference with Revans on 153–4; context, leadership and 161; contracting 165–7; conversation, absence of agenda and ebb and flow of 149; critical approaches to 153; dominant discourse, shortcomings of 169; dynamic administration, effective exercise of 160–61; dynamic administration, exchange (learning) conditions and 159; dynamic administration, positivity in 159–60; dynamic administration, principles of 158–9; dynamic group administration 158–61; endings 165–7; group administration, practicalities and time-keeping 158–67; group analytic conductor, paradox in role of 161; group analytic thinking/practice 148; group

analytic thinking/practice, elements of 157; group analytic tradition, potential of methods derived from 169–70; group dynamics, Revans' concern about explorations of 154–5; group dynamics, sensitivity to 168; group work, tangible differences between 149; group working, adaptation to fit context 163–5; groups and teams, working with 148–9; Institute of Group Analysis (IGA) 149, 150, 151, 155, 157, 163, 167; journalling 162–3; Leadership Experience Groups (LEGs), from Community Meetings to 150; Leadership Experience Groups (LEGs), role of convener 150–52; Leadership Experience Groups (LEGs), what they are not 150; learning, goals and richness of 165; letting go 163, 164–5; mainstream understandings of leadership, disillusionment with 151–2; Making Sense of Leading (MSOL) 149, 150, 151, 153, 157, 159–60, 163, 170n3; management as science, academic conceptions of 169; methodical exploration of meaning of leadership 150; micro-management 164; note taking 161–2; object choice, participative encouragement and 163–4; one size does not fit all 165; *The Paradox of Control in Organisations* (Streatfield, P.J.) 160; practical judgment 160–61; programmed knowledge and questioning insight in 168–9; psychodynamic approach to

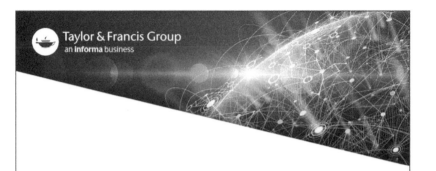

Taylor & Francis eBooks

www.taylorfrancis.com

A single destination for eBooks from Taylor & Francis
with increased functionality and an improved user
experience to meet the needs of our customers.

90,000+ eBooks of award-winning academic content in
Humanities, Social Science, Science, Technology, Engineering,
and Medical written by a global network of editors and authors.

TAYLOR & FRANCIS EBOOKS OFFERS:

A streamlined
experience for
our library
customers

A single point
of discovery
for all of our
eBook content

Improved
search and
discovery of
content at both
book and
chapter level

REQUEST A FREE TRIAL
support@taylorfrancis.com